THE
EVERYTHING.
EATING CLEAN COOKBOOK
FOR VEGETARIANS

Dear Reader,

Finding a great vegetarian cookbook can require a little bit of work, but finding a vegetarian cookbook that uses clean ingredients and keeps things simple can be downright challenging! I'm happy to bring you this collection of amazing recipes that makes eating clean vegetarian meals easy and enjoyable . . . whether you're a seasoned chef or a kitchen newbie. The goal of this book is to help you create meals that taste amazing, adhere to your vegetarian guidelines, and include clean ingredients that pack every bite with the right nutrition your body needs to thrive!

Eating clean vegetarian foods should be an experience you enjoy, an experience that never leaves you feeling like you're missing out. Getting in a "recipe rut," when you feel like you're eating the same ingredients every day or that your meals lack pizzazz, will only lead you to skip meals or opt for unhealthy alternatives. This cookbook is designed to give you plenty of ideas for delicious breakfasts, snacks, lunches, dinners, and desserts, while also covering specialty areas like raw food diets and kid-friendly recipes so every possible want is met.

Enjoy eating! And, never forget to enjoy the great life your clean foods help you live to the fullest!

Britt Brandon

Welcome to the EVERYTHING® Series!

These handy, accessible books give you all you need to tackle a difficult project, gain a new hobby, comprehend a fascinating topic, prepare for an exam, or even brush up on something you learned back in school but have since forgotten.

You can choose to read an Everything® book from cover to cover or just pick out the information you want from our four useful boxes: e-questions, e-facts, e-alerts, and e-ssentials.

We give you everything you need to know on the subject, but throw in a lot of fun stuff along the way, too.

We now have more than 400 Everything® books in print, spanning such wide-ranging categories as weddings, pregnancy, cooking, music instruction, foreign language, crafts, pets, New Age, and so much more. When you're done reading them all, you can finally say you know Everything®!

QUESTION

Answers to common questions

FACT

Important snippets of information

ALERT

Urgent warnings

ESSENTIAL

Quick handy tips

PUBLISHER Karen Cooper

MANAGING EDITOR, EVERYTHING® SERIES Lisa Laing

COPY CHIEF Casey Ebert

ASSOCIATE PRODUCTION EDITOR Mary Beth Dolan

ACQUISITIONS EDITOR Lisa Laing

SENIOR DEVELOPMENT EDITOR Brett Palana-Shanahan

EVERYTHING® SERIES COVER DESIGNER Erin Alexander

Visit the entire Everything® series at *www.everything.com*

THE EVERYTHING®

EATING CLEAN COOKBOOK FOR VEGETARIANS

Britt Brandon, CFNS, CPT

Avon, Massachusetts

For my loves: Jimmy, Lilly, Lonni, and JD!
You make my life better than I ever could have
imagined it . . . every single day!

An Everything® Series Book.
Everything® and everything.com® are registered trademarks of F+W Media, Inc.

Published by Adams Media, a division of F+W Media, Inc.
57 Littlefield Street, Avon, MA 02322 U.S.A.
www.adamsmedia.com

ISBN 10: 1-4405-5140-5
ISBN 13: 978-1-4405-5140-6
eISBN 10: 1-4405-5211-8
eISBN 13: 978-1-4405-5211-3

The Everything® Eating Clean Cookbook for Vegetarians contains material adapted and abridged from *The Everything® Eating Clean Cookbook* by Britt Brandon, CFNS, CPT, copyright © 2012 by F+W Media, Inc., ISBN 10: 1-4405-2999-X, ISBN 13: 978-1-4405-2999-3; *The Everything® Vegetarian Slow Cooker Cookbook* by Amy Snyder and Justin Snyder, copyright © 2012 by F+W Media, Inc., ISBN 10: 1-4405-2858-6, ISBN 13: 978-1-4405-2858-3; and *The Everything® Raw Food Recipe Book* by Mike Snyder with Nancy Faas, MSW, MPH and Lorena Novak Bull, RD, copyright © 2010 by F+W Media, Inc., ISBN 10: 1-4405-0011-8, ISBN 13: 978-1-4405-0011-4.

Printed in the United States of America.

10 9 8 7 6 5 4 3 2 1

Nutritional statistics by Nicole Cormier, RD.

Always follow safety and common-sense cooking protocol while using kitchen utensils, operating ovens and stoves, and handling uncooked food. If children are assisting in the preparation of any recipe, they should always be supervised by an adult.

Many of the designations used by manufacturers and sellers to distinguish their products are claimed as trademarks. Where those designations appear in this book and Adams Media was aware of a trademark claim, the designations have been printed with initial capital letters.

This book is available at quantity discounts for bulk purchases.
For information, please call 1-800-289-0963.

Contents

Introduction 9

1 Vegetarianism and Clean Eating 11

Why Be a Clean Vegetarian? 12

Classes of Vegetarians 12

The Clean Vegetarian Diet 14

The Benefits of a Clean Vegetarian Diet 18

The Protein Question 21

Soy-Based and Other Meatless Products 22

2 Getting Started 25

Defining Your Goals 26

Plan Your Path 27

Essentials for Your Eating Clean Kitchen 29

Stocking the Pantry 32

Staying Motivated 35

Tips for Eating Clean Away from Home 37

Vegan Option 39

3 Breakfasts 41

4 Smoothies 61

5 Snacks 73

6 Sandwiches and Wraps 91

7 Soups 109

8 Salads 127

9 Appetizers 141

10 Vegetarian Entrées 159

11 Grains and Pastas 183

12 Splendid Sides 203

13 Delightful Desserts 223

14 Radiant Raw Foods 241

15 Healthy Holidays 259

16 Kid-Friendly Fun 277

Appendix: Eating Clean Meal Plan 294
Standard U.S. Metric Measurement Conversions 295

Index 296

Acknowledgments

This book has been an absolute adventure to write, and it would not have been possible to create without the love and support of some extraordinary people I am very lucky to have in my life.

First, and foremost, I would like to thank my husband, Jimmy, for being an amazing source of support and strength that never seems to waver. My life has become an even more wonderful road to travel since we've started enjoying it together. I love you so very much for each and every way you help make my life all I've ever dreamed for and more!

To my wonderful children, Lilly, Lonni, and JD: I thank you for making every day so much more special than the last. I love you guys so much, and can't thank you enough for inspiring me to do great things, motivating me to always be better, and loving me unconditionally as I do you!

To Neal: Thank you for protecting our country each and every day! Your fearless drive to accomplish great things and be the best (. . . always!) is nothing short of inspirational and amazing! I love you very much!

To my amazing Dad: thank you for being the wisest person I have ever met! I feel extremely blessed to have been given the gift of having someone as caring and special as you to be my source of . . . everything . . . always!

To my very special Mom who has given me love and lessons that I am lucky to carry with me each and every day: I thank you for being you and always encouraging me to "shoot for the stars" without fear. I love you so very much!

For my lovely Miss Pam: I treasure every wonderful moment we have that lifts my spirits, enlightens my thoughts, and helps me realize new and wonderful things about myself and my life. I am truly blessed to have been given the gift of you . . . and I thank you.

Introduction

CONGRATULATIONS TO YOU! Making the choice to be proactive in bettering your health through a better diet is a life-altering decision that can have a profound impact on the quality of your life each and every day. One meal at a time, you have the power to improve everything from the quality of your skin to the quality of your blood, the efficiency of your thought processes to the efficiency of your digestion, your immunity to the common cold to your immunity against certain cancers. Improving energy levels, mental clarity, and overall health and well-being, a well-balanced diet of clean vegetarian foods provides your body with all of the essential vitamins, minerals, antioxidants, and macronutrients your body needs to thrive!

A large majority of the American population has succumbed to a diet that is commonly (and quite appropriately) referred to by its acronym: SAD. The Standard American Diet has gone from one of "home-grown," natural foods with a flare of multicultural influences to one that revolves around prepackaged, takeout, and fast-food meals designed to be more efficient, not more nutritious. Studies have long shown the disastrous health consequences that result from a diet that consists of heavily processed foods high in sodium, sugar, and unhealthy fats; these "foods" may provide temporary sustenance, but they also promote disease and illness rather than health and well-being. New research that becomes available more and more readily every day continues to show that the chemicals used to promote the growth of meats, fruits, vegetables, and grains can have dramatically devastating effects on consumers' quality of life. Luckily, these foods are not the only options available, and those who choose to maintain and promote a healthy lifestyle can do so by choosing to eat clean foods, vegetarian foods, foods that will protect, promote, and provide for the health sought by so many.

With the revolution of health-focused eating, Americans can now take control of their own health by choosing to eat foods that provide great nutrition with every bite. Beautiful, vibrant, fresh foods that deliver vitamins, minerals, powerful plant chemicals, and essential protein, carbohydrates, and healthy fats are the foods that comprise the clean vegetarian diet. Easy to find in the local grocery store, fresh market, or produce stand, these delicious foods can be at anyone's fingertips regardless of their location, time of year, or amount of money available. Better yet, eating a diet of clean vegetarian meals can be a simple change that will (sometimes surprisingly) save you time, money, and energy. That's right! In the same time it would take you to sit and wait in the drive-through or order take-out, you can enjoy a delicious meal that's healthy right in your own kitchen or on the go.

The keys to getting healthy, staying healthy, and living a life that is full of energy, focus, and satisfaction are available to us all. When faced with the question, "What should I eat?" first ask yourself, "What does my body need . . . right now?" and let your answer guide you to a choice that will help your health . . . not hurt it. Disengage from the multimillion-dollar marketing campaigns designed to confuse consumers with buzzwords like "low-fat," "non-fat," "heart-healthy," or "no trans fats," and recognize the danger-free zone of natural foods you can enjoy in their natural states. Deliver powerful nutrition to your body, eat free of chemicals and synthetics, and relish the positive results that can be seen, felt, and lived!

CHAPTER 1

Vegetarianism and Clean Eating

Vegetarians have enjoyed the plentiful benefits of their meatless ways for centuries, and in recent decades, a progressive group has improved upon the meat-free diet to include additional standards that improve one's health, wellness, and quality of life. By fusing a diet that focuses on the elimination of meat products and the inclusion of fruits, vegetables, nuts, beans, and grains, with a lifestyle that maximizes health benefits by the elimination of harmful additives and processing, the *clean vegetarian lifestyle* was born. This new and improved way of life provides the best of both worlds in a collaboration that is far better than either original on its own.

Why Be a Clean Vegetarian?

From the beginning of mankind, the earth was the sole provider for the sustenance of life. Hunting and gathering a variety of fruits, vegetables, and grains, the first people to walk the earth had to depend on these natural food sources in order to survive. While variety may have been limited depending upon a multitude of factors, the fact remains that natural foods composed the diets of the earliest eaters. Not only did this all-natural diet make it possible for mankind to survive, it allowed mankind to thrive!

Over the span of time that has brought us from those earliest years to the present, modern cultures have learned how to develop a more streamlined system to provide the necessary amounts and types of foods to satisfy the needs of the masses. While markets, restaurants, and fast-food drive-throughs are the predominate sources of our "sustenance" now, the foods we consume still start in the same place as they did so many years ago. The major difference between now and then, though, is the process through which foods travel from the earth to your plate. While today's farming and production may have the same original ideals, these processes have had to adapt to modern needs. As the population has amplified, food manufacturers have had to increase supply in order to satisfy the ensuing demand. Manufacturers have turned to modern methods of promoting the growth of their crops and livestock, reducing the cost of production, and preventing loss of their products. While these modern marvels achieve the goals of boosting production, most of the objectives have been achieved by using antibiotics, hormones, fertilizers, pesticides, and methods that, while improving production, have led consumers to question the safety of consuming these heavily processed manufactured foods. In short, it is this modern "processing" that *clean* vegetarians strive to remove from their diet in order to preserve and promote their health and well-being.

Classes of Vegetarians

While vegetarians can be classified into groups with different goals and motives that drove them to choose vegetarian living, there is one commonality that unites them all: Their diets are free of meat. Beyond the "meat-free" element, though, vegetarian diets fall into a broad spectrum between those who only exclude specific meats to those who consume a diet void of all animal products and byproducts and maintain their foods be prepared at or below certain temperatures. Regardless of where on the spectrum of vegetarian diets one falls, clean eating guidelines can promote health and well-being by focusing on the potential nutrition of the foods that are included in the diet, and structuring them in such a way that the body benefits from each and every food consumed in the best way possible. The most common classifications of vegetarians are lacto-ovo vegetarians, lacto-vegetarians, ovo-vegetarians, vegans, and raw vegans. Following are a few short descriptions of each classification, and how they differ.

Lacto-Ovo Vegetarians

When most people think of vegetarian diets, lacto-ovo vegetarianism is what most commonly comes to mind. This diet is one that consists of all of the fruits, vegetables, beans, nuts, and grains, while also including dairy products and eggs. There is no meat in the lacto-ovo diet, and there is no restriction on food temperature or preparation.

Lacto-Vegetarians

Vegetarians who choose to adopt the commonly thought of vegetarian diet with the exclusion of eggs and egg products fall into this category. An allergy to eggs and products that contain them is the most common motive in modifying the traditional vegetarian diet this way. Egg and egg white substitutes are readily available at most grocery stores, and the nutritional content is very similar to that of a natural egg or egg white.

Ovo-Vegetarians

Like lacto-vegetarians, ovo-vegetarians adhere to the commonly thought of vegetarian diet with the exception of one element: ovo-vegetarians exclude dairy products. Lactose intolerant individuals (those who have difficulty digesting dairy products or products containing lactose) and those who prefer to eliminate dairy products for ethical reasons or other various health concerns would fall into this category. Dairy substitutes like almond milk, rice milk, soy milk, and nut and soy cheeses are great alternatives to conventional dairy products excluded in this diet.

Vegans

Sometimes termed "extreme vegetarians," those who choose to eliminate all animal products—as well as their byproducts—from their diet would fall into the category of "vegans." Vegans not only exclude dairy and eggs, but also refrain from consuming (and sometimes purchasing) products that are manufactured in such a way that animals are adversely affected (directly or indirectly) in the process. Vegan alternatives are extremely popular due to the increasing demand over the past few years, so substitutions for everything from eggs to sausage can be found at a grocery store near you.

Raw Vegans

Raw vegans, sometimes referred to as "extreme vegans," adhere to the same diet as a vegan with an added (and extremely important) focus on *how* their foods are prepared. Maintaining that foods are cooked to a temperature at, or below, 145°F, raw vegans consume their foods in this "raw" form in order to preserve the natural nutrition of foods that would otherwise be compromised in cooking processes that use higher temperatures.

The Clean Vegetarian Diet

Simply put, a clean vegetarian diet is one that embraces both the vegetarian ideals as well as the principles of clean eating. Designed to optimize the overall health of the body's parts, processes, and functions, the clean vegetarian lifestyle is a simple way to enjoy a variety of nutritious, delicious foods in a way that can better your life! Including all of the foods that comprise a vegetarian diet, "clean vegetarianism" adheres to the simple guidelines of clean eating that focus on consuming foods as close to their natural state as possible in order to maximize their nutritional benefits, eating consistent snacks and meals, and consuming a variety of foods to ensure that the body is fueled with adequate amounts and types of nutrients. For example, while vegetarians consume a diet that includes fruits, vegetables, beans, legumes, nuts, and grains, the clean eating standards eliminate their processed forms, embrace a variety of foods for each meal and snack, and divide these foods equally to provide a daily diet of five to six balanced meals and snacks consumed every three to four hours for constant delivery of nutrition. While it may sound complicated, the combination of these two healthy lifestyles gives its followers an inspiring number of benefits that improve the individual, as well as the environment.

Clean eating guidelines are designed to utilize each meal and snack as an opportunity to consume the most beneficial nutrition possible while keeping the body free of toxins and harmful chemicals. Such eating promotes a healthy metabolism and optimal system functioning, maintains higher energy levels, improves fat loss and muscle gain, betters brain function and mental clarity, and advances immunity. The guidelines are easy to understand and simple to implement seamlessly into any lifestyle.

Drink Clean

By drinking more than enough water throughout the day, you can ensure your body is receiving all it needs for hydration. Studies have shown that, on average, the human body requires a minimum of sixty-four ounces of clean water each day just to perform its *basic* daily functions. Consuming adequate amounts of water, you can help your body's cells and systems detoxify, hydrate with pure fluids free of chemicals and additives, and promote a steady concentration of much-needed fluids that can be utilized for every process of the body.

FACT

A rumble in your tummy may not be your body telling you food is needed; instead, cravings, headaches, fatigue, stomachaches, and "tummy talking" can all be signs of dehydration. Before you reach for your next planned snack, think about your water intake in the three hours prior, and if you think you think your body's SOS is for water, try to quench your thirst and wait thirty minutes before quenching your palate.

Avoid Processed Foods

Too often, processed foods are marketed under the guise of "healthy" because of their seemingly low content of fat, calories, sugar, or sodium. However the additives used to preserve processed foods in order to extend their shelf life, improve their taste, or maintain their "freshness" can wreak havoc on your body and gets them excluded from the clean diet. By opting for natural foods, you can avoid the questionable prepackaged alternatives that have long lists of ingredients that most people can hardly pronounce, let alone identify.

Eliminate Refined Sugars

Refined sugars can be found in almost every prepackaged food available. While this ingredient may improve the taste of a product, this is one element that has no place in a clean diet. The disastrous consequences of a diet high in refined sugar only begin with the sugar-highs and sugar-crashes that lead to roller coaster rides of "fake" energy followed by foggy minded exhaustion; studies are now showing that illnesses and diseases are striking people of all ages as a result of diets too high in sugar. Always pay attention to the grams of sugar per serving size of a product, and identify the types of sugar used in the product by locating them in the ingredients list. The best bet when it comes to sweetening things up is to opt for pure maple syrup or other all-natural alternatives.

ESSENTIAL

Just because a drink says it contains no sugar doesn't make it a healthy option. From fruit juices to artificially sweetened beverages, you have to think, "If it's sweet, something sweet is in it." Play detective and find naturally sweetened drink alternatives if water isn't appealing right off the bat. Keep in mind, though, there are no sugar concerns when it comes to pure water.

Eat Every Three to Four Hours

The body's metabolism is designed to run similarly to a car engine. With fuel, you can run, but without fuel, you can't. Expecting your body to run on little or no food for long periods of time would be like expecting your car to drive long distances at high speeds on nothing but fumes. Fueling up your body every three to four hours with adequate nutrition promotes a speedy metabolism and provides your body with the energy it needs to function properly. As an added benefit, eating every couple of hours helps satisfy hunger and keeps the temptation to binge on unhealthy foods at bay.

Balance Daily Calories Into Five to Six Equal Meals and Snacks

While some people skip breakfast or go long hours without eating under the misconception that fewer meals will result in consuming fewer calories, the reality is that dangerous consequences can result from this short-term starvation. When your body is forced to function on little or no food, it turns to a sort of "hibernation mode" and begins to burn its own sources of fuel for energy. Because muscle mass provides more energy pound-per-pound compared to fat, the body burns the meatier muscle mass for fuel *and* starts to store consumed calories in preparation for upcoming "hibernation" periods. Breaking the day's total calories into five or six equal meals and snacks allows the body's metabolism to increase and the bodily systems to run at peak performance.

ALERT

People who eat most of their calories at night after hours of deprivation have weight gain and other negative, and sometimes serious, consequences. By overloading the metabolism at night, sugar spikes in the blood, digestive enzymes overload in a reclined position, and excessive calories get stored while sleeping rather than utilized. All these troubles can be avoided by simply redistributing calories evenly throughout the day.

Max Out Nutrition

Every macronutrient (carbohydrates, proteins, and fats) and micronutrient (vitamins and minerals) is utilized by the body in different ways. Without even one of these essential elements, one or more of the body's systems can pay a heavy price. Each meal and snack should contain foods that supply ample amounts of complex carbohydrates, clean protein, and healthy fats; vitamins and minerals are plentiful in natural foods, so eating a variety of natural nutritious options makes micronutrient consumption a no-thought-required part of the diet. By including a variety of foods that contain balanced provisions of macronutrients and micronutrients, you can promote optimal system functioning . . . with the added benefit of delicious meals that have a variety of colors, textures, and flavors.

Variety and Vibrancy!

The vibrant colors of foods signify their high content of great, unique nutrition. From blueberries' blue anthocyanins to broccoli's green chlorophyll and phytochemicals, foods you choose to include in your diet should be appealing to the eyes as well as the palate. By focusing your diet on foods that make your plate (or your glass) as colorful as possible, you can benefit from the variety of nutrients contained within each and every food you enjoy.

Plan Ahead

Knowing what your body will be doing for the hours following your meals and snacks can help guide your food choices in such a way that you can maximize the fueling potential and resulting benefits of choosing the best foods for the job. If you're going to be inactive following your meal (for example, sitting at work, driving, or sleeping), a meal or snack that provides heavy doses of energy fueling carbohydrates would be futile. Those carbohydrate-packed meals and snacks should, instead, be consumed prior to strenuous activities, workouts, etc., in order to provide adequate fuel to be used in the process. On the same note, protein intake should be higher following bouts of activity in order to provide necessary nutrition for the recovery process that follows.

The Benefits of a Clean Vegetarian Diet

Almost as amazing as the delicious, nutritious meals and snacks that comprise the clean vegetarian diet are the plentiful benefits that result! The positive effects on the health of body and mind are only the beginning. Clean vegetarians not only improve their own health and preserve their own vitality, but they live a lifestyle that resonates in the animals and environment that benefit from advantages resulting from a "meat-free" way of life.

Top-Notch Metabolism

By fueling your body with maxed out nutrition every three to four hours, your metabolism becomes a more efficient fat-burning machine. Able to burn the fuel you consume, and expecting the upcoming meal in your new routine, your body no longer hoards stores of fat or depends on its own mass for energy. By eating more consistently in terms of time and amounts, you actually help your body become a fat-burning, muscle-building machine that no longer starves for hours on end!

Long-Lasting Energy

Gone are the days that you hit the 3:00 P.M. energy crash! Because of the constant routine of meals and snacks that optimize nutrition content, your body is able to function better and have ample sources of energy (food) around the clock. The energy spikes and crashes that result from your body "shutting down" to preserve energy are no longer part of your day!

Improved Performance

Balanced meals that contain complex carbohydrates, perfect proteins, and beneficial fats allow your body to function at peak performance. Athletes focus so much of their attention on the quality and consistency of their diet because eating an optimal diet means the body is able to be pushed farther, faster, and harder . . . and responds better! In the body, food equals fuel; the quality of your fuel promotes quality work. Eating balanced and consistent meals makes for maxed out nutrition and maxed out performance.

Better Brain Functioning

Who couldn't use better focus, better memory, or simply better thinking capabilities? The clean foods that provide amazing nutritional benefits not only keep your body functioning at its best but also make for a better brain that performs at its best. The fogginess and forgetfulness that come hand in hand with hours of starvation and sugar spikes and dips get the boot when you start delivering necessary nutrients where and when they're needed. Healthy fats, particularly, help promote better brain functioning by directly serving the nerve cells that house so much of one's brain activity; by consuming nuts and oils that provide healthy fats to the body, you feed your brain the food it needs to thrive.

Stronger Immunity

A clean diet provides the body with quality vitamins and minerals; promotes healthier, cleaner, quality blood and system functioning; and improves the body's defenses against illnesses and diseases all while promoting the health of each of the body's components. By eating healthier, your body is able to *be* healthier!

Quality Hydration

Keeping your body clear and clean of toxins, chemicals, and waste are the prized performance markers of hydration. Water is the purest form of hydration and helps deliver essential fluids to the body's cells; by receiving quality fluids free of additives, the body's cells (of *all* of the body's systems) are able to function optimally and more effectively free themselves of waste products that would otherwise be stored and built up over time. Water is the body's best friend, and the bountiful benefits range from clearer skin to improved cancer-fighting capabilities.

ALERT

Recent studies have shown that dehydration of even the most seemingly insignificant amount can cause staggering effects on everything from mood to sleep quality. While mental clarity and hunger are the two most commonly recognized consequences of dehydration, dehydration can adversely affect mood significantly, and a normal pattern of sleep can be disrupted and disturbed far more than when one is adequately hydrated throughout the day.

More Meals!

Cravings, stomachaches, and hunger pains are the downside to almost every diet. With all of the meals and snacks to choose from in your clean vegetarian lifestyle, you get to enjoy all kinds of foods constantly and consistently throughout the day! Eating every three to four hours, the feeling of hunger can be satisfied with delicious foods that deliver amazing nutrition! More meals for better health . . . who knew?

Recognize True Portion Sizes

Because of the average American's history with food servings being oversized and supersized, it can be astounding for someone to see what constitutes a true serving size. Simplified by using natural foods that easily fit the "quick guide to serving sizes" (see list that follows), clean vegetarian eating helps to alleviate the need to measure everything . . . though sometimes a scale is still helpful.

ESSENTIAL

Try to find ways to keep your favorite meals to a size that will satisfy without going overboard. Enjoy your favorite foods with new additions that will help fill you up and add essential nutrition. Vegetables contain a lot of nutrients that promote health-boosting effects, but they also contain more water than other foods, which helps you feel full faster and stay satisfied longer!

Here is a quick guide to serving sizes:

- **Dairy:** 1 serving is equal to 1 cup of milk or yogurt, 1 ounce of cheese
- **Vegetables:** 1 serving is equal to 1 cup of raw leafy greens, or about the size of your fist; ½ cup cooked vegetables, or about the size of a deck of cards
- **Fruits:** 1 serving is equal to 1 medium-sized fruit the size of a tennis ball, or ½ cup sliced fruit

The Protein Question

One aspect of the vegetarian diet that has come under fire over past decades has been protein intake. Because meat is the main protein provision in non-vegetarian diets, many people mistakenly believe that a diet without meat would inevitably lack protein. This is simply not the case. By focusing a diet's protein component on plant-based ingredients like eggs, milks, beans, nuts, soy, and other protein alternatives like tempeh and miso, a vegetarian is able to consume adequate amounts of protein with the added benefit of no saturated fats.

Meat-free does not lead to protein deficiency, but meat-free *does* constitute a diet that is free of ingredients that may, or may not, contain harmful chemicals and additives used in the manufacturing of those products. As previously explained, many vegetarians opt for a diet free of meat because of health concerns related to the production of animals raised for consumers' meat products. By eliminating meat from their diets, vegetarians can enjoy protein-packed meals without the concern of antibiotics and hormones used in the manufacturing process.

While some question vegetarian diets out of concern for inadequate protein intake, the real surprise may be held in the results of a diet that contains too much protein. Diets providing too much protein, resulting in dangerous and uncomfortable health conditions like kidney stones, brittle bones, and possibly heart disease and certain cancers, can be just as dangerous (if not more so) than a diet that contains too little.

Soy-Based and Other Meatless Products

With the goal of developing and adhering to a clean vegetarian diet intended to promote one's health and well-being, a discussion of soy is a must. When it comes to the decision to include or exclude soy from your diet, arming yourself with as much information about the topic as possible will ensure you make the best decision for you. With more and more information becoming available on this topic, seemingly every day, this choice is one best made by analyzing the current information available and making a decision that is, ultimately, best for you.

The History of Soy Foods

Asia is credited with providing the world with soybeans. Long before written records of their use for production, eastern Asia had been cultivating soybeans for a variety of uses with a primary focus on dietary consumption. While the soybean has been a staple of life for many other parts of the world for thousands of years, only in the eighteenth century did the soybean make its American debut. As a multitasking crop, the soybean was originally grown in the states for its use as a soil-correcting agent that was able to balance the nitrogen levels of farmers' crop soils. Shortly following the soybean's introduction to American industries, it became a staple of the automotive business as an oil used in every step of the car manufacturing process from the production of paint to car parts.

How Soy Products Are Made

Early on in the 1920s, the soybean broke through the barrier of the American diet and is now used in a variety of products as a "healthy" alternative to protein-packed animal foods that contain higher levels of saturated fats. Soy is considered to be a "complete protein" because of its provision of all of the essential and nonessential amino acids required by the human body. In order to produce the most well-known soy foods like tofu, tempeh, natto, miso, textured vegetable protein (TVP), and soy milks, soybeans are mixed with grains (normally rice) and fermented; following the fermentation process, different products are created depending on the additional ingredients used in the processing or the duration of time the products are fermented. Because of the wide variety of soy products available today, one can now find soy alternatives to animal-based products such as milks, yogurts, cheeses, mayonnaise, meats, and even infant formulas.

Benefits of Soy

Soy's benefits became widely accepted once the Food and Drug Administration (FDA) promoted soy as a heart-healthy food, mainly due to its cholesterol lowering capabilities. As an alternative to saturated fat- and cholesterol-laden foods like animal products, soy became popular in populations choosing diets with the specific goal to improve heart-health. With the added benefits of high omega-3 and omega-6 content, soy also gained recognition as a brain-boosting food that even outranked the fatty coldwater fish previously credited with contributing these essential acids to a healthy diet. Low in calories and saturated fat, and fitting the lifestyle of health-focused vegetarians nationwide, soy food production became a lucrative industry in America.

ESSENTIAL

With eating clean becoming more popular, manufacturers are developing new products to appeal to the growing number of clean consumers. Vegan varieties of your favorite foods are now available in a surprisingly widespread number of grocery stores. Just beware that processing is still required, so read labels and do research to determine if a new products meets your specific criteria.

The Questionable Consequences of Soy

Today, health concerns focus on the genetic modification of soybeans that are grown for human consumption. The genetic modifications used to prevent soybean plants from falling vulnerable to farmers' uses of a strong herbicide known as Roundup have led to questions and concerns about the health consequences that may result from this "biotech" food. With the FDA's withdrawing its claim of soy as a "heart-healthy" food, the questions concerning soy's health risks rose at an alarming rate. Studies have started to focus on the consequences of soy on mental functioning, cancer promotion, and limitations of the body's ability to absorb certain vitamins and minerals and to create and replenish essential blood vessels. High levels of phytoestrogens and the well-known omega-6 fatty acid have become the focus of many studies trying to determine the cancer-causing effects that may result from the high doses of these particular components inevitably elevated in soy-based diets. Even infant formulas that had previously been considered healthier alternatives to cows' milk or goats' milk formulas have been falling under criticism and claims that the phytoestrogen and allergy stimulating components of soy products may cause more harm than good.

Soy Alternatives

Whether you choose to include soy in your diet or not, it never hurts to educate yourself about the varieties of healthy protein alternatives available. From whey protein shakes to protein-packed cereals and grains, the options and combinations are infinite. Seaweeds and spirulina, quinoa and buckwheat, and almost all nuts, seeds, and beans provide protein. By pairing protein-rich foods in a clean meat-free meal or snack, you can boost your average protein intake to surpass that of a meat-packed meal.

CHAPTER 2

Getting Started

Making the change to a clean vegetarian diet is simple and easy when you set yourself up for success by first defining your goals for choosing to eat clean vegetarian and deciding how extreme you plan to be. Preparing your kitchen with all of the necessary tools and stocking your pantry with all of the wondrous ingredients you'll need, you can set yourself up for quick and easy cuisine creations that will help you eat healthfully at home or away.

Defining Your Goals

By asking yourself one simple question, you can quickly define your goals for choosing clean vegetarian living: "Why do I want to live the clean vegetarian lifestyle?" Maybe you're tired of being tired, sick of being sick, ethical or moral reasons resound with you, the preservation of the environment is important, or all of the above. Whatever your reasons may be, knowing what they are can hone your focus on the types of foods you'll want to include in and exclude from your clean vegetarian diet.

Improving Health and Immunity

There's no doubt that diet can improve or deteriorate your health. If your goal is to change your health for the better, you'll want your diet to focus on vibrancy. Colorful foods should cover your plate (or fill your glass) at each and every meal in order to ensure you're receiving plentiful vitamins and minerals from every bite you eat (or drink you sip). Remember that colorful foods are those that contain the highest concentration of micronutrients that help to promote and preserve your body's health and vitality. Eat and drink the rainbow, and enjoy the bountiful health benefits that result!

Losing Weight

Because eating clean vegetarian is not a diet, you can eliminate the stigma of "crash diets" right off the bat. With a goal to lose weight, clean vegetarians have high success because of the boost in metabolism, the consistent schedule of meals and snacks that satisfies hunger and curbs cravings, and the variety of food that can be eaten in just one day. By enjoying five to six meals of flavorful foods that deliver the utmost nutrition, you'll feel less tired, be less hungry, have more energy, be more focused, and have a more efficient metabolism that helps your body burn fat and build muscle. By eliminating refined carbohydrates and sugars, you're able to choose from a variety of foods that will help you reach your weight-loss goals instead of sabotaging them!

Increasing Energy

You can easily eat for energy by knowing when you start to feel fatigue throughout your normal day and planning meals that will perk you up during those times. If you need help getting moving in the morning, a fruit-packed smoothie is perfect for you. If the midafternoon feels like naptime, a high-protein snack like nuts will smooth out any slump. All it takes to have more energy is to pay attention to your body's cues and give it what it needs, when it needs it.

Better Variety

From juicy fruits to flavorful vegetables, great grains to scrumptious soy, the foods that comprise the clean vegetarian diet leave no craving uncurbed. Even with a long list of foods you choose not to include, there is an even longer list of delicious alternatives from which to choose. Each and every meal and snack is a new opportunity to enjoy different flavors and textures. So, get choosy and start enjoying the plentiful variety that is clean vegetarian eating!

Avoiding Specific Ingredients

If your vegetarian ideals lead you to eliminate certain elements of the common vegetarian diet, you can actually pick and choose recipes that adhere to your diet goals quickly and easily. Products that contain soy, milk, and eggs being just a few examples of those some vegetarians choose to avoid, diets with eliminated ingredients shouldn't be limiting when it comes to delicious taste and nutritional benefits. The recipes contained in this book offer ideas for vegan substitutions in order to help keep recipe options open to all readers.

Plan Your Path

With your goals in mind, you can start brainstorming about your average day and how you can utilize the guidelines of clean vegetarian eating to help you reach those goals. If you're willing to make the change, you can change your life for the better! If you spend the time to figure out how to make the most out of this diet for your needs and wants, you can design a plan that's perfect for you, and in no time at all, it will be second nature and require no thought at all.

Your Personal Meal Plan

Take a moment to think of your average day. From the time you wake up to the time you fall asleep, what comprises your day? When do you wake up? When do you fall asleep? At what times do you eat your meals? What do you normally eat? When are you most active? When are you least active? When are you hungriest? When are you the most tired? What kind of cravings do you get? When do those cravings strike? How much water do you drink on an average day?

All of these questions can help you design a meal schedule that gives you the general time frames for when you should have your first meal (when you wake up), your last meal (sometime before you go to bed), and every one in between (every three to four hours). For example, if someone wakes up at 5:00 A.M. and goes to sleep at 10:00 P.M., their meal schedule would be designed accordingly: breakfast at 5:30 A.M., snack number one at 9:00 A.M., lunch at 12:30 P.M., snack number two at 4:00 P.M., and dinner at 7:30 P.M. This meal schedule allows for five complete meals and snacks, thirty minutes between wake up time and the first meal, three and a half hours between each meal, and two and a half hours between dinner and bedtime.

Your Vegetarian Diet

"What should a clean vegetarian diet consist of?" This question is one of the most important when it comes to creating a lifestyle that both fits your needs as well as your tastes. Everyone has likes and dislikes, and your personal diet should include foods that not only deliver nutrition but also fit flavor combinations that you'll enjoy and look forward to. You can't take advantage of food's health benefits if you don't eat the foods, right? Once you have a general idea of the times at which you'll enjoy your meals and the foods you know you'll enjoy, you can move on to establishing which macronutrients your meals will focus on heavily. For example, knowing you need a pick-me-up at your first morning meal and your midafternoon meal, you might plan to include fruits and grains for energy boosting complex carbohydrates and sugars. Protein-packed meals would better fit your body's needs at snack and meal times that follow exercise, more active periods, and prior to bed. It is this meal component planning that can help deliver the most beneficial nutrition to your body at exactly the right times.

Fit In Hydration

Hydration is imperative to any healthy lifestyle! Just as important as the nutrition in your foods, water is absolutely essential to promoting the best health of your body. With a minimum goal of 64 ounces of water per day, the easiest way to ensure you're meeting and exceeding your minimum is to drink up as much and as often as you can. Keeping in mind that thirst is a sign of dehydration, don't wait until your mouth is dry to quench your body's thirst. Drinking water at every meal time and snack time is an easy way to consume those essential sixty-four, and sipping throughout the day will get you to that water goal even faster.

More or Less?

Balance! Balance! Balance! Between the scheduling, planning, and perfecting of your personal meal plan, try to focus on the clean eating guideline of equal proportions. The varying amounts of macronutrients (carbohydrates, proteins, and fats) will change depending on the meal times and your body's needs at those times, but the calorie component of those meals and snacks should stay similar throughout the day. If your goal is to consume 1,500 calories per day, your five meals would consist of an average of 300 calories each. Keeping the calorie content in mind can help you plan your meals in such a way that you avoid "heavy" meals and "light" meals that can put your metabolism (and your energy level) through the wringer!

Essentials for Your Eating Clean Kitchen

For every job, there is a perfect tool. When it comes to creating delicious, nutritious meals, having the necessary hardware can make life a lot easier. While some of these essentials can be found in most kitchens, there are a couple must-have items that can cut prep time, minimize mess, and make on-the-go eating simple and easy. Set yourself up for success by setting up your kitchen first!

Assorted Knives

Peeling a pineapple requires a far more heavy-duty knife than slicing tofu. By having a variety of knives available, you can make meal prep much more efficient. Don't set limitations on yourself when it comes to the time, simplicity, or presentation of your meals. Having an assortment of knives that are best for particular jobs can make your meals as simple to create as they are delicious to eat!

Cutting Boards

From keeping your kitchen free of messes to quickening cleaning time, cutting boards can make meal prep a breeze. Having cutting boards that are designated for specific types of foods is also beneficial for keeping strong tastes of foods like garlic and onions from seeping into others like sweet fruits. Glass cutting boards can also ensure that the chemicals used in manufacturing plastic alternatives stay out of foods; a quick rinse in a dishwasher is completely safe with glass cutting boards, but can be questionable with plastics.

Glass Containers

On the same note of safety when it comes to possible chemical contamination, the containers you use for storing or reheating foods should be glass. A wide variety of inexpensive glass containers that are free of harmful chemicals can now be purchased at most home stores and even local grocery stores. Using glass containers to store foods, you also avoid the cross-contamination of tastes from strong foods stored at one time to other foods stored immediately after. Simply by soaking or washing glass containers, the cleanup between uses is far easier when using glass instead of plastic.

ESSENTIAL

With the importance of glass containers for heating and storing foods being a priority, it is essential to make sure you have enough containers of various sizes to be prepared for any job necessary. Inexpensive and readily available at superstores, discount stores, and local grocery stores, you can find what you need at just the right price.

Immersion Blender

From soups and dips to sauces and nut butters, an immersion blender is a wonderful tool that can save you time and energy. Rather than hand mashing or puréeing foods, an immersion blender allows you to quickly and easily emulsify any softened foods with the added benefit of quick cleanup. Inexpensive and available in a variety of stores, immersion blenders are handy, helpful, portable tools that make food prep and smoothie making a breeze.

Blender or Food Processor

For countertop tools, blenders and food processors take the top prize when it comes to efficiency and ease of cleanup. Available at every home store are new and improved versions of blenders that can double duty as a food processor as well. Glass blenders and food processors with a wide spectrum of speeds and intensities can help turn solid foods into every consistency from puréed smoothies to chunky sauces with the added simplicity of quick, soapy rinses being the only cleanup needed. Fairly inexpensive and long-lasting, these handy countertop tools can keep your time spent in the kitchen to a minimum.

Scale and Measuring Cups

It can be surprising to relearn what a true portion size is. While you're getting your lifestyle back to one that maxes out nutrition per serving, measuring cups and scales can be handy tools that can ensure your measurements are correct. Eyeballing your measurements can be misleading and turn healthful helpings into diet-busting disasters. Simple to use and inexpensive, liquid and dry measuring cups can help you create delicious, nutritious meals that keep your diet on track and your goals within reach.

Insulated Cooler

For on-the-go eaters, an insulated cooler can be a lifesaver! Whether you're looking forward to a trip or spending the day trapped in the office, an insulated cooler can keep your foods hot or cold for long periods of time. With a wide variety of styles and sizes, insulated coolers can be an inexpensive way to keep your meal schedule simple to adhere to, and your foods delicious.

Notebook

One of the most handy tools to keep in your clean kitchen is a notebook where you can keep "notes-to-self." With recipe changes, ideas for ingredient substitutions, and grocery lists or lists of favorites all in the same place, your kitchen notebook can be a helpful tool that will save you time and energy. Rather than relying on your memory, keeping your notes and lists written down in one place can help you keep your focus.

Stocking the Pantry

The beautiful beginnings of homemade clean vegetarian meals can all be found in your refrigerator and pantry. By ridding your clean kitchen of unhealthy, processed foods and restocking with fresh fruits, vegetables, nuts, grains, beans and legumes, and milks and yogurts, you can set yourself up for cuisine-creating success that will be simple, as well as enjoyable and fun! Here are a few lists of the best ingredients to keep on hand:

CLEAN PROTEINS: DAIRY, SOY, AND BEANS

- Beans (all, dried or fresh—not canned)
- Raw nuts and seeds
- Natural nut butters
- Eggs and vegan egg substitutes
- Fat-free, plain yogurt (regular or Greek style)
- Low-fat cottage cheese
- Nondairy milks (almond, rice, and soy)
- Kefir
- Tofu
- Tempeh
- Quinoa, hemp seed, and flax-seed (considered proteins and carbohydrates)

ALERT

Because of phytoestrogens (naturally occurring plant estrogens) in soy, the soy products that are marketed as healthy vegetarian options have come under scrutiny as possibly contributing to certain types of cancers and illnesses. No studies have proven or disproved the theories thus far, but educating yourself as much as possible and staying up to date on research will help you make informed decisions about soy products and your diet.

CLEAN COMPLEX CARBOHYDRATES: WHOLE GRAINS

- Bran cereal
- Rolled oats
- Cream of Wheat
- Buckwheat
- 100% whole-wheat bread
- Sprouted grain bread
- 100% whole-wheat pasta
- 100% whole-wheat tortillas
- Bulgur
- Quinoa
- Millet
- Wheat germ

CLEAN COMPLEX CARBOHYDRATES: VEGETABLES

- Beets
- Broccoli
- Cabbage
- Carrots
- Cauliflower
- Celery
- Corn
- Green beans
- Kale
- Onions
- Peas
- Peppers
- Potatoes
- Romaine lettuce
- Spinach
- Squash
- Sweet potatoes
- Zucchini

ESSENTIAL

If you're going to spend the time and money to stock your fridge with fresh vegetables, you can make it easier to use them up by prepping them ahead. Rather than letting vegetables go bad because you feel like it will take forever to prep them, chop, dice, and slice the vegetables within twenty-four to forty-eight hours after bringing them home. You'll save money, save time, and save the guilt of wasting precious foods.

CLEAN COMPLEX CARBOHYDRATES: FRUITS

- Apples
- Avocado
- Bananas
- Blackberries
- Blueberries
- Cantaloupe
- Grapefruit
- Grapes
- Honeydew melons
- Kiwi
- Lemons
- Limes
- Mango
- Oranges
- Papayas
- Peaches
- Pears
- Pineapple
- Pomegranates
- Raspberries
- Strawberries
- Tomatoes

ESSENTIAL

One of the best tricks to keep your fruit intake on track is to keep your favorite fruit choices in your fridge and on your countertop. If you find yourself looking for a snack or meal and can't decide what would satisfy your hunger, a long stare in the fridge that's packed with an assortment of beautiful and delicious fruit is, more often than not, going to result in a healthy choice that will satisfy your hunger, your sweet tooth, *and* suggested fruit servings.

CLEAN FATS

- Almonds
- Avocado oil
- Bee pollen
- Canola oil
- Cashews
- Coconut oil
- Flaxseeds
- Hemp seeds
- Olive oil
- Pistachios
- Walnuts

CLEAN SWEETENERS

- Agave nectar
- Fruit sugar
- Organic honey
- Rapadura (sugar cane juice)
- Sucanat (whole cane sugar)
- Turbinado sugar (cane extract)

ALERT

In your trek to find the perfect alternative to refined white sugar, keep in mind that many sugars that are marketed as natural may not meet your standards for limited refinement. By doing a little bit of research or spending some time in the grocery store comparing and contrasting certain brands and types available, you can make a decision that fits your needs.

THE WORST OFFENDERS: NONCLEAN INGREDIENTS

- Artificial sweeteners
- Brown sugar
- "Natural" artificial sweeteners
- "Refined" ingredients
- Solid oils and fats
- White flour
- White sugar

QUESTION

What is choline?
Choline is a nutrient that has recently received great attention. Studies have suggested that this nutrient is essential for almost every system's proper functioning—including promoting healthy brain and nerve development in fetuses and improving the impulses and connections of nerve cells. While meats are the most well-known providers of choline, vegetarians and vegans can reap the benefits of added choline with eggs or dried soy beans, respectively.

Staying Motivated

The worst part of any diet is the terrible stigma that comes from being on one, and the limitations and sacrifice you feel as soon as you start. As with almost everything in life, there can be times when your lifestyle and/or diet momentarily lose their appeal. For whatever reasons you may have to sway from your clean vegetarian eating, there are far more to stick with it! The clean vegetarian lifestyle is designed with health-focused guidelines that are intended to help you eat and live in a new way that will help you to maximize your health potential and improve your quality of life. This novel way of thinking of food as fueling your body is not a diet, though, it's a lifestyle!

When you feel those momentary lapses in judgment or temptations coming on, keep the following points in mind to help you stay motivated.

Remember Your Reasons

Whether you decided to start your clean vegetarian lifestyle for moral reasons or weight loss, improving one aspect of your health or the total package, your initial motivations can be excellent keys in keeping you motivated. If you start to feel discouraged, you can refocus your energy to maintain healthy food choices by simply remembering the initial incentives that led you to your new way of eating and living.

Eat What You Like

There's nothing worse than feeling like your food choices are limited to only a few bland food options. That's why the clean vegetarian lifestyle is a lifestyle and not a diet; the wide variety of food choices from which you can choose to create five or six meals a day provides different flavors and textures that can stand alone or be combined with others to make for enjoyable eating around the clock! Eating delicious foods closest to their natural forms is the goal of this lifestyle, so all of your favorites are still options you can include . . . just without undesirable additives and processing.

Experiment with New Ingredients

If you've never tried certain foods, an amazing taste adventure awaits! You can keep things fresh and exciting by aiming to experiment with new foods that can lend fresh flavors and tantalizing textures to any recipe. While you know your likes and dislikes, venturing outside the confines of your traditional taste preferences can open up your dietary world to include new favorite foods you may never have even considered. Keep your mind open to trying new foods.

Don't Keep Bad Foods Around

Temptation can be the worst distraction from good intentions. If you stock your pantry and fridge with delicious, nutritious foods, you set yourself up for success. But, if those healthy options are next to unhealthy alternatives, temptation to indulge in not-so-clean foods can strike. The easiest way to avoid a situation like this is to eliminate the not-so-clean foods from your space. By surrounding yourself with delicious meal and snack options, you can allow yourself to pick and choose freely, rather than make a difficult decision between good and bad.

Keep Water on Hand

By keeping water at your side at all times, you can keep yourself on track by quenching hunger pains that are actually caused by thirst, fill your need for "filling up" with something that's actually clean and beneficial, and calm cravings for unhealthy foods by occupying your mouth and your mind with a quality, life-sustaining clean ingredient. When boredom, cravings, and temptation start tricking you into indulging in foods you'd otherwise avoid, reach for the clear, clean liquid alternative and enjoy the benefits of health that result from sticking to something that's always the best choice!

If You Fall Off, Get Right Back On

If you do succumb to temptation or find yourself in a situation where clean options just aren't available, the world is not over! If you fall off track by choice or circumstance, all you have to do is get right back on. The clean, vegetarian lifestyle is not one that backfires with a "bad day." Unlike diets that require you adhere to strict rules and guidelines or suffer the consequences of your hard work's benefits unraveling or completely disappearing altogether, the clean vegetarian lifestyle is one that is all about choices; with more good choices, you enjoy more benefits that positively affect your health and your life . . . but the sliding scale will not explode because of bad choices.

Tips for Eating Clean Away from Home

Whether it's a quick trip or extended vacation, the clean vegetarian lifestyle can be enjoyed as easily away from home as it is in your regular routine. By setting yourself up for success with preparation and planning, you can utilize some simple solutions ahead of time to avoid some common setbacks posed by on-the-road obstacles. Simply and easily, you can enjoy the ways of your clean vegetarian lifestyle and continue eating healthy even while traveling.

Plan Ahead

Knowing the duration of your time away from home, what will be available to you, and when, you can plan your healthy meals and snacks ahead of time and avoid getting stuck in situations where unhealthy alternatives are your only options. Arm yourself with information about stores in the area on your travels and at your destination, what foods will be available, what foods you'll need to bring, and a general idea of what meals and snacks would be ideal for in the car, on a plane, or at your final destination. For a seven-day excursion with market-fresh pit stops along the way, your plan for food prep would be far different than one for even a two-day trip with no fresh foods available in sight.

Shop Smart

A quick trip to the grocery store or fresh market is essential prior to hitting the road. Formulate a list based on your preplanned meals and snacks, and include all of the ingredients you'll need. From fresh fruits and vegetables to great grains, beans, and legumes, you'll want to make sure all of the ingredients you'll need for prepping ahead are on hand.

Prep Ahead

There are a wide variety of meals and snacks that can be prepped ahead of time for any trip. Prepared pastas, fruits, vegetables, grains, and almost every combination of them can be made ahead of time and simply stored so they're readily available for each and every meal and snack you'll want on-the-go. From ready-on-the-fly packaging to requiring a little more involved preparation, you can cut, chop, and precook individual ingredients and store them to be eaten alone or combined when needed. Sauces and additions can also be added to your nutritional arsenal to be used at just the right time.

Pack It Up

A small cooler, a large cooler, glass containers, small zip-tight baggies, and other handy to-go containers can hold your foods safely while preserving their tastes and textures. Not only can these travel-food essentials house your on-the-go ingredients, but the simplicity of your packing and storing can keep foods that you'll need sooner than later separate from those you'll need later than sooner. Preparing, planning, and packing your foods in a simple way that makes them easily accessible will help make your clean vegetarian lifestyle as easy on-the-go as it is at home.

Don't Forget the Water

There's nothing worse than being stuck without water! Whether it's a dehydration headache, a dry mouth, or stomach pains, the uncomfortable physical consequences of going stretches of time without water can be terrible. Being held captive in a car, plane, or room without the water you're dying for is the only thing that could make it worse! So, don't let the fears of frequent bathroom trips, lugging extra baggage, or the label of being that person who's bringing along tons of water sway you from adding an adequate water supply to your travel needs.

Vegan Options

One of the most appealing aspects of the clean vegetarian lifestyle is that it can be adapted to almost every alternative lifestyle with simple alterations or substitutions. The recipes that are contained within this book are different than those in other cookbooks that focus specifically on a clean diet or a vegetarian diet because they fully encompass both lifestyles with the added benefit of including the necessary information you'll need to transform each recipe into a vegan option. As with all great things in life, the clean vegetarian lifestyle comes with choices and options. For vegans who choose to use this book, take note of the vegan ingredients in most recipes, and the suggested substitutions available for those that are not. Keep this simple list of dairy and egg substitutes to use for future reference:

INGREDIENT	VEGAN SUBSTITUTION
1 cup cows' milk	1 cup plain, unsweetened almond milk or soy milk
1 cup buttermilk	1 cup plain, unsweetened almond milk or soy milk + 2 tablespoons lemon juice (mixed and allowed to sit for 5–10 minutes before use)
1 cup sour cream	1 cup soy yogurt or 1 cup dairy free yogurt or 1 cup silken tofu
1 cup ricotta cheese	1 cup mashed soft tofu + ½ tablespoon lemon juice
1 cup butter	¾ cup canola oil
1 egg	¼ cup vegan egg substitute
1 egg	1½ tablespoons Ener-G Egg Replacer (vegan egg replacement) + 2 tablespoons water
1 egg	¼ cup mashed apple or banana (works well for binding purposes in baking, as in pies and custards)
1 egg	¼ cup water + 1 tablespoon ground flaxseed (works well for thickening/binding purposes in baking, as in breads, and cakes)
1 egg	¼ cup plain, unsweetened almond milk or soy milk + 1 tablespoon lemon juice (leavening purposes in baking, as in cookies, cakes, and muffins)
1 egg white	½ tablespoon Ener-G Egg Replacer (vegan egg replacement) + 2 tablespoons water
1 egg yolk	½ tablespoon Ener-G Egg Replacer (vegan egg replacement) + 2 tablespoons water

The best way to determine which substitutions work best for specific foods is to experiment. Through trial and error, you can perfect any recipe's taste and texture to appeal to your desires. With the added benefit of new vegan products becoming available consistently, you can also check out your local supermarket or health food retailer for the newest vegan options and alternatives that could better fit your needs for simple substitutions.

CHAPTER 3

Breakfasts

Spinach, Red Onion, and
Mushroom Frittata
42

Protein-Packed Breakfast
Burritos
43

Clean Huevos Rancheros
44

Clean Black Bean
Huevos Rancheros
45

Apple-Cinnamon Pancakes
46

Simple Sweet Potato Pancakes
47

Best-Ever Breakfast Bars
48

Clean Protein Power Bars
49

Fruity French Toast Sandwiches
50

Protein-Packed Parfaits
51

Fast Fruit-Oatmeal Bowls
52

Fruity Egg White Frittata
53

Homemade Scallion
Hash Brown Cakes
54

Baked Fruit with Cinnamon
and Spice
55

Toasted Almond Butter
Banana Sandwiches
55

Over-the-Top Cinnamon
Walnut Oatmeal
56

Banana Bread with Walnuts
and Flaxseed
57

Veggie and Egg White Omelets
58

Sunshine Corn Muffins
59

Poached Eggs with
Spicy Chive Cream
60

Spinach, Red Onion, and Mushroom Frittata

A delicious combination of iron-rich spinach and antioxidant-packed red onion and mushrooms, this frittata delivers loads of tasty nutrition.

INGREDIENTS | SERVES 6

6 eggs, or vegan egg substitute
2 tablespoons water
½ cup sliced or diced red onion
1 cup sliced mushrooms
1 cup fresh spinach
1 teaspoon all-natural sea salt
1 teaspoon cracked black pepper

Bone Benefits of Spinach

While spinach has long been recognized as a nutritious green for its high content of iron and complex carbohydrates, the vitamin K content of this superfood is far more impressive. With each cup of cooked spinach comes more than 181 percent of the daily recommendation for vitamin K, which has the primary role of preventing bone loss and promoting bone strength. By inhibiting the activity of *osteoclasts* (cells that act to deteriorate bone) and providing nourishment to *osteoblasts* (cells that build bone and support their structure), spinach's heavy dose of vitamin K is an essential part of any diet in need of bone-supporting benefits.

1. Preheat the oven to 350°F.

2. In a mixing bowl, thoroughly combine the eggs (or egg substitute) and 1 tablespoon of water.

3. Preheat a large, ovenproof skillet over medium heat, and spray with nonstick spray.

4. Add 1 tablespoon of water and the red onion to the skillet and sauté until slightly softened, about 2 minutes.

5. Add the mushrooms to the skillet and sauté for 2 minutes.

6. Add spinach to the skillet and sauté for 1 minute before adding the egg mixture.

7. Place entire skillet into the oven and bake for 20 minutes, or until firm to touch.

8. Season with salt and pepper.

PER SERVING Calories: 82 | Fat: 5 g | Protein: 7 g
Sodium: 468 mg | Fiber: 0.5 g | Carbohydrates: 2 g
Sugar: 1 g

Protein-Packed Breakfast Burritos

Spicy Clean Refried Beans take the starring role in this delicious breakfast, providing healthy amounts of protein in every scrumptious bite! With ingredients that appeal to both vegetarians and vegans, this is the perfect long-lasting, energy-providing meal for all!

INGREDIENTS | SERVES 2

½ red pepper, diced

1 small jalapeño, seeds removed, and sliced or chopped

½ yellow onion, diced

4 eggs, or 1 cup vegan egg substitute

2 tablespoons water

2 100% whole-wheat tortillas

1 cup Spicy Clean Refried Beans (see Chapter 9)

2 tablespoons Greek-style nonfat yogurt, or vegan sour cream

¼ cup shredded romaine lettuce

¼ cup diced tomatoes

1. Coat a large skillet with olive oil spray and place over medium heat.

2. Add the red pepper, jalapeño, and onions to the pan and sauté until cooked, but not soft, about 5 minutes.

3. In a mixing bowl, beat together the eggs and water and pour over the vegetables. Scramble together until light and fluffy.

4. Lay out 2 tortillas and spread ½ cup of the Spicy Clean Refried Beans on each.

5. Top beans on each with 1 tablespoon of the yogurt, and layer egg mixture on top.

6. Sprinkle lettuce and tomato on top of each tortilla, and wrap tightly.

PER SERVING Calories: 375 | Fat: 14 g | Protein: 23 g | Sodium: 877 mg | Fiber: 8.5 g | Carbohydrates: 41 g | Sugar: 5.5 g

Clean Huevos Rancheros

Packed with clean ingredients that all provide quality nutrition, these huevos rancheros are a healthier version that you can actually feel good about eating.

INGREDIENTS | SERVES 4

4 whole-wheat tortillas
8 eggs, or 2 cups vegan egg substitute
1 tablespoon water
2 cups Fresh Salsa (see Chapter 5)
2 tablespoons chopped fresh cilantro

1. In a large skillet prepared with nonstick spray over medium heat, warm tortillas individually, about 1–2 minutes. Quickly wrap with tinfoil to keep warm until use.

2. Spray skillet with more nonstick spray and add the eggs carefully, not breaking the yolks. Cook for about 3 minutes, or until the whites turn white.

3. Add the tablespoon of water and cover. Continue cooking for 3–5 minutes, until desired doneness is achieved.

4. Lay 1 tortilla on each of 4 plates, top with 2 eggs each.

5. Return skillet to heat and add salsa to skillet, stirring constantly for 1–2 minutes or until heated through.

6. Top each tortilla's eggs with ½ cup of salsa, and garnish with chopped cilantro.

PER SERVING Calories: 271 | Fat: 12 g | Protein: 17 g | Sodium: 1,108 mg | Fiber: 3 g | Carbohydrates: 24 g | Sugar: 5 g

Clean Black Bean Huevos Rancheros

Quick and easy, these huevos rancheros pack a double-dose of protein from the eggs and black beans. Substitute the eggs with egg whites for a cholesterol-light alternative.

INGREDIENTS | SERVES 4

4 whole-wheat tortillas

2 cups prepared black beans

8 eggs, or 2 cups vegan egg substitute

1 tablespoon water

2 cups Fresh Salsa (see Chapter 5)

2 tablespoons chopped fresh cilantro

Black Beans for Fiber *and* Protein

While most fiber-rich foods predominately belong in the complex carbohydrate category (vegetables and fruits), black beans are one of the few exceptions. In a single cup of black beans, there is enough protein to satisfy nearly ⅓ of your daily protein requirement with the added benefit of nearly ⅔ your daily recommended amount of fiber! Providing benefits that range from improved muscle performance and repair to quality digestion and reduced colon cancer risk, black beans serve up satisfying health benefits and taste.

1. In a large skillet prepared with nonstick spray over medium heat, warm tortillas individually for 1–2 minutes. Quickly wrap with tinfoil to keep warm until use.

2. Add black beans to skillet and stir for about 3 minutes, or until heated through.

3. Lay 1 tortilla on each of 4 plates, and top each with ½ cup black beans.

4. Spray the pan with cooking spray again, and add the eggs to skillet carefully, not breaking the yolks. Cook for about 3 minutes, or until the whites turn white.

5. Add the tablespoon of water and cover. Continue cooking for 3–5 minutes, until desired doneness is achieved.

6. Remove eggs from heat and top each tortilla's black beans with 2 eggs.

7. Return skillet to heat and add salsa, stirring constantly for 1–2 minutes or until heated through.

8. Top each tortilla's eggs with ½ cup of salsa, and garnish with chopped cilantro.

PER SERVING Calories: 379 | Fat: 13 g | Protein: 23 g | Sodium: 1,487 mg | Fiber: 10 g | Carbohydrates: 42 g | Sugar: 7.5 g

Apple-Cinnamon Pancakes

*Sweet apples spiced with cinnamon swirl throughout these light, fluffy pancakes.
A clean carbohydrate option that's packed with delicious nutrition, these pancakes can be
enjoyed fresh at home, on the go, or reheated later for a scrumptious snack!*

INGREDIENTS | SERVES 4

1 apple, cored and chopped (peel, if desired)
1 cup whole-wheat flour
¼ cup unsweetened applesauce
1 tablespoon Rapadura or Sucanat
¾ cup plain or vanilla almond milk
2 teaspoons baking powder

1. Prepare a large skillet with olive oil spray over medium heat.

2. Sauté the chopped apples until slightly softened, about 2 minutes.

3. In a large mixing bowl, combine the whole-wheat flour, softened apples, applesauce, Rapadura or Sucanat, almond milk, and baking powder, and mix well.

4. In skillet (sprayed again with olive oil spray to prevent sticking), pour ¼ cup of batter to form each pancake. Cook for 4 minutes or until bubbles appear on surface; flip and continue cooking for 2–3 minutes until pancakes are firm.

PER SERVING Calories: 153 | Fat: 1.5 g | Protein: 6 g | Sodium: 268 mg | Fiber: 4.5 g | Carbohydrates: 32 g | Sugar: 7 g

Simple Sweet Potato Pancakes

Sweet, fluffy, and packed with clean complex carbohydrates, this brightly colored breakfast option is quick, easy, nutritious, and delicious!

INGREDIENTS | SERVES 10

1 cup sweet potato purée

1 cup plain low-fat Greek-style yogurt, or vegan sour cream

1 cup unsweetened applesauce

2 egg whites, or vegan egg white substitute

2 whole eggs, or ½ cup vegan egg substitute

2 teaspoons vanilla

2 tablespoons Sucanat

¼ cup 100% whole-wheat flour

1 teaspoon baking powder

1 teaspoon pumpkin pie spice

1 teaspoon cinnamon

2 tablespoons agave nectar

1. Coat a nonstick skillet with olive oil cooking spray and place over medium heat.

2. In a large bowl, combine all ingredients except the agave nectar and mix well.

3. Scoop the batter onto the preheated skillet, using approximately ½ cup of batter per pancake.

4. Cook 2–3 minutes on each side, or until golden brown. Remove from heat, plate, and drizzle all pancakes with the agave nectar.

PER SERVING Calories: 78 | Fat: 1 g | Protein: 7 g | Sodium: 52 mg | Fiber: 1 g | Carbohydrates: 13 g | Sugar: 6 g

Best-Ever Breakfast Bars

Delivering scrumptious crunch and fruity sweetness, these breakfast bars will load you up with clean carbohydrates without weighing you down with processed ingredients.

INGREDIENTS | SERVES 9

4 cups rolled oats

½ cup whole-wheat flour

1 cup assorted natural, unsweetened dried fruits of choice, chopped

2 eggs, or ½ cup vegan egg substitute

½ cup plain or vanilla almond milk or soymilk

1 tablespoon all-natural maple syrup

1 teaspoon cinnamon

Dangerous Sugar Substitutes

Marketed as healthier alternatives to natural sugars, synthetic sugar substitutes may be the more questionable ingredient of the two. While a diet high in refined sugar has been directly attributed with contributing to dangerous diseases, disabilities, and illnesses, the chemical concoction that provides consumers with a variety of sugar substitutes is just that: a chemical concoction. Beware of sugar substitutes, or avoid them altogether, by keeping in mind that natural is always the better alternative!

1. Spray a 9" × 9" glass pan with olive oil spray and preheat oven to 350°F.

2. In a large bowl, combine oats, flour, dried fruit, eggs, almond or soymilk, and maple syrup, and blend thoroughly.

3. Pour the mixture into the prepared pan and spread evenly. Sprinkle with cinnamon.

4. Bake for 25–35 minutes, or until firm.

5. Allow to set for 1 hour before slicing into 9 equal squares.

PER SERVING Calories: 211 g | Fat: 4 g | Protein: 7.5 g | Sodium: 33 mg | Fiber: 5 g | Carbohydrates: 38 g | Sugar: 8 g

Clean Protein Power Bars

Rather than opting for a store-bought version, try these delicious homemade power bars. Not only are they the perfect provision of muscle-promoting protein, there's the added benefit of a burst of delicious flavor in every bite.

INGREDIENTS | SERVES 9

4 cups rolled oats

¼ cup whole-wheat flour

¼ cup ground flaxseed

2 eggs, or ½ cup vegan egg substitute

1 cup all-natural almond butter

½ cup plain or vanilla almond milk or soymilk

2 tablespoons chopped or slivered almonds

1. Spray a 9" × 9" glass pan with olive oil spray and preheat oven to 350°F.

2. In a large bowl, combine oats, flour, flaxseed, eggs or egg substitute, almond butter, and almond or soymilk, and blend thoroughly.

3. Pour the mixture into the prepared pan and spread evenly. Top with chopped or slivered almonds, pressing them lightly into the top of the mixture.

4. Bake for 25–35 minutes, or until firm.

5. Allow to set for 1 hour before slicing into 9 equal squares.

PER SERVING Calories: 382 | Fat: 26 g | Protein: 8 g | Sodium: 27 mg | Fiber: 4.5 g | Carbohydrates: 28 g | Sugar: 1 g

Anti-inflammatory Benefits of Flaxseed

When it comes to great sources of omega-3 fatty acids, most people think of fish as being the best provider. Flaxseed is one of the lesser known foods that packs enough of this essential acid to greatly reduce inflammation and debilitating conditions that result. In just 2 tablespoons of flaxseeds, more than 130 percent of the recommended daily intake for omega-3s is provided. Asthma, osteoporosis, osteoarthritis, rheumatoid arthritis, and even migraines can all be improved with the daily inclusion of delicious flaxseeds in any diet.

Fruity French Toast Sandwiches

French toast has gotten a bad reputation from traditional recipes requiring loads of butter, unhealthy cream cheese, and sugar. This cleaner version satisfies the sweet tooth and suggested fruit servings with a punch of nutrition and flavor!

INGREDIENTS | SERVES 2

4 eggs (beaten), or 1 cup vegan egg substitute

2 tablespoons vanilla almond milk

2 tablespoons agave nectar

4 slices sprouted grain bread

8 tablespoons sugar-free fruit spread

1 cup nonfat Greek-style yogurt, or vegan sour cream

½ cup sliced strawberries

1 sliced banana

Sprouted Grain Bread

Sprouted grain breads are located in the frozen section of most grocery stores. They're a great option for the clean lifestyle because of their immense nutrition per slice—they contain about half the carbohydrate count of a slice of white bread. They use the sprouted germ of the wheat berry, thus the need for refrigeration.

1. Spray a large skillet with olive oil cooking spray and place over medium heat.

2. In a medium bowl, whisk together the eggs, almond milk, and agave nectar.

3. Dip each bread slice in the egg mixture and place in heated skillet.

4. Cook each slice for 2–4 minutes, or until lightly browned on each side and remove from heat.

5. Spread fruit spread evenly on one side of all bread slices, followed by a thin layer of yogurt. Layer the strawberries and bananas on two slices, and close the sandwiches by placing the other slices over the fruit.

6. Return the sandwiches to the heated frying pan and press down slightly.

7. Cook for 2–3 minutes and turn over. Continue cooking for 2–3 minutes or until both sides of the sandwiches are browned.

PER SERVING Calories: 452 | Fat: 12 g | Protein: 25 g | Sodium: 548 mg | Fiber: 3.5 g | Carbohydrates: 68 g | Sugar: 37 g

Protein-Packed Parfaits

Using ingredients that provide essential clean protein and complex carbohydrates, this recipe boosts the nutrition content of a simple breakfast favorite by focusing on natural fruits and nuts, and protein-packed yogurt that's not only delicious and creamy but healthy too!

INGREDIENTS | SERVES 2

2 cups plain low-fat yogurt, or vegan yogurt
1 cup All-Natural Granola (see Chapter 5)
2 sliced bananas
½ cup blueberries
½ cup sliced strawberries

Yogurt for All

Whatever your taste and consistency preferences, there's a yogurt out there that you'll like. This protein-packed, probiotic snack helps promote a healthy metabolism, fuels the body and mind, and builds up protection against harmful bacterial growth. Plus, soy, soy free, and other vegan yogurts are now readily available at most grocery stores.

1. Place ⅓ cup of yogurt in the bottom of 2 (16-ounce) glasses.

2. Top each with ¼ cup granola, ½ sliced banana, and ¼ cup blueberries.

3. Layer another ⅓ cup of yogurt, followed by ¼ cup granola, ½ sliced banana, and ¼ cup strawberries.

4. Top with remaining yogurt.

PER SERVING Calories: 397 | Fat: 2.5 g | Protein: 19 g | Sodium: 307 mg | Fiber: 7 g | Carbohydrates: 80 g | Sugar: 50 g

Fast Fruit-Oatmeal Bowls

By using fresh ingredients that add taste, texture, and a kick of spice, you can turn a bland bowl of oatmeal into a creative, delicious, nutritious meal or snack that's as appealing to the eyes as it is to the taste buds!

INGREDIENTS | SERVES 4

4 cups quick-cooking rolled oats

2 cups vanilla almond milk or soymilk

1 teaspoon cinnamon

1 teaspoon ground cardamom

1 cup blueberries

1 cup strawberries, tops removed and quartered

1 cup sliced peaches

1. In a large glass bowl, combine the oats and almond or soymilk with the cinnamon and cardamom. Blend well and microwave for 3–4 minutes, or until thickened.

2. Pour the oatmeal evenly into 4 separate dishes.

3. Top each serving with ¼ cup each of blueberries, strawberries, and peaches.

PER SERVING Calories: 423 | Fat: 8 g | Protein: 15.5 g | Sodium: 67 mg | Fiber: 11 g | Carbohydrates: 75 g | Sugar: 14 g

Oats for Better Blood Quality

Oats are a great clean ingredient to be included in any diet. Whether blood health is a concern because of family history, individual experience, or to maintain overall wellness, a diet rich in quality fiber sources is key to improving or maintaining quality blood composition. Studies have shown drastic improvements in cholesterol levels from the daily inclusion of oats, and it's all due to the type of fiber contained in each individual oat. Rich in a specific fiber called *beta-glucan*, oats are able to act as blood-cleaning agents that can effectively remove wastes like cholesterol from the blood.

Fruity Egg White Frittata

Fresh fruits combine with luscious spices and sweetness for an all-natural dish of protein-packed, flavorful enjoyment . . . for breakfast or any other meal!

INGREDIENTS | SERVES 6

1 cup sliced strawberries

1 cup blueberries

1 cup raspberries

10 egg whites, or vegan egg white substitute

1 teaspoon vanilla extract

1 tablespoon agave nectar

Essential Vanilla Extract

When a recipe calls for vanilla, use *real* vanilla extract. Although real vanilla extract is more expensive than imitation, the flavor is far superior. Store it in a cool, dark place.

1. Preheat oven to 350°F and spray an oven-safe frying pan with olive oil cooking spray.

2. Over medium heat, sauté all fruit together for about 1–2 minutes, until lightly heated and softened.

3. While fruit is heating, whisk together the egg whites, vanilla, and agave nectar briskly until well blended. Add to the frying pan, covering fruit completely.

4. Continue cooking for 2–4 minutes, or until the center solidifies slightly and bubbles begin to appear.

5. Remove pan from heat and place into preheated oven.

6. Cook for 10–15 minutes, or until frittata is firm in the center.

PER SERVING Calories: 70 | Fat: 0.5 g | Protein: 6.5 g | Sodium: 92 mg | Fiber: 2.5 g | Carbohydrates: 11 g | Sugar: 7.5 g

Homemade Scallion Hash Brown Cakes

Traditional fat-laden recipes of this breakfast favorite get cleaned up in this new and improved version by using heart-healthy olive oil and fresh ingredients that provide clean complex carbohydrates and antioxidants in every crispy cake!

INGREDIENTS | SERVES 6

3 Idaho potatoes, shredded

1 cup chopped scallions

1 egg, or vegan egg substitute

2 tablespoons 100% whole-wheat flour

1 teaspoon garlic powder

1 tablespoon extra-virgin olive oil

1 teaspoon all-natural sea salt

½ teaspoon cracked black pepper

Better Your Brain Functioning with Better Potatoes

Because potatoes have received a bad reputation as an unhealthy starchy carbohydrate, it's important to clarify that there are bountiful benefits of including clean potato recipes in your diet. With a single potato providing a whopping 20 percent of your daily recommended vitamin B_6 intake, a meal including a baked, sautéed, steamed, or mashed potato contributes to the health of your brain's processes by focusing on the most intricate of all its parts: the cell. Promoting cell production, cell regeneration and repair, and cell functioning and communication, potatoes' provision of B_6 can help your mind be clear and your brain function as it's intended.

1. Spray a large skillet with olive oil spray and place over medium heat.

2. In a large mixing bowl, combine shredded potatoes, scallions, egg, flour, and garlic powder.

3. Form potato mixture into 6 even servings, and mold into dense patties.

4. Heat the olive oil in the skillet for 1 minute and swirl to evenly coat.

5. Add patties to skillet, 3 at a time, cooking 5–7 minutes per side or until golden brown and cooked through. Season with salt and pepper.

PER SERVING Calories: 131 | Fat: 3 g | Protein: 4 g | Sodium: 412 mg | Fiber: 2 g | Carbohydrates: 22 g | Sugar: 1.5 g

Baked Fruit with Cinnamon and Spice

A great way to spruce up any old fruit plate, this recipe bakes a beautiful variety of fruit to accentuate their sweet, natural flavors. This is one delicious way to enjoy the healthy fruits you love!

INGREDIENTS | SERVES 6

1½ teaspoons cinnamon

1½ teaspoons ground ginger

1 teaspoon ground cardamom

2 apples, cored and sliced into ¼" slices (peeled, if desired)

2 pears, cored and sliced into ¼" slices (peeled, if desired)

2 peaches, pitted and sliced into ¼" slices (peeled, if desired)

1. Preheat oven to 350°F and prepare a 13" × 9" glass baking dish with olive oil spray.

2. In a large mixing bowl, combine all spices thoroughly. Add fruit slices to spice mixture and toss to coat.

3. Arrange the fruit slices evenly throughout the baking dish, and bake for 15–20 minutes or until fork tender.

PER SERVING Calories: 80 | Fat: 0 g | Protein: 1 g | Sodium: 1 mg | Fiber: 3.5 g | Carbohydrates: 21 g | Sugar: 15 g

Toasted Almond Butter Banana Sandwiches

Packed with potassium, complex carbohydrates, and protein, this clean breakfast sandwich is the perfect meal or snack with just the right nutrition to be enjoyed at any time of the day you need a little natural pick-me-up!

INGREDIENTS | SERVES 2

2 100% whole-wheat English muffins, halved and toasted

4 tablespoons almond butter

1 banana, sliced

1. Spread each English muffin half with 1 tablespoon almond butter.

2. Top 2 muffin halves with banana slices.

3. Place other English muffin half on top and enjoy.

PER SERVING Calories: 316 | Fat: 9 g | Protein: 7.5 g | Sodium: 267 mg | Fiber: 4.5 g | Carbohydrates: 53 g | Sugar: 17 g

Over-the-Top Cinnamon Walnut Oatmeal

A simple recipe that adds tons of flavor and texture to the traditional bowl of oatmeal, this is a delicious way to indulge in a carbohydrate-fueled meal that provides plentiful antioxidants, omega-3s, omega-6s, and protein!

INGREDIENTS | SERVES 4

4 cups quick-cooking rolled oats

2 cups plain or vanilla almond milk or soymilk

2 teaspoons cinnamon

1 cup walnuts, crushed

Walnuts for a Slimmer Waistline

Walnuts are a well-known provider of fat. While some people may be dissuaded from including this tree nut in their daily diet because of that fact alone, there is more to consider when it comes to the fat found in walnuts. Rich in omega-3 fatty acids, the walnut's fat content has actually been shown to reduce the severity of metabolic conditions like high blood pressure, high blood fats (triglycerides), and obesity. In addition to improving the severity of metabolic conditions, walnuts have also been shown to reduce the waistline of those who include at least one ounce in their diet per day.

1. In a large glass bowl, combine the oats and almond or soymilk with the cinnamon. Blend well and microwave for 3–4 minutes, or until thickened.

2. Pour oatmeal evenly into 4 separate dishes.

3. Top each dish with ¼ cup crushed walnuts and stir to combine thoroughly.

PER SERVING Calories: 566 | Fat: 26 g | Protein: 19 g | Sodium: 67 mg | Fiber: 11 g | Carbohydrates: 67 g | Sugar: 6 g

Banana Bread with Walnuts and Flaxseed

Created using natural fruits and clean alternatives to unhealthy additions, this banana bread has all the flavor of your favorite classic with impressive amounts of health-boosting nutrients.

INGREDIENTS | SERVES 12

½ cup 100% whole-wheat baking flour

½ cup oat flour

¾ cup ground flaxseed

½ cup Sucanat

1 teaspoon cinnamon

1 teaspoon baking soda

½ teaspoon baking powder

3 cups mashed bananas (about 3–4 medium-large bananas)

½ cup unsweetened applesauce

3 egg whites, or egg white substitute

1 egg, or ¼ cup vegan egg substitute

1 teaspoon vanilla extract

1 cup chopped natural walnuts

1. Preheat oven to 350°F.

2. Spray a loaf pan with olive oil cooking spray and cover with a thin coating of wheat flour.

3. In a large mixing bowl, combine flours, flaxseed, Sucanat, cinnamon, baking soda, and baking powder.

4. Add bananas, applesauce, egg whites, egg, and vanilla. Mix to combine.

5. Incorporate walnuts evenly throughout the batter.

6. Pour batter into the prepared pan and bake for 45–60 minutes, or until a knife inserted in the middle comes out clean.

PER SERVING Calories: 215 | Fat: 10 g | Protein: 6.5 g | Sodium: 146 mg | Fiber: 5 g | Carbohydrates: 28 g | Sugar: 14 g

An Entire Day's Serving?

Just ¼ cup of natural walnuts has almost an entire day's recommended value of omega-3s, an essential fatty acid our bodies can't produce. Omega-3s are an important element of any daily diet because it is absolutely critical for optimal brain and body system functioning. By gobbling up just a handful of these portable tasty treats, you're quickly and easily fueling your brain and your body.

Veggie and Egg White Omelets

Perfect for a quick meal or snack that delivers quality nutrition and tons of great taste, this is the perfect recipe for an omelet that's low in fat and calories, and high in clean protein and complex carbohydrates.

INGREDIENTS | SERVES 1

¼ cup red onion, chopped

¼ cup broccoli florets, chopped

2 tablespoons water

¼ cup mushrooms, chopped

1 cup egg whites, or vegan egg white substitute

¼ cup tomato, chopped

1 teaspoon all-natural sea salt

½ teaspoon cracked black pepper

1. Prepare an omelet pan with olive oil spray and place over medium heat.

2. Add the chopped red onion, broccoli, and water to the skillet, and sauté until vegetables are slightly softened, about 2 minutes.

3. Add mushrooms to the skillet, and sauté until slightly softened, about 1 minute.

4. Pour the egg whites or vegan egg white substitute over the vegetable mixture to cover completely. Cook until edges are set, about 3–4 minutes, flip and continue cooking for 3–4 minutes or until cooked through.

5. Remove from heat and slide onto a plate. Top with tomatoes, season with salt and pepper, and fold over.

PER SERVING Calories: 155 | Fat: 1 g | Protein: 28 g | Sodium: 277 mg | Fiber: 2 g | Carbohydrates: 10 g | Sugar: 5 g

Sunshine Corn Muffins

The uniquely sweet bursts of crunchy corn kernels explode in every bite of these perfectly proportioned powerhouse muffins that provide your body with energy-fueling carbohydrates, protein, and fat to get you going and keep you moving!

INGREDIENTS | SERVES 12

1 cup 100% whole-wheat flour

1 cup cornmeal

2 teaspoons baking soda

2 teaspoons baking powder

2 eggs, or ½ cup vegan egg substitute

2 egg whites, or ½ cup vegan egg white substitute

½ cup unsweetened applesauce

3 tablespoons agave nectar

2 cups vanilla almond milk

½ cup plain nonfat yogurt

2 tablespoons canola oil

1 cup kernel corn (fresh or frozen)

1. Preheat oven to 425°F. Grease a 12-cup muffin pan or line with paper baking cups.

2. In a large bowl, combine the flour, cornmeal, baking soda, and baking powder, and mix thoroughly. Add the eggs, egg whites, applesauce, agave nectar, almond milk, yogurt, and canola oil. Mix well.

3. Fold in the corn kernels, and spoon evenly into muffin cups.

4. Bake for 30–45 minutes, or until golden brown and inserted fork comes out clean.

PER SERVING Calories: 166 | Fat: 5 g | Protein: 5 g | Sodium: 386 mg | Fiber: 2.5 g | Carbohydrates: 26 g | Sugar: 6 g

Crunchy Cornmeal

Cornmeal can jazz up foods with a unique crunchy texture and taste. Try adding vegetables (raw or sautéed) to cornmeal breads and muffins for a new way to eat your vegetables! Low in fat, and a great source of energy, cornmeal is versatile, delicious, and nutritious.

Poached Eggs with Spicy Chive Cream

This clean version of eggs Benedict provides all of the great flavors without the mess of empty calories and unhealthy ingredients.

INGREDIENTS | SERVES 4

2 cups water

1 teaspoon all-natural sea salt

8 eggs, or 2 cups vegan egg substitute

2 cups low-fat Greek-style yogurt, or vegan sour cream

1 tablespoon lemon juice

½ cup chopped chives

¼ teaspoon cayenne pepper

Spice Up Your Metabolism

Hot spices not only add unique flavors to your favorite dishes, but they can speed up your metabolism as well! Sprinkling these spicy additions into your creative cuisines improves your fat-burning potential by raising your internal temperature just enough that your body is forced to work harder to bring it back to a normal level. This extra work requires a temporary spike in your metabolism's speed, resulting in more calories burned.

1. In a large saucepan over medium heat, bring the water and salt to a boil. Reduce heat to low until bubbles are no longer surfacing.

2. Crack eggs directly over water, careful to keep yolks intact and enough space between each so that the yolks don't touch.

3. Cook eggs until the whites are set and the yolks are firm, about 5–7 minutes.

4. While eggs are cooking, combine yogurt, lemon juice, and chives in a small bowl and set aside.

5. Carefully scoop the eggs from saucepan and set 2 each on 4 separate plates.

6. While eggs are hot, spoon ¼ cup of yogurt mixture over top, and sprinkle with cayenne.

PER SERVING Calories: 220 | Fat: 14 g | Protein: 17 g | Sodium: 790 mg | Fiber: 0 g | Carbohydrates: 7 g | Sugar: 6.5 g

CHAPTER 4

Smoothies

Tofu Berry Smoothie
62

Blueberry Cobbler Smoothie
62

Cherry-Pineapple Pucker
63

Sweet Citrus Smoothie
63

Pear Paradise
64

Crunchy Chai Confection
64

Perfect Pineapple-Banana Blend
65

Peachy Protein Smoothie
65

Spicy Cinnamon-Almond
Smoothie
66

Mango Medley
66

Savory Spinach, Tomato, and
Garlic Smoothie
67

Simple Strawberry-Banana
Smoothie
67

Spiced Apple Surprise
68

Dreamy Melon Cream Smoothie
68

Crazy for Cranberry-Orange
69

Sweet Potato Pie Smoothie
69

Banana-Nut Smoothie
70

Clean "Chocolate"–Almond
Butter Smoothie
71

Clean Green Go-Getter
71

Clean Piña Colada
72

Tofu Berry Smoothie

This smoothie creates a beneficial blend of powerful antioxidants that act to promote the health of all of the body's cells while providing the essential protein needed to promote the chemical reactions that take place within them.

INGREDIENTS | SERVES 4

1 cup silken tofu
1 cup blueberries
1 cup strawberries, tops removed
1 cup raspberries
1 cup ice
1 cup water

1. Combine the tofu, blueberries, strawberries, raspberries, ½ cup of ice, and ½ cup of water in a blender. Blend until thoroughly combined.

2. Add remaining ice and water as needed while blending until desired consistency is achieved.

PER SERVING Calories: 83 | Fat: 2 g | Protein: 5 g | Sodium: 22 mg | Fiber: 3.5 g | Carbohydrates: 13 g | Sugar: 7.5 g

Blueberry Cobbler Smoothie

Rather than baking up a clean blueberry cobbler, you can blend one up instead! A great way to add some clean protein and carbohydrates to your favorite blueberry smoothie, this recipe includes All-Natural Granola for added flavor.

INGREDIENTS | SERVES 4

2 cups blueberries
1 cup All-Natural Granola (see Chapter 5)
1 cup organic apple juice, not from concentrate
1 cup ice

1. Combine the blueberries, granola, apple juice, and ½ cup of the ice in a blender, and blend until thoroughly combined.

2. Add remaining ice while blending until desired consistency is achieved.

PER SERVING Calories: 147 | Fat: 1.5 g | Protein: 3 g | Sodium: 4 mg | Fiber: 4 g | Carbohydrates: 31 g | Sugar: 13.5 g

Cherry-Pineapple Pucker

This recipe will satisfy your cravings for sweet and tangy while providing unique antioxidants like bromelain and anthocyanins to protect and promote your overall health and well-being.

INGREDIENTS | SERVES 4

2 cups cherries, pitted

2 cups pineapple chunks

1 cup organic apple juice, not from concentrate

1 cup ice

1. Combine the cherries, pineapple, ½ cup apple juice, and ½ cup of the ice in a blender, and blend until thoroughly combined.

2. Add remaining apple juice and ice while blending until desired consistency is achieved.

PER SERVING Calories: 118 | Fat: 0 g | Protein: 1 g | Sodium: 33 mg | Fiber: 3 g | Carbohydrates: 30 g | Sugar: 24 g

Pineapple's Many Benefits

The vibrant yellow tropical fruit we all know and love gets its beautiful coloring from its high content of *beta-carotene*. Combined with *bromelain*—a specific phytochemical unique to pineapples—vitamin A, and vitamin C help to promote the body's immune system functioning while also boosting the cells' defenses against foreign invaders like free radicals.

Sweet Citrus Smoothie

Forego the traditional morning glass of orange juice and opt for this fiber-packed citrus smoothie instead. This recipe is brimming with essential fiber and vitamin C for energy-boosting power and immunity protection in every delicious sip!

INGREDIENTS | SERVES 4

2 oranges, peeled and deseeded

1 cup pineapple chunks

2 red grapefruits, peeled and deseeded

1 cup ice

1. Combine the oranges, pineapple, grapefruits, and ½ cup of the ice in a blender. Blend until thoroughly combined.

2. Add remaining ice while blending until desired consistency is achieved.

PER SERVING Calories: 92 | Fat: 0 g | Protein: 1.5 g | Sodium: 0 mg | Fiber: 3.5 g | Carbohydrates: 23 g | Sugar: 19 g

Pear Paradise

Filled with fiber, antioxidants, and protein, this smoothie packs loads of cancer-preventing benefits in a simple, sweet, creamy treat!

INGREDIENTS | SERVES 4

4 pears, cored

1 cup low-fat Greek-style yogurt, or vegan soy yogurt

1 cup organic apple juice, not from concentrate

1 teaspoon cinnamon

1 cup ice

1. Combine the pears, yogurt, ½ cup apple juice, cinnamon, and ½ cup of the ice in a blender. Blend until thoroughly combined.

2. Add remaining apple juice and ice while blending until desired consistency is achieved.

PER SERVING Calories: 163 | Fat: 2 g | Protein: 3 g | Sodium: 32 mg | Fiber: 5.5 g | Carbohydrates: 36 g | Sugar: 25 g

Crunchy Chai Confection

A coffeehouse chai confection packs loads of calories, fat, and sugar with few healthy ingredients. This smoothie is loaded with all-natural ingredients that provide clean carbohydrates and protein, B vitamins, and potassium.

INGREDIENTS | SERVES 2

2 bananas, peeled

1 cup All-Natural Granola (see Chapter 5)

1 cup vanilla almond milk

1 teaspoon ground cardamom

1 teaspoon ground ginger

½ teaspoon ground cloves

1 cup ice

1. Combine the bananas, granola, almond milk, cardamom, ginger, cloves, and ½ cup of the ice in a blender. Blend until thoroughly combined.

2. Add remaining ice while blending until desired consistency is achieved.

PER SERVING Calories: 332 | Fat: 5 g | Protein: 10 g | Sodium: 67 mg | Fiber: 8 g | Carbohydrates: 63 g | Sugar: 19 g

Perfect Pineapple-Banana Blend

This smoothie is a perfect treat to enjoy morning, noon, or night! Brimming with powerful nutrients like bromelain, vitamin C, and potassium that boost your immunity, this smoothie is far more than just a delicious indulgence.

INGREDIENTS | SERVES 4

3 bananas, peeled

2 cups pineapple chunks

1 cup water

1 cup ice

1. Combine the bananas, pineapple, ½ cup water, and ½ cup of the ice in a blender, and blend until thoroughly combined.

2. Add remaining water and ice while blending until desired consistency is achieved.

PER SERVING Calories: 120 | Fat: 0 g | Protein: 1 g | Sodium: 2 mg | Fiber: 3.5 g | Carbohydrates: 31 g | Sugar: 18 g

Peachy Protein Smoothie

This sweet, creamy, protein-packed peach smoothie will remind you of the delectable nectar you can only get from a juicy peach.

INGREDIENTS | SERVES 4

4 peaches, pitted

2 cups low-fat Greek-style yogurt or silken tofu

1 cup ice

1 cup water

1. Combine the peaches, yogurt or tofu, and ½ cup of the ice in a blender. Blend until thoroughly combined.

2. Add water gradually, as needed, and remaining ice while blending until desired consistency is achieved.

PER SERVING Calories: 132 | Fat: 4 g | Protein: 5.5 g | Sodium: 56 mg | Fiber: 2 g | Carbohydrates: 20 g | Sugar: 18 g

Spicy Cinnamon-Almond Smoothie

Providing powerful antioxidants to this sweet almond smoothie, a double dose of strong spices kick this smoothie's intensity up a notch!

INGREDIENTS | SERVES 2

2 cups vanilla almond milk
½ cup whole, natural almonds
1 tablespoon cinnamon
⅛ teaspoon cayenne pepper
1½ cups ice

1. Combine the almond milk, almonds, cinnamon, cayenne pepper, and 1 cup of the ice in a blender, and blend until thoroughly combined.

2. Add remaining ice while blending until desired consistency is achieved.

PER SERVING Calories: 276 | Fat: 16 g | Protein: 13 g | Sodium: 124 mg | Fiber: 6 g | Carbohydrates: 23 g | Sugar: 10 g

Mango Medley

The vitamin C–packed mango has immense flavor and nutrition that's well worth including in your diet on a regular basis. Simple and easy, this is an all-natural way to savor the flavor of mangoes any time.

INGREDIENTS | SERVES 4

3 cups mango, peeled and cubed
1 cup coconut water
1 cup ice

1. Combine the mangoes, coconut water, and ½ cup of the ice in a blender, and blend until thoroughly combined.

2. Add remaining ice while blending until desired consistency is achieved.

PER SERVING Calories: 151 | Fat: 7 g | Protein: 1 g | Sodium: 6 mg | Fiber: 4 g | Carbohydrates: 24 g | Sugar: 19 g

Savory Spinach, Tomato, and Garlic Smoothie

Rather than satisfying that midafternoon craving for salt with unhealthy snacks that are loaded with preservatives and sodium, opt for this delicious blend of spinach and garlic that will calm your cravings with the added benefit of powerful vitamins, minerals, and antioxidants.

INGREDIENTS | SERVES 2

2 cups spinach

1 large tomato, cored

3 cloves garlic, peeled

1 teaspoon cracked black pepper

1 cup ice

1 cup water

1. Combine the spinach, tomato, garlic, black pepper, and ½ cup of the ice in a blender. Blend until thoroughly combined.

2. While blending, gradually add water and remaining ice until desired consistency is achieved.

PER SERVING Calories: 27 | Fat: 5.5 g | Protein: 2 g | Sodium: 28 mg | Fiber: 2 g | Carbohydrates: 5.5 g | Sugar: 2 g

Simple Strawberry-Banana Smoothie

While the ingredients may be simplistic, the protein, complex carbohydrates, and essential vitamins, minerals, and antioxidants in this smoothie make it an amazingly powerful recipe that only tastes simple!

INGREDIENTS | SERVES 4

2 cups strawberries, tops removed

2 bananas, peeled

1 cup coconut water

1 cup ice

1. Combine the strawberries, bananas, coconut water, and ½ cup of the ice in a blender, and blend until thoroughly combined.

2. Add remaining ice while blending until desired consistency is achieved.

PER SERVING Calories: 146 | Fat: 7 g | Protein: 2 g | Sodium: 5 mg | Fiber: 5 g | Carbohydrates: 22 g | Sugar: 12 g

Spiced Apple Surprise

The nostalgic aroma of apple pie swirls through this smoothie and tantalizes the taste buds with its amazing flavors.

INGREDIENTS | SERVES 4

4 apples, cored and sliced

½ cup All-Natural Granola (see Chapter 5)

2 teaspoons cinnamon

1 cup organic apple juice, not from concentrate

1 cup ice

1. Combine the apples, granola, cinnamon, and ½ cup apple juice with ½ cup of the ice in a blender. Blend until thoroughly combined.

2. Gradually add remaining apple juice and ice while blending until desired consistency is achieved.

PER SERVING Calories: 146 | Fat: 1 g | Protein: 2 g | Sodium: 3 mg | Fiber: 4 g | Carbohydrates: 35 g | Sugar: 22 g

Dreamy Melon Cream Smoothie

Unique flavors of cantaloupe and honeydew melons stand alone in the wide spectrum of fruit taste sensations. Dripping with super sweet vitamin C–packed juice, these melons get boosted with protein benefits by the addition of Greek-style yogurt.

INGREDIENTS | SERVES 4

1 cup cantaloupe, peeled and deseeded

1 cup honeydew melon, peeled and deseeded

1 cup nonfat Greek-style yogurt, or 1 cup silken tofu

½ cup organic apple juice, not from concentrate

1 cup ice

1. Combine the cantaloupe, honeydew, Greek-style yogurt or silken tofu, and ¼ cup of apple juice with ½ cup of the ice in a blender. Blend until thoroughly combined.

2. Add remaining apple juice and ice, gradually, while blending until desired consistency is achieved.

PER SERVING Calories: 80 | Fat: 2 g | Protein: 3 g | Sodium: 43 mg | Fiber: 1 g | Carbohydrates: 13 g | Sugar: 12 g

Crazy for Cranberry-Orange

Avoiding the confectionary consequences of manufactured products, you can enjoy the amazing flavors of cranberries and oranges in this simple smoothie. Packed with tons of beneficial nutrition, you can indulge in the sweet, tangy flavors and avoid the guilt.

INGREDIENTS | SERVES 4

4 oranges, peeled and deseeded

2 cups cranberries

1 cup ice

½ cup organic apple juice, not from concentrate

1. Combine the oranges, cranberries, and ½ cup of the ice in a blender, and blend until thoroughly combined

2. Add apple juice and remaining ice while blending until desired consistency is achieved.

PER SERVING Calories: 98 | Fat: 0 g | Protein: 1.5 g | Sodium: 2 mg | Fiber: 5.5 g | Carbohydrates: 24 g | Sugar: 17 g

Sweet Potato Pie Smoothie

While most wouldn't think to use sweet potatoes as a smoothie ingredient, the beta-carotene and vitamin C–packed vegetable adds valuable nutrition and a sweet creaminess to any smoothie.

INGREDIENTS | SERVES 2

2 large baked sweet potatoes, peeled and cooled

1 cup vanilla almond milk

1 teaspoon ground ginger

1 teaspoon cinnamon

½ teaspoon ground cloves

1 cup ice

1. Combine the sweet potatoes, almond milk, ginger, cinnamon, cloves, and ½ cup of the ice in a blender. Blend until thoroughly combined.

2. Add remaining ice while blending until desired consistency is achieved.

PER SERVING Calories: 185 | Fat: 2 g | Protein: 6 g | Sodium: 135 mg | Fiber: 5.5 g | Carbohydrates: 35 g | Sugar: 10 g

Banana-Nut Smoothie

When you're seeking that unique banana-nut flavor but want to avoid the weigh-you-down sensation of heavy breads, blend up this light, nutritious smoothie that packs in all the flavors you want without the ingredients you don't.

INGREDIENTS | SERVES 4

1 cup vanilla almond milk

½ cup whole natural almonds

½ cup shelled walnuts

1 teaspoon cinnamon

2 bananas, peeled

1 cup ice

Easy, All-Natural Homemade Almond Milk

If you're not able to find your favorite almond milk, or simply run out, your favorite smoothie base is easily created in your very own home using nothing more than two ingredients and your trusty blender. By combining 1 cup of whole, natural almonds and 1 cup of water in your blender, and blending until emulsified and no bits remain, you can create completely natural homemade almond milk for a fraction of the price. Plus, you can add subtle flavors like vanilla bean by adding the pulp of one bean to the concoction while blending.

1. Combine the almond milk, almonds, walnuts, and cinnamon in a blender and emulsify until no nut bits remain.

2. Add bananas and ½ cup of the ice in a blender, and blend until thoroughly combined.

3. Add remaining ice while blending until desired consistency is achieved.

PER SERVING Calories: 250 | Fat: 16 g | Protein: 7 g | Sodium: 32 mg | Fiber: 4.5 g | Carbohydrates: 22 g | Sugar: 10 g

Clean "Chocolate"–Almond Butter Smoothie

A clean substitute for chocolate, dates provide a great "chocolaty" flavor with immense nutrition and without unnecessary fat, calories, and sugar. If you like the taste of chocolate and peanut butter, you're going to love this delicious smoothie!

INGREDIENTS | SERVES 2

1 banana, peeled
4 dates, pitted
¼ cup raw cocoa
½ cup natural almond butter
2 cups vanilla almond milk
2 cups ice

1. Combine the banana, dates, cocoa, almond butter, and almond milk in the blender with ½ cup of the ice and blend until thoroughly combined.

2. Add remaining ice gradually while blending until desired consistency is reached.

PER SERVING Calories: 473 | Fat: 25 g | Protein: 10.5 g | Sodium: 411 mg | Fiber: 11 g | Carbohydrates: 63 g | Sugar: 38 g

Clean Green Go-Getter

Clearing your mind out of the morning fog or perking you up from the midday slump, this smoothie's ingredients are the perfect blend of carbohydrates, protein, vitamins, minerals, phytochemicals, and antioxidants that will give you the lasting blast of energy you're looking for.

INGREDIENTS | SERVES 2

1 cup spinach
½ cup broccoli florets
½ cup cauliflower florets
2 garlic cloves
2 cups water
2 cups ice

1. Combine spinach, broccoli, cauliflower, garlic, and 1½ cups of water in the blender with 1 cup of the ice. Blend until thoroughly combined.

2. Add remaining water and ice gradually while blending until desired consistency is reached.

PER SERVING Calories: 21 | Fat: 0.2 g | Protein: 2 g | Sodium: 34 mg | Fiber: 1.5 g | Carbohydrates: 4 g | Sugar: 1 g

Clean Piña Colada

Avoiding alcohol doesn't mean you can't still enjoy the scrumptious drinks you've always adored! This smoothie uses simple, all-natural ingredients that will satisfy even the most intense piña colada cravings!

INGREDIENTS | SERVES 2

2 cups pineapple chunks

1 cup coconut water

1 cup ice

1. Combine the pineapple, coconut water, and ½ cup of the ice in a blender, and blend until thoroughly combined.

2. Add remaining ice while blending until desired consistency is achieved.

PER SERVING Calories: 224 | Fat: 13 g | Protein: 2 g | Sodium: 10 mg | Fiber: 6 g | Carbohydrates: 27 g | Sugar: 18 g

CHAPTER 5

Snacks

Colorful Cabbage Rolls
74

Roasted Red Pepper and
Pine Nut Hummus
75

Roasted Red Pepper Pesto
75

Fresh Salsa
76

Fruit Salsa
76

Sweet and Spicy Sesame
Tofu Strips
77

Mediterranean Couscous–
Stuffed Tomato Poppers
78

All-Natural Granola
79

Tangy Tomatillo Salsa Verde
79

Tex-Mex Quesadillas
80

Garlic and Herb Tortilla Chips
80

Spicy Spanish Egg Quesadilla
81

Creamy Cashew Dipping Sauce
82

Tasty Tomato Sauce
82

Zucchini Bread
83

Crunchy Garlic Eggplant Chips
84

Roasted Eggplant Dip
85

Baked Potato Chips
86

Tasty Tostadas
87

Lime-Avocado Dipping Sauce
87

Perfect Pumpkin Pie Snack Bars
88

Apricot, Cranberry, Almond Bars
89

Peppy Pesto
90

Colorful Cabbage Rolls

A delicious and nutritious way to use vibrant red cabbage, these cabbage rolls are wrapped with the deep purple leaves that provide tons of vitamins and minerals.

INGREDIENTS | SERVES 6

1 tablespoon canola oil
½ cup diced white onion
½ cup chopped celery
½ cup chopped carrot
1 garlic clove, minced
2 cups red kidney beans, cooked
1½ cups cooked brown rice
4 cups Tasty Tomato Sauce (recipe in this chapter), divided
1 head red cabbage

Opt for Red When It Comes to Cabbage

Although the sheer inclusion of any cabbage in your regular diet will increase your daily intake of great vitamins and minerals like vitamin K and folic acid, this fiber-rich food is far more beneficial when you choose the vibrant violet variety. Red cabbage gets its extraordinary coloring from its rich concentration of *polyphenols* called *anthocyanins,* which help protect and promote the health of cells within the body.

1. In a large saucepan over medium heat, combine the canola oil, onion, celery, carrot, and minced garlic. Sauté for 5–7 minutes, or until slightly softened.

2. In a large mixing bowl, combine the kidney beans, rice, 2 cups tomato sauce, and cooked vegetable mixture. Combine well.

3. From the head of cabbage, remove 6 outer leaves and trim the thick vein on the underside until flush with the cabbage leaf.

4. Spoon about ¾ cup of mixture into center of each leaf. Carefully tuck in each filled cabbage leaf's sides, and roll until completely enclosed.

5. In a 9" × 9" baking dish, spoon 1 cup tomato sauce to cover pan, add cabbage rolls, top with remaining sauce, cover with aluminum foil, and bake for 30–45 minutes in a 375°F oven, or until leaves are soft.

PER SERVING Calories: 234 | Fat: 3.5 g | Protein: 10 g | Sodium: 1,118 mg | Fiber: 12 g | Carbohydrates: 44 g | Sugar: 14 g

Roasted Red Pepper and Pine Nut Hummus

Everyday hummus gets kicked up a notch with the vibrant addition of roasted red peppers. The amazing combination of peppers, pine nuts, and garlic add a depth of flavor and variety of nutrients and antioxidants to your favorite dip or spread.

INGREDIENTS | SERVES 4

1 cup chickpeas (soaked for 48 hours)
½ cup roasted red peppers
¼ cup pine nuts, toasted
2 garlic cloves, crushed
¼ cup extra-virgin olive oil
¼ cup freshly squeezed lime juice
1 teaspoon all-natural sea salt

1. Combine chickpeas, roasted red pepper, pine nuts, garlic cloves, ⅛ cup of the olive oil, lime juice, and salt in a blender or food processor.

2. Emulsify ingredients into a thick paste.

3. Add remaining ⅛ cup of oil gradually until desired consistency is achieved.

PER SERVING Calories: 218 | Fat: 16 g | Protein: 4 g | Sodium: 597 mg | Fiber: 4 g | Carbohydrates: 14 g | Sugar: 3 g

Roasted Red Pepper Pesto

The traditional pesto that's loaded with fat and calories gets a healthy spin with this clean alternative. With the addition of roasted red peppers, this classic concoction gains the added benefit of powerful antioxidants that will promote your body's overall health and vitality.

INGREDIENTS | SERVES 12

2 cups roasted red peppers
2 cups fresh basil leaves, washed and dried
½ cup toasted unsalted pine nuts
6 garlic cloves, peeled
2 tablespoons lemon juice
1 cup extra-virgin olive oil, divided
1 teaspoon all-natural sea salt
1 teaspoon cracked black pepper

1. In a food processor, combine the roasted red peppers, basil, pine nuts, garlic cloves, lemon juice, and ¼ cup of the olive oil. Process until well blended.

2. Drizzle remaining olive oil until desired consistency is achieved.

3. Add sea salt and pepper.

PER SERVING Calories: 223 | Fat: 24 g | Protein: 1.5 g | Sodium: 208.5 mg | Fiber: 1.25 g | Carbohydrates: 3 g | Sugar: 0 g

Fresh Salsa

Salsa is so versatile—why not learn how to make it at home with fresh ingredients? After all, poor ingredients are packed into the store-bought varieties: sugar, sodium, and preservatives. Opting for homemade salsa saves money, keeps it clean, and skips out on unhealthy additives.

INGREDIENTS | SERVES 8

2 large beefsteak tomatoes, chopped
2 avocados, peeled and chopped
½ large red onion, peeled and chopped
½ large red pepper, chopped
½ small jalapeño, chopped and seeded
2 garlic cloves, crushed
¼ cup freshly squeezed lime juice
3 tablespoons chopped cilantro
1 teaspoon chili powder
¼ cup olive oil

1. Combine all ingredients in a medium bowl.

2. Cover and refrigerate for 2–12 hours before serving.

PER SERVING Calories: 163 | Fat: 15 g | Protein: 2 g | Sodium: 9 mg | Fiber: 5 g | Carbohydrates: 8.5 g | Sugar: 1.5 g

Fruit Salsa

Perfect for a quick energy burst due to its high complex carbohydrate content and all-natural sugars, this is a healthy option for any time of the day you feel you need a little helpful fuel to keep you moving!

INGREDIENTS | SERVES 12

1 cup chopped strawberries
1 cup chopped mango
1 cup chopped pineapple
2 kiwis, peeled and chopped
2 tablespoons chopped fresh mint
¼ cup freshly squeezed lime juice

Combine all the fruits with mint and lime juice in a covered container. Chill for 1 hour.

PER SERVING Calories: 28 | Fat: 0 g | Protein: 0.5 g | Sodium: 1.5 mg | Fiber: 1 g | Carbohydrates: 7 g | Sugar: 4 g

Sweet and Spicy Sesame Tofu Strips

This "pan-fried" tofu recipe can be enjoyed hot or cold, which makes it the perfect snack at home or on the go. Eaten alone or wrapped in a tortilla with vibrant vegetables, these sweet and spicy tofu strips pack a nutritious pick-me-up punch.

INGREDIENTS | SERVES 4

2 tablespoons sesame oil

1 (12-ounce) package extra-firm tofu

2 tablespoons agave nectar

1 teaspoon red pepper flakes

¼ cup black sesame seeds

Sesame Seeds for Liver Longevity

The natural wonders contained within the sesame seed are seemingly infinite. While the vitamin and mineral content of the sesame seed can be surprising, even more exciting is the provision of two phytonutrients that are unique to the sesame seed: *sesamin* and *sesamolin*. These two nutrients act primarily to protect the quality and condition of the blood and cardiovascular system; by normalizing blood pressure and keeping the blood clear of oxidative invaders, sesamin and sesamolin are just two more reasons to enjoy sesame seeds in your diet each and every day!

1. In a large skillet, heat 1 tablespoon of sesame oil over medium heat.

2. Cut the tofu block in half lengthwise, cut into ⅛" strips.

3. In a small mixing bowl, combine the agave nectar, remaining tablespoon of sesame oil, and red pepper flakes, and mix well.

4. Toss the tofu strips in the agave mixture until well coated, and roll in the sesame seeds.

5. Gently place the tofu strips into the skillet and sauté for 2–3 minutes, turn, and sauté another 2–3 minutes until cooked through.

PER SERVING Calories: 213 | Fat: 14 g | Protein: 9 g | Sodium: 41 mg | Fiber: 1 g | Carbohydrates: 13 g | Sugar: 10 g

Mediterranean Couscous–Stuffed Tomato Poppers

These tomato poppers are a quick and easy way to enjoy a delightful combination of tastes and flavors. Packed with clean complex carbohydrates, you can enjoy as many of these little savory snacks as you'd like . . . without any guilt!

INGREDIENTS | SERVES 10

10 plum tomatoes, tops removed

2 cups prepared Mediterranean Couscous (see Chapter 12)

6 ounces crumbled goat cheese, or vegan crumbled cheese substitute

1. Scoop out the insides of the tomatoes, and reserve them in a large mixing bowl.

2. Add the prepared couscous to the mixing bowl that holds the reserved tomato seeds and juice, mix thoroughly until couscous mixture is wet and well blended.

3. Arrange the hollow tomatoes on a platter with open sides up, and scoop the couscous mixture into the tomatoes pressing mixture gently into the tomatoes until firmly packed.

4. Sprinkle the tops of the tomatoes with crumbled goat cheese, and serve.

PER SERVING Calories: 217 | Fat: 6 g | Protein: 10 g | Sodium: 64 mg | Fiber: 2 g | Carbohydrates: 30 g | Sugar: 2 g

All-Natural Granola

Quick, easy, and less expensive than manufactured options, this recipe will quickly become your multipurpose go-to for great granola!

INGREDIENTS | SERVES 20

½ cup all-natural organic maple syrup

½ cup natural organic honey or agave nectar

½ cup canola oil

1 teaspoon vanilla extract

8 cups natural rolled oats

1 cup toasted, unsalted sunflower seeds

1 cup natural pecans, measured then chopped

1 cup natural walnuts, measured then chopped

1 teaspoon cinnamon

2 cups honey wheat germ

1. Preheat the oven to 325°F and prepare a baking sheet with aluminum foil and olive oil spray.

2. In a large mixing bowl, combine the syrup, honey or agave, oil, and vanilla, and mix well.

3. Add the oats, sunflower seeds, chopped nuts, cinnamon, and wheat germ. Toss to coat evenly.

4. Spread the mixture on the prepared baking sheet, and bake for 15 minutes. Shake the mixture or turn with a spatula, return to the oven, and continue baking for 10–15 minutes, or until crispy.

PER SERVING Calories: 378 | Fat: 20 g | Protein: 10 g | Sodium: 5 mg | Fiber: 6 g | Carbohydrates: 43 g | Sugar: 12 g

Tangy Tomatillo Salsa Verde

Tangy tomatillos make this beautiful salsa a bright green and give it a unique taste. You can use this delightful salsa as a side for chips or as a topping on enchiladas, tofu, or almost any Mexican-inspired dish.

INGREDIENTS | SERVES 8

2 cups water

1 pound tomatillos, husks removed

½ cup chopped red onion

1 serrano chile pepper, seeded and minced

1 garlic clove, minced

2 tablespoons cilantro, chopped

1 tablespoon oregano, chopped

½ teaspoon cumin

1 teaspoon all-natural sea salt

1. In a large pot over medium heat, combine all ingredients except the sea salt, (but including the water), and bring to a boil.

2. Reduce the heat to low, and simmer until tomatillos are cooked through and fork tender, about 15 minutes. Remove from heat and allow to cool for 5–10 minutes. Add sea salt.

3. Transfer tomatillo mixture from the pot to a blender or food processor, and blend or process until the mixture reaches desired consistency.

PER SERVING Calories: 26 | Fat: 0 g | Protein: 1 g | Sodium: 296 mg | Fiber: 2 g | Carbohydrates: 5 g | Sugar: 3 g

Tex-Mex Quesadillas

Packed with clean ingredients, these quick and easy quesadillas are the perfect snack option when you're craving something a little spicy! Serve with the Lime-Avocado Dipping Sauce (recipe in this chapter) for a clean, cool accompaniment!

INGREDIENTS | SERVES 4

1 cup cooked black beans
1 cup corn
1 cup chopped tomato
½ cup chopped green pepper
½ cup chopped red onion
1 teaspoon cumin
1 teaspoon garlic powder
2 whole-wheat tortillas

1. Preheat the oven to 400°F and prepare a baking sheet with tinfoil and extra-virgin olive oil spray.

2. In a mixing bowl, combine the black beans, corn, tomato, green pepper, red onion, and spices.

3. Lay the tortillas on the baking sheet and spoon the black bean mixture onto ½ of each tortilla, folding the empty half over. Press lightly to close.

4. Bake for 5 minutes, turn, and continue baking for 5 minutes or until golden brown.

PER SERVING Calories: 164 | Fat: 2 g | Protein: 7 g | Sodium: 291 mg | Fiber: 6 g | Carbohydrates: 31 g | Sugar: 5.5 g

Garlic and Herb Tortilla Chips

While your grocery store may provide you with tons of tortilla chip options, you can save your health and money by creating homemade chips. Using only a few ingredients you can whip up some clean tortilla chips you'll actually feel good about eating!

INGREDIENTS | SERVES 10

4 100% whole-wheat tortillas
1 teaspoon all-natural sea salt
2 teaspoons garlic powder
2 teaspoons sodium-free Italian seasoning

1. Preheat the oven to 350°F. Cut each tortilla into 8 pizza-shaped slices.

2. Line a baking sheet with aluminum foil and spray with olive oil spray.

3. Arrange the tortilla pieces evenly on the baking sheet, spray with olive oil, and sprinkle with the salt, garlic powder, and Italian seasoning.

4. Bake for 10–15 minutes, or until crispy.

PER SERVING Calories: 39 | Fat: 1 g | Protein: 1 g | Sodium: 312 mg | Fiber: 0.5 g | Carbohydrates: 6.5 g | Sugar: 0 g

Spicy Spanish Egg Quesadilla

This recipe packs a wide variety of antioxidants and nutrients in every soft, spicy bite. Crunchy peppers and onions make the perfect texture complement to the soft eggs, and the kick of cayenne makes for a subtle spice sensation.

INGREDIENTS | SERVES 4

½ red pepper, chopped
½ green pepper, chopped
½ cup yellow onion, chopped
2 tablespoons water
4 eggs or 1 cup vegan egg substitute
2 whole-wheat tortillas
⅛ teaspoon cayenne pepper

1. Prepare a skillet with olive oil spray over medium heat. Sauté peppers and onion in 1 tablespoon of water until slightly softened, about 2–3 minutes.

2. In a small mixing bowl, beat together the eggs and 1 tablespoon of water, and pour over pepper and onions.

3. With a spatula, circle the edge of the pan, keeping the edges of the egg from sticking. Cook for 4–5 minutes, or until the eggs seem slightly firm. Top the egg mixture with a tortilla and flip completely so the tortilla is underneath the egg mixture in the skillet.

4. Sprinkle the eggs with the cayenne and place the second tortilla on top, pressing down slightly. Continue cooking for about 4–5 minutes or until eggs are cooked through.

5. Flip again, toasting the uncooked tortilla for about 1 minute. Remove from heat, allow to set for 5 minutes, and slice into 8 equal wedges.

PER SERVING Calories: 129 | Fat: 6 g | Protein: 8 g | Sodium: 166 mg | Fiber: 1 g | Carbohydrates: 10 g | Sugar: 2 g

Creamy Cashew Dipping Sauce

This quick and easy recipe uses natural ingredients that add a deep flavor and creamy texture to this delightful dipping sauce. Perfectly paired with your favorite Asian cuisine, this is a sweet, salty, creamy dip that packs tons of protein in every delicious bite!

INGREDIENTS | SERVES 4

3 cups cashews, roasted
¼ cup light sesame oil
1¼ cups coconut milk
2 tablespoons agave nectar
1 teaspoon all-natural sea salt

1. In a blender or food processor, grind the roasted cashews until fine; add sesame oil gradually while processing until mixture becomes a paste.

2. In a saucepan over medium heat, combine the cashew paste with coconut milk and agave nectar until smooth consistency is reached.

3. Remove from heat, allow to cool, and add salt.

PER SERVING Calories: 765 | Fat: 65 g | Protein: 16 g | Sodium: 609 mg | Fiber: 3 g | Carbohydrates: 36 g | Sugar: 13 g

Tasty Tomato Sauce

No need to purchase the store-bought varieties of preservative-packed tomato sauce any more. This is a delicious recipe for your favorite tomato topping that can be made right in your own kitchen.

INGREDIENTS | SERVES 8

2 yellow onions, chopped
2 green bell peppers, chopped
1 tablespoon extra-virgin olive oil
8 large tomatoes, peeled and crushed
2 tablespoons minced garlic
1 (6-ounce) can organic tomato paste
1 teaspoon dried basil
1 teaspoon dried oregano
1 teaspoon Sucanat
2 teaspoons all-natural sea salt
2 teaspoons cracked black pepper

1. In a large skillet over medium heat, sauté the onions and green peppers in the olive oil for 5 minutes, or until softened.

2. In a large pot over medium-low heat, combine the tomatoes (and their juice), sautéed onions and peppers, garlic, tomato paste, basil, and oregano. Stir the sauce and cover.

3. Simmer the sauce for about 1 hour.

4. Add the Sucanat, sea salt, pepper, and stir.

PER SERVING Calories: 88.5 | Fat: 2 g | Protein: 3 g | Sodium: 767 mg | Fiber: 4 g | Carbohydrates: 16.5 g | Sugar: 10 g

Zucchini Bread

Packed with vibrant zucchini and fresh ingredients that fill every slice with beneficial nutrition like complex carbohydrates and vitamins, this is a delicious snack that will boost your energy levels while satisfying your sweet tooth.

INGREDIENTS | SERVES 4

1 large zucchini

1 cup vanilla almond milk

2 eggs (beaten), or ½ cup vegan egg substitute

½ cup all-natural organic agave nectar

4 tablespoons canola oil

2 cups 100% whole-wheat flour

1 tablespoon baking powder

1 teaspoon all-natural sea salt

1 teaspoon cinnamon

1 teaspoon pumpkin pie spice

Zucchini: Get a Lot with Just a Little

Zucchini is one of those superfoods that provides a lot of essential nutrition with very few calories. For every cup of this scrumptious summer squash, the cost is a mere 18 calories, but the benefits are from the clean complex carbohydrates and essential vitamins and minerals like vitamins C and B_6 and magnesium that act to promote the health of the whole body as well as its many parts.

1. Preheat the oven to 375°F and prepare a loaf pan with olive oil spray and a light coating of flour.

2. In a food processor or blender, process the zucchini until shredded. Add the almond milk, eggs or egg substitute, agave nectar, and oil to the zucchini and pulse until well blended.

3. In a large mixing bowl, combine the dry ingredients and spices and mix well.

4. Add the zucchini mixture to the dry ingredients and stir until combined.

5. Pour the batter into the prepared loaf pan, and bake for 40–45 minutes, or until a knife inserted into the center of the loaf comes out clean.

PER SERVING Calories: 556 | Fat: 18 g | Protein: 12 g | Sodium: 1,028 mg | Fiber: 3 g | Carbohydrates: 89 g | Sugar: 38 g

Crunchy Garlic Eggplant Chips

Who knew eggplant could be transformed into delicious chips that satisfy your salt cravings but also provide tons of essential nutrition? Now, you can use your favorite purple vegetable for far more than just roasting and grilling!

INGREDIENTS | SERVES 4

1 eggplant, cut into ⅛" slices
2 teaspoons all-natural sea salt
2 teaspoons garlic powder
1 teaspoon cracked black pepper

Eggplant's Flavorful Fiber

The versatility of eggplant makes it an excellent option for an amazing main dish or side dish star, but its healthy dose of fiber makes it an even better health decision. The fiber contained in every bite of eggplant remains the same regardless of how it's cooked. If you can include this nutritious, delicious superfood in your diet, you'll boost your cancer-fighting capabilities and enjoy a wide variety of eggplant-focused foods!

1. Place the eggplant slices on ½ of a towel, cover with remaining ½ of towel, and press down firmly to remove excess moisture.

2. Salt top sides of eggplant slices with 1 teaspoon of salt and allow to set for about 5 minutes. Perform towel-press again to remove any excess moisture, and sprinkle with 1 teaspoon of garlic powder and ½ teaspoon of pepper.

3. Preheat an oven to broil at 400°F and spray an oven rack with olive oil spray.

4. Arrange the eggplant slices on the oven rack with salted sides down. Sprinkle remaining salt, garlic powder, and pepper on slices.

5. Broil for 5 minutes, checking frequently, or until golden brown. Turn chips and continue broiling for another 5 minutes, or until golden brown.

6. Remove from heat and allow to cool for 5 minutes before serving.

PER SERVING Calories: 39 | Fat: 0 g | Protein: 2 g | Sodium: 1,182 mg | Fiber: 5 g | Carbohydrates: 9 g | Sugar: 3 g

Roasted Eggplant Dip

Adding a flavorful creaminess to sandwiches and wraps, or a chunky dip for your favorite vegetable assortment, this recipe delivers all the taste and nutrients you desire with the added benefit of versatility.

INGREDIENTS | SERVES 8

2 large eggplants
4 garlic cloves peeled
1 tablespoon lemon juice
1 cup goat cheese or soft vegan cheese
1 cup nonfat Greek-style yogurt, or soy yogurt
1 teaspoon all-natural sea salt

1. Preheat the oven to 400°F and prepare a baking sheet with foil and olive oil spray.

2. Pierce the skins of the eggplants with a fork, and cut in half lengthwise.

3. Place eggplant halves on the baking sheet with insides facing up, and place the 4 garlic cloves on the same sheet. Bake for 30 minutes or until eggplant and garlic cloves are soft.

4. Remove from heat. Spoon out eggplant into chunks and set in a strainer to allow excess juices to drip away, and allow to cool.

5. In a blender, combine the eggplant, garlic cloves, lemon juice, goat cheese, and ½ cup yogurt. Blend until thoroughly combined, adding remaining ½ cup yogurt until desired consistency is reached. Add salt.

PER SERVING Calories: 111 | Fat: 6 g | Protein: 6 g | Sodium: 399 mg | Fiber: 4.5 g | Carbohydrates: 10 g | Sugar: 4.5 g

Baked Potato Chips

Bag the store-bought potato chips that are packed with fat, calories, and sodium, and opt for these homemade crispy chips instead!

INGREDIENTS | SERVES 8

2 Idaho potatoes, cut into ⅛" slices
1 tablespoon extra-virgin olive oil
2 teaspoons all-natural sea salt
2 teaspoons garlic powder
1 teaspoon cracked black pepper

1. Preheat the oven to broil at 400°F and prepare an oven rack with olive oil spray.

2. Toss the potato slices in the olive oil until evenly coated.

3. Spread the potato slices flat on the prepared oven rack, salt top sides of slices with 1 teaspoon of salt, and sprinkle with 1 teaspoon of garlic powder and ½ teaspoon of pepper.

4. Broil for 5 minutes, checking frequently, or until golden brown.

5. Remove rack, flip chips, sprinkle with remaining salt, garlic powder, and pepper, and return to oven to continue broiling for another 5 minutes, or until golden brown.

6. Remove from heat and allow to cool for 5 minutes before serving.

PER SERVING Calories: 59 | Fat: 2 g | Protein: 1 g | Sodium: 592 mg | Fiber: 1 g | Carbohydrates: 10 g | Sugar: 0 g

Tasty Tostadas

Serving up clean protein has never been easier! Using clean refried beans, protein-packed yogurt, and healthy, fresh vegetables, you can create a crunchy snack that packs in flavor without packing on the pounds.

INGREDIENTS | SERVES 2

2 whole-wheat tortillas

1 cup Spicy Clean Refried Beans (see Chapter 9)

1 cup shredded lettuce

1 whole tomato, diced

2 tablespoons low-fat Greek-style yogurt, or soy yogurt

1. Preheat the broiler to 400°F and bake tortillas for 3 minutes, or until golden and crispy. Flip, continue broiling for 2 minutes, or until golden brown and crispy.

2. Remove from heat and place each tortilla on separate serving plates.

3. Spread ½ cup of Spicy Clean Refried Beans on each tortilla, and top with ½ cup each shredded lettuce and tomato.

4. Garnish with 1 tablespoon yogurt in center of the toppings.

PER SERVING Calories: 225 | Fat: 4 g | Protein: 10 g | Sodium: 740 mg | Fiber: 8 g | Carbohydrates: 37 g | Sugar: 3.5 g

Lime-Avocado Dipping Sauce

With a spicy citrus kick, this smooth avocado sauce serves up valuable nutrition in a dish that can be served as a cool complement to your favorite finger foods or the perfect pairing to your spicy entrées.

INGREDIENTS | SERVES 4

2 Hass avocados

1 teaspoon lemon juice

2 tablespoons lime juice

1 teaspoon all-natural sea salt

1 teaspoon agave nectar

1. Remove seeds from avocados, and remove avocado flesh from skin.

2. In a mixing bowl, combine the avocado, lemon juice, and lime juice. With a fork, mash together and blend until combined and desired texture is achieved.

3. Add salt and agave, mixing well and carefully keeping desired texture consistent.

PER SERVING Calories: 166 | Fat: 15 g | Protein: 2 g | Sodium: 596 mg | Fiber: 7 g | Carbohydrates: 10 g | Sugar: 2 g

Perfect Pumpkin Pie Snack Bars

Indulging in a sweet piece of pumpkin pie is now a good thing! This recipe maxes out nutrition by using clean ingredients and spicing things up with the antioxidant-packed flavors that make pumpkin pie an extraordinary taste sensation!

INGREDIENTS | SERVES 9

3 cups All-Natural Granola (see recipe in this chapter)

2 tablespoons coconut oil

2 cups pumpkin purée

1 egg, or ¼ cup vegan egg substitute

1 cup almond milk

1 teaspoon cinnamon

1 teaspoon ground ginger

½ teaspoon ground cloves

1. Preheat the oven to 350°F and prepare a 9" × 9" pan with olive oil spray.

2. In a mixing bowl, combine the granola and coconut oil. Mix well and pour into pan, pressing firmly to pack into a crust. Bake for 15–20 minutes, or until firm and crispy.

3. While crust is baking, add the pumpkin, egg (or egg substitute), almond milk, cinnamon, ginger, and cloves to a large mixing bowl and combine well.

4. Pour pumpkin mixture into prepared crust and bake for 25–30 minutes, or until set and inserted fork comes out clean.

PER SERVING Calories: 155 | Fat: 5 g | Protein: 5 g | Sodium: 24 mg | Fiber: 3 g | Carbohydrates: 22 g | Sugar: 2 g

Apricot, Cranberry, Almond Bars

These quick granola bars are perfect for the kids! Not only can they enjoy them, but they can get their hands dirty by helping to make them, too!

INGREDIENTS | SERVES 12

4 cups All-Natural Granola (see recipe in this chapter)

1½ cups all-natural creamy almond butter

½ cup unsweetened dried cranberries, chopped

½ cup unsweetened dried apricots, chopped

⅓ cup natural almonds (crushed, sliced, or slivered)

2 tablespoons agave nectar

1. Prepare a 9" × 9" pan with olive oil spray.

2. In a mixing bowl, combine the granola, almond butter, dried fruit, and almonds, and mix well.

3. Pour mixture into prepared pan, pressing slightly to set.

4. Drizzle agave nectar over top of bars and serve.

PER SERVING Calories: 336 | Fat: 26 g | Protein: 4 g | Sodium: 5 mg | Fiber: 3 g | Carbohydrates: 23 g | Sugar: 4 g

Apricots: The See-Easy Fruits

When it comes to great sources of vitamin A, apricots rank high on the list. Fresh, frozen, or dried, these delicious fruits add a sweet flavor and delicious texture to smoothies, sweet treats, and even savory entrées. Packed with an abundance of vitamins and minerals, the apricot's vitamin A content and ability to prevent free radical damage to the cells, tissues, and lenses of the eyes make it a delightful fruit that packs fun flavor *and* eye-health benefits into every juicy bite!

Peppy Pesto

*Spinach makes this pesto a very vibrant green that can't
be achieved with the traditional recipe's basil alone.*

INGREDIENTS | SERVES 12

2 cups baby spinach leaves, washed and dried

1 cup fresh basil leaves, washed and dried

½ cup toasted unsalted pine nuts

6 garlic cloves, peeled

2 tablespoons lemon juice

½ cup extra-virgin olive oil, divided

1 teaspoon all-natural sea salt

1 teaspoon cracked black pepper

1. In a food processor, combine the spinach, basil, pine nuts, garlic cloves, lemon juice, and ¼ cup of the olive oil. Process until well blended.

2. Drizzle remaining olive oil until desired consistency is achieved.

3. Add sea salt and pepper.

PER SERVING Calories: 223 | Fat: 24 g | Protein: 1.5 g | Sodium: 208.5 mg | Fiber: 1 g | Carbohydrates: 3 g | Sugar: 0 g

Luscious Lemons: Nature's Immunity Promoting Powerhouses

Did you know that just ¼ cup of lemon juice contains almost half of your daily recommendation for vitamin C? By adding this flavor-boosting juice to your favorite foods, you're not just intensifying the taste, you're adding essential vitamins to your diet. Try adding lemon juice to your water, foods, sauces, and desserts, and you'll benefit from the immune system–supporting vitamin C that dazzles every drop.

CHAPTER 6

Sandwiches and Wraps

Waldorf Wrap
92

Black Bean and Yellow
Rice Wraps
92

Sweet Pepper Sandwich Stacker
93

Grilled Veggie Wrap-Up
94

Asian-Infused Tofu Burgers
95

Perfect Portobello Burgers
96

Sweet Carrot, Cabbage, and
Cucumber Wraps
97

Black Bean-Garbanzo Burgers
97

Spicy Zucchini Stacker
98

Marvelous Mediterranean Wraps
99

Tomato, Basil, and
Mozzarella Wraps
99

Artichoke-Mozzarella Wraps
100

Eggplant, Portobello, Spinach,
and Mozzarella Stacks
101

Veggie Burgers
102

Quick Quinoa and
Black Bean Burger
103

Lean, Mean Sloppy Joes
104

Roasted Red Pepper and Onion
Wrap with Spicy Chickpea Sauce
105

Sweet and Spicy
Avocado Burger
106

Italian Eggplant Sandwiches
107

Chick Patties
108

Waldorf Wrap

This creamy combination of sweet fruit, smooth yogurt, and crunchy walnuts makes for a sweet snack with a crunch. Loaded with intense nutrition and beneficial phytochemicals, this is a healthy wrap that will quickly become your go-to.

INGREDIENTS | SERVES 2

½ red apple, minced

½ cup chopped celery

½ cup grapes, quartered

½ cup walnuts, crushed

2 tablespoons plain nonfat yogurt, or soy yogurt

1 teaspoon nutmeg

2 100% whole-wheat tortilla wraps

1. In a mixing bowl, combine the minced apple, celery, grapes, walnuts, yogurt, and nutmeg, and blend well.

2. Lay the tortillas flat, and spoon half of the mixture down the center of each wrap.

3. Wrap tightly, and enjoy!

PER SERVING Calories: 331 | Fat: 21 g | Protein: 7 g | Sodium: 223 mg | Fiber: 4 g | Carbohydrates: 32 g | Sugar: 13 g

Black Bean and Yellow Rice Wraps

A fragrant yellow rice with a spicy kick gets all wrapped up with smooth black beans for a delicious snack or meal that packs clean complex carbohydrates, protein, and fiber in every delightful bite.

INGREDIENTS | SERVES 2

2 cups water

2 cups instant brown rice, uncooked

1 teaspoon turmeric

¼ teaspoon cumin

⅛ teaspoon cayenne

1 teaspoon all-natural sea salt

2 cups cooked black beans, room temperature

2 100% whole-wheat tortillas

2 tablespoons low-fat Greek-style yogurt or soy yogurt

1. In a large saucepan, bring the water to a boil and stir in brown rice, spices, and sea salt. Continue stirring for 1 minute, cover, and reduce heat to simmer rice for 5 minutes, or until cooked through.

2. To the rice, add black beans and blend well.

3. Prepare tortillas by spreading 1 tablespoon of yogurt on each.

4. Spoon equal amounts of rice and black bean mixture down the center of each tortilla and fold to enclose.

PER SERVING Calories: 878 | Fat: 7 g | Protein: 31 g | Sodium: 1,423 mg | Fiber: 23 g | Carbohydrates: 175 g | Sugar: 2 g

Sweet Pepper Sandwich Stacker

This simple sauté of sweet bell peppers makes for a quick, tasty sandwich you can enjoy for lunch or dinner. The vibrant variety of red, yellow, and orange peppers makes this nutritious treat a feast for the eyes as well as for the stomach.

INGREDIENTS | SERVES 2

1 red bell pepper

1 yellow bell pepper

1 orange bell pepper

2 tablespoons water

2 tablespoons balsamic vinegar

1 teaspoon sea salt

4 slices whole-wheat or sprouted grain bread

2 lettuce leaves

1. Remove tops, ribs, and seeds from bell peppers, and cut into strips.

2. In a saucepan over medium heat, combine the water and pepper strips, and cook for 1 minute, or until water has evaporated.

3. Add the balsamic vinegar to the peppers and sauté for about 3–5 minutes, or until slightly soft and vinegar has absorbed. Add salt.

4. Remove the peppers from the heat and place ½ of the peppers on each of 2 slices of bread. Top the peppers with 1 lettuce leaf for each sandwich, and top with remaining bread slice.

PER SERVING Calories: 192 | Fat: 2 g | Protein: 6 g | Sodium: 1,436 mg | Fiber: 5 g | Carbohydrates: 37 g | Sugar: 10 g

Grilled Veggie Wrap-Up

The colorful variety of red and white onions, green zucchini, yellow squash, and orange bell pepper in this wonderful wrap signifies the rich nutritional array packed into every bite.

INGREDIENTS | SERVES 2

1 large orange bell pepper
1 large zucchini
1 yellow squash
½ large red onion
½ large white onion
2 tablespoons water
1 teaspoon garlic powder
1 teaspoon all-natural sea salt
1 teaspoon cracked black pepper
2 100% whole-wheat tortillas

Eat the Rainbow Every Day

If you're looking to expand your vitamin, mineral, and antioxidant intake, aim for including all of the colors of the rainbow in your daily diet . . . every day. By including a variety of colors in your meals and snacks, you're actually adding a variety of color-specific phytochemicals that give those vibrant fruits and vegetables their amazing hues. For example, concord grapes have rich *anthocyanins* while red peppers are packed with *lutein*; these phytochemicals create very different colors and perform very different functions. So, eat the colors of the rainbow and benefit from each in their own unique ways.

1. Prepare the vegetables by removing the tops from the bell pepper, zucchini, squash, and onions, as well as the ribs and seeds from the pepper. Slice the pepper into ¼" slices, the zucchini and squash into lengthwise strips ¼" thickness, and the onions in very thin slices.

2. In a skillet over medium heat, combine 1 tablespoon of the water with the peppers and onions. Sauté about 2 minutes, or until water is evaporated and onions and peppers are slightly soft.

3. Add the remaining tablespoon of water, zucchini, and squash, and sprinkle with garlic powder, salt, and pepper. Sauté for another 3–4 minutes or until zucchini and squash are slightly softened. Remove from heat and allow to cool.

4. Set tortillas on plates, and fill each with an equal amount of the assorted vegetables, roll, and serve.

PER SERVING Calories: 148 | Fat: 1.5 g | Protein: 6 g | Sodium: 1,211 mg | Fiber: 7 g | Carbohydrates: 29 g | Sugar: 10 g

Asian-Infused Tofu Burgers

With powerful aromatic ingredients that combine to pack tons of delicious flavor and healthy nutrients into every inch, this vegetarian burger makes for a low-fat, low-calorie meal or snack that will satisfy cravings you never even knew you had!

INGREDIENTS | SERVES 2

¼ cup sesame oil

¼ cup agave nectar

1 clove garlic, crushed

½ cup scallions, chopped

1 tablespoon freshly grated gingerroot, peeled

1 pound extra-firm tofu

2 whole-wheat ciabatta rolls

2 large leaves of bib lettuce

Ginger for Gastrointestinal Issues

What is it about ginger ale that can make a stomach ache completely disappear? Ginger! For centuries, ancient Chinese medicine has used ginger to alleviate stomach issues that range from slight discomfort to extreme nausea. This sweet, spicy root not only alleviates gastrointestinal issues, it adds a distinctive kick to favorite dishes and has become a staple in Asian cuisine across the globe.

1. In a large mixing bowl, combine the sesame oil, agave nectar, garlic, scallions, and ginger. Combine thoroughly.

2. Slice the tofu into ½"-thick slices, and set inside marinade. Cover and refrigerate for 1 hour, turning to coat every 20 minutes.

3. Prepare a large skillet with olive oil spray over medium heat, and add the tofu slices. Pour 2 tablespoons of marinade over slices while cooking, and cook for 4–5 minutes or until golden and crispy. Turn, pour 2 tablespoons of marinade over top of tofu again, and continue cooking for 4–5 minutes, or until golden and crispy.

4. Set 1 slice of tofu on each ciabatta roll and top with bib lettuce.

PER SERVING Calories: 582 | Fat: 31 g | Protein: 20 g | Sodium: 281 mg | Fiber: 3 g | Carbohydrates: 52 g | Sugar: 36 g

Perfect Portobello Burgers

Thick, flavorful portobello mushroom caps pack a punch of deliciousness that gets heightened when grilled and topped with fresh and flavorful ingredients. Thanks to my Dad and Miss Pam for bringing this recipe to our attention, this has become a wonderful meat-free burger recipe the whole family enjoys!

INGREDIENTS | SERVES 2

2 large portobello mushroom caps

2 tablespoons extra-virgin olive oil

1 teaspoon garlic powder

1 teaspoon cracked black pepper

2 100% whole-wheat hamburger buns

½ cup crumbled goat cheese, or soft vegan cheese

4 strips roasted red pepper

Mistaken for Meat?

While portobello mushroom caps can be described as "meaty," the extent of their "meatiness" is in the heartiness of their flavor and taste. The biggest benefit for vegetarians who choose to opt for meatless meal options like portobello burgers, rather than traditional hamburgers, is the vast difference in saturated fat. Unlike beef, portobello mushrooms pack loads of healthy nutrients like complex carbohydrates, protein, vitamins, minerals, and phytochemicals (chemicals specific to plants), without unhealthy elements like saturated fats.

1. Prepare a grill with olive oil spray over medium heat.

2. Paint the underside of the mushroom caps with ¼ tablespoon of olive oil each. Sprinkle each cap with the garlic powder and black pepper.

3. Set the caps on the grill with the gills facing down, and paint the tops with remaining olive oil.

4. Grill for 4–6 minutes, flip, and continue grilling for 5 minutes.

5. Remove the mushrooms from the grill and set one on each bun bottom, with gills facing up.

6. Sprinkle gills with the crumbled goat cheese, and lay roasted red pepper strips on top.

7. Cover with bun tops and enjoy.

PER SERVING Calories: 579 | Fat: 35 g | Protein: 27 g | Sodium: 620 mg | Fiber: 3.5 g | Carbohydrates: 43.5 g | Sugar: 5.5 g

Sweet Carrot, Cabbage, and Cucumber Wraps

Store-bought coleslaw gets left on the shelf after you discover how simple and delicious this homemade version is. This wrap provides all the energy-producing carbohydrates you need to keep you going with the added benefits of crunch and sweetness!

INGREDIENTS | SERVES 2

¼ cup red wine vinegar

2 tablespoons agave nectar

1 cup grated carrot

1 cup grated red cabbage

1 large cucumber, seeds removed and grated

1 teaspoon all-natural sea salt

2 100% whole-wheat tortillas

1. In a mixing bowl, whisk together the vinegar and agave nectar until thoroughly combined. Add the grated carrot, cabbage, cucumber, and salt. Cover and refrigerate for 1 hour, turning every 15–20 minutes.

2. Spoon half of mixture onto each tortilla and fold to enclose.

PER SERVING Calories: 168 | Fat: 1 g | Protein: 3 g | Sodium: 1,139 mg | Fiber: 4 g | Carbohydrates: 35 g | Sugar: 20 g

Black Bean-Garbanzo Burgers

With omega-rich flaxseeds, fiber-packed beans, and ample amounts of antioxidants from the red onion, these burgers are filled with heart- and brain-healthy ingredients that combine to create a meal of delicious, health-promoting nutrition.

INGREDIENTS | SERVES 4

1 cup cooked black beans, whole

1 cup cooked black beans, mashed

1 cup cooked garbanzos, mashed

¼ cup red onion, diced

½ cup ground flaxseed

2 teaspoons garlic powder

½ teaspoon all-natural sea salt

1 teaspoon cracked black pepper

4 100% whole-wheat, whole-grain rolls

1. In a large mixing bowl, combine the black beans, garbanzos, and red onion. Combine thoroughly until mixture is thickened. Add flaxseed, garlic powder, salt, and pepper. Mix well until thick.

2. Form mixture into 4 even patties.

3. Prepare skillet with olive oil spray over medium heat. Place the burgers in the skillet, cooking for 2 minutes on each side until slightly crusted and heated through.

PER SERVING Calories: 322 | Fat: 7 g | Protein: 16 g | Sodium: 830 mg | Fiber: 17 g | Carbohydrates: 48 g | Sugar: 3 g

Spicy Zucchini Stacker

Brightening the flavors of zucchini with the delightfully fresh addition of goat cheese, garlic, and balsamic vinegar, this stacked-high sandwich is a zippy snack that will add some zing to your step!

INGREDIENTS | SERVES 2

1 large zucchini
1 tablespoon balsamic vinegar
4 slices sprouted grain bread
2 tablespoons crumbled goat cheese, or soft vegan cheese

1. Prepare a skillet with olive oil spray over medium heat.

2. Cut the zucchini in half, and slice thin lengthwise slices.

3. Arrange the zucchini slices in the skillet and cook for 3 minutes, turning frequently.

4. Sprinkle the slices with the balsamic vinegar and continue cooking until slightly soft. Remove from heat.

5. Lay 2 slices of the bread on 2 plates. Sprinkle ¼ of the goat cheese on each slice and cover each with ½ of the zucchini slices.

6. Sprinkle remaining goat cheese on each sandwich and cover with remaining bread.

PER SERVING Calories: 192 | Fat: 4 g | Protein: 7 g | Sodium: 459 mg | Fiber: 3 g | Carbohydrates: 32 g | Sugar: 8 g

Marvelous Mediterranean Wraps

With fresh ingredients that add tons of taste and a variety of rich nutrients, you can quickly create the filling for this wrap to eat on the spot with enough left over to allow the flavors to marry overnight for an on-the-go option the following day.

INGREDIENTS | SERVES 2

4 tablespoons plain low-fat Greek-style yogurt, or silken tofu

1 package extra-firm tofu, cut into bite-sized pieces

½ cup sun-dried tomatoes

½ cup roasted red peppers

½ cup sliced pitted green olives

½ cup artichoke hearts, chopped

1 teaspoon garlic powder

1 teaspoon all-natural sea salt

2 100% whole-wheat tortillas

1. In a mixing bowl, combine the yogurt, tofu, sun-dried tomatoes, red peppers, olives, artichokes, and garlic powder. Add salt.

2. Lay tortillas on a flat surface and spoon half of the mixture down the center of each wrap.

3. Wrap tightly and enjoy!

PER SERVING Calories: 352 | Fat: 9 g | Protein: 33 g | Sodium: 1,587 mg | Fiber: 6 g | Carbohydrates: 35 g | Sugar: 10 g

Tomato, Basil, and Mozzarella Wraps

While the ingredient list is short and the directions are simple, this bright wrap of flavorful ingredients is nothing short of amazing! This is a perfect wrap to enjoy when you're short on time but still want big taste!

INGREDIENTS | SERVES 2

4 beefsteak tomato slices

2 (¼") slices of fresh mozzarella cheese, or vegan mozzarella

2 100% whole-wheat tortillas

2 tablespoons balsamic vinegar

1 teaspoon cracked black pepper

4 tablespoons chopped fresh basil leaves

1. Cut tomato slices and cheese slices into thin strips.

2. Lay tortillas flat, and layer half of the mozzarella strips down the center of each tortilla, followed by the tomato slices on top.

3. Drizzle the balsamic vinegar and cracked black pepper over the mozzarella and tomato, and cover with the chopped basil.

4. Wrap tightly, and enjoy!

PER SERVING Calories: 213 | Fat: 9.5 g | Protein: 10 g | Sodium: 213 mg | Fiber: 2 g | Carbohydrates: 21 g | Sugar: 4.5 g

Artichoke-Mozzarella Wraps

This wrap is creamy, crunchy, and absolutely delicious! This simple and quick treat is a satisfying, clean alternative to store-bought snack options when you're craving something salty.

INGREDIENTS | SERVES 2

¾ cup extra-virgin olive oil

¼ cup red wine vinegar

4 cloves garlic, crushed

2 teaspoons all-natural sea salt

¼ teaspoon red pepper flakes

12 artichoke hearts, quartered

2 100% whole-wheat tortillas

4 ounces buffalo mozzarella or vegan mozzarella, sliced into 4 even slices

The Whole Truth about Whole-Wheat

When you purchase products that are labeled "wheat," beware that these may not be what you think they are. U.S. guidelines for labeling wheat products as such are that the products use 60 percent of the wheat berry, which leaves more than enough wiggle room for undesirable ingredients that "enrich" these products. If you prefer to have your whole-wheat products actually be "whole-wheat," then "100 percent whole-wheat" is the label you're looking for.

1. In a mixing bowl, whisk together the olive oil, vinegar, garlic, 1 teaspoon of the salt, and the red pepper flakes. Submerge the artichoke hearts, cover, and refrigerate 8 hours or overnight.

2. Remove artichokes from oil, and squeeze to remove excess oil. Move the artichokes to a dry bowl, and gently crush the artichoke hearts.

3. Prepare each tortilla with 2 slices of the mozzarella, and top with equal amounts of the artichokes. Sprinkle with remaining teaspoon of salt and fold tortillas to enclose.

PER SERVING Calories: 937 | Fat: 83 g | Protein: 21 g | Sodium: 2,157 mg | Fiber: 9 g | Carbohydrates: 31 g | Sugar: 2 g

Eggplant, Portobello, Spinach, and Mozzarella Stacks

Combining the thick portobello and eggplant slices with vibrant spinach and creamy mozzarella, the delightful combination of all-natural ingredients takes this clean flavor sensation to the next level.

INGREDIENTS | SERVES 2

1 large eggplant, cut into ¼"–½" full-length slices

2 tablespoons extra-virgin olive oil

1 teaspoon all-natural sea salt

1 teaspoon cracked black pepper

4 large portobello mushrooms

1 cup baby spinach leaves

2 slices fresh buffalo mozzarella, or vegan mozzarella

Excellent Eggplant for Brain Food

Eggplant is not only delicious, nutritious, and extremely versatile, it contains a powerful *anthocyanin* (the cancer-fighting chemicals that cause the deep, vibrant colors in fruits and vegetables) called *nasunin* that make it a powerful brain food. Nasunin acts as a powerful protector against free radical damage (which wreaks havoc on cells, causing dangerous changes like cancer) in the brain by protecting the fats that are so important to the brain's optimal functioning and the conveyance of messages to the rest of the body. By enjoying eggplant, you're not only satisfying your hunger and your taste, you're doing your brain a world of good.

1. Prepare a grill with olive oil spray and bring to medium heat.

2. Paint the eggplant slices with olive oil, sprinkle with salt and pepper, and place on the grill. Grill for 8–10 minutes, or until the eggplant is cooked through.

3. Paint the portobello mushroom caps' gills with olive oil, sprinkle with salt and pepper, and place on the grill. Paint the tops, and flip to grill the tops after about 5–7 minutes.

4. Toss the spinach leaves in the remaining olive oil, and sprinkle with remaining salt and pepper.

5. While still on the heat, immediately after flipping the caps so gills are facing up, place ½ of the spinach on each of the 2 caps and 1 slice of mozzarella on each of the other 2 caps. Continue cooking until the spinach is wilted and the cheese is slightly melted.

6. Remove the caps from the grill, and stack the eggplant slices on the 2 caps with spinach. Top with the mozzarella caps, and enjoy!

PER SERVING Calories: 313 | Fat: 21 g | Protein: 13 g | Sodium: 1,390 mg | Fiber: 12 g | Carbohydrates: 24 g | Sugar: 11 g

Veggie Burgers

This vibrant vegetarian burger option combines a variety of vegetables that add intense flavor and crunchy texture to every delightful bite . . . without the preservatives and additives of the boxed versions!

INGREDIENTS | SERVES 4

2 slices sprouted grain bread

2 teaspoons garlic powder

2 teaspoons onion powder

1 pound garbanzo beans, soaked and drained

½ red pepper, minced

½ green pepper, minced

½ zucchini, minced

¼ cup black or green olives, minced

½ red onion, minced

2 eggs, or ½ cup vegan egg substitute

1 teaspoon all-natural sea salt

1 teaspoon cracked black pepper

Don't Buy Into the Fast-Food Health-Food Hype

Catching on to the clean revolution that's taking the country to a healthier place, fast-food restaurants are now offering their own varieties of "veggie burgers." Buyer beware, though, because these "healthy" options may be healthier than other fast-food alternatives, but probably don't measure up to your expectations of healthy food. Packed with who knows what, made who knows when, and made who knows how, these unhealthy "health-food" imposters don't fit the bill of clean eating, definitely don't provide the nutrition you're looking for, and thus, don't belong anywhere in your clean lifestyle.

1. In a food processor, reduce bread slices to crumbs with the garlic and onion powders, and move to a large mixing bowl.

2. Process the garbanzo beans, red pepper, green pepper, zucchini, olives, and onion until finely minced, and add to bread crumbs.

3. Add the eggs to the mixture, and blend well. Form into 4 even patties and sprinkle with the salt and pepper.

4. Prepare a skillet over medium heat with olive oil spray, and place the patties into the skillet. Cook for 4–6 minutes on each side, or until golden brown and slightly crispy.

PER SERVING Calories: 522 | Fat: 11 g | Protein: 28 g | Sodium: 834 mg | Fiber: 21 g | Carbohydrates: 83 g | Sugar: 14 g

Quick Quinoa and Black Bean Burger

Crunchy quinoa blends with smooth black beans and flavorful vegetables for a black bean burger like no other! Packed with essential nutrition like complex carbohydrates, complete proteins, fiber, and powerful antioxidants, this is an all-natural way to enjoy the best of what nature has to offer!

INGREDIENTS | SERVES 4

2 tablespoons water

½ green bell pepper, chopped

½ cup red onion, chopped

½ cup celery, chopped

2 garlic cloves, crushed and chopped

1 cup prepared quinoa

1 cup cooked black beans, whole

1 cup cooked black beans, mashed

1 teaspoon cumin

1 teaspoon smoked paprika

¼ teaspoon cayenne

½ teaspoon all-natural sea salt

4 100% whole-wheat, whole-grain rolls

1. In a large skillet over medium heat, combine the water, bell pepper, onion, and celery, and sauté 2–3 minutes or until slightly softened. Add garlic, and continue sautéing for 2 minutes or until water has evaporated completely and vegetables are soft.

2. In a large mixing bowl, combine the quinoa, black beans, sautéed vegetables, spices, and sea salt. Combine thoroughly until mixture is thickened.

3. Form mixture into 4 even patties.

4. Prepare skillet with olive oil spray and return to medium heat. Place the burgers in the skillet, cooking for 2 minutes on each side until slightly crusted and heated through.

PER SERVING Calories: 250 | Fat: 2 g | Protein: 12 g | Sodium: 843 mg | Fiber: 11 g | Carbohydrates: 43 g | Sugar: 2 g

Quinoa for Complete Protein

This clean kitchen staple gets far less recognition than it deserves. Providing a slightly nutty crunch to your favorite dishes, this amazing seed packs tons of protein into every serving. Not a grain, quinoa is actually a seed that contains all nine essential amino acids that the body is unable to produce on its own. Rather than having to food combine in order to consume the full spectrum of proteins, quinoa is the one-stop-shop for all of your essential amino acid needs.

Lean, Mean Sloppy Joes

With all of the flavor-filled ingredients that pack these sloppy sandwiches with delicious nutrition, you'll never miss the classic fat-filled version again.

INGREDIENTS | SERVES 6

1 tablespoon extra-virgin olive oil

1 onion, minced

1 green pepper, minced

1 pound extra-firm tofu, crumbled

½ teaspoon garlic powder

1½ teaspoons dry mustard

1 teaspoon vegan Worcestershire sauce

3 tablespoons water

6 100% whole-wheat hamburger buns

High-Fructose Corn Syrup Is Where?

The next time you're searching for a healthy whole-wheat bread or bun, take a good look at the ingredient lists. While you're making sure that "stone-ground whole-wheat" or "whole-wheat flour" is the first ingredient (of which there shouldn't be too many), be on the lookout for "high-fructose corn syrup." Adding flavor and richness to breads inexpensively and easily, blood-sugar barraging high-fructose corn syrup has now crept into even the bread aisle! Save yourself the blood sugar spike and crash, and opt for a healthier alternative free of this overprocessed sweetener.

1. In a large skillet over medium heat, drizzle the olive oil and sauté the onion and pepper for 3–5 minutes, or until slightly soft. Add the tofu and sauté until brown, about 8–10 minutes.

2. In a large mixing bowl, combine the tofu, sautéed onion and green pepper, garlic powder, mustard, and Worcestershire, and mix until thoroughly combined.

3. Return the mixture to the skillet and continue to cook over medium heat, stirring constantly.

4. If the tofu seems to be drying out before completely done, add water, 1 tablespoon at a time, and continue cooking until the mixture has your preference for the perfect sloppy Joe consistency and all "meat" is browned, between 5–15 minutes.

5. Remove from heat and scoop 6 even servings onto each of the whole-wheat buns.

PER SERVING Calories: 161 | Fat: 4.5 g | Protein: 8 g | Sodium: 243 mg | Fiber: 2 g | Carbohydrates: 28 g | Sugar: 3 g

Roasted Red Pepper and Onion Wrap
with Spicy Chickpea Sauce

Accented with a creamy sauce that delivers a spicy kick, the roasted red peppers and onions in this wrap make for an intense flavor combination that's sweetly delicious and nutritious!

INGREDIENTS | SERVES 2

2 large red peppers, sliced

1 large Vidalia onion, sliced

2 garlic cloves, mashed

4 tablespoons extra-virgin olive oil

1 teaspoon all-natural sea salt

½ cup chickpeas, cooked

1 teaspoon smoked paprika

⅛ teaspoon cayenne (optional)

2 100% whole-wheat tortillas

Roast for Robust Flavors

If you're looking for flavor-packed ingredients, but have only the normal everyday ingredients like peppers, onions, and tomatoes in your fridge, you can bring out amazing flavors in your favorite foods just by roasting them. Covering a sheet pan with aluminum foil and preheating an oven or broiler to 450°F are your only prep steps; spread the sliced vegetables of your choice evenly over the pan, drizzle extra-virgin olive oil over the vegetables, and sprinkle with sea salt and pepper if you choose. Broil the vegetables for 10–15 minutes, flip or toss, and continue broiling until they've reached the desired texture, flavor, etc., of your choosing.

1. Preheat broiler to 450°F; line a baking sheet with aluminum foil and spray with olive oil spray. Scatter the red pepper strips, onion slices, and garlic cloves evenly over pan. Drizzle 2 tablespoons of olive oil over all and sprinkle with salt.

2. Broil for 20 minutes, paying close attention to prevent burning, turning as needed throughout cooking.

3. Line a plate with paper towels, and transfer the peppers and onions to the towels to drain excess oil.

4. In a blender or food processor, combine the roasted garlic, chickpeas, paprika, and cayenne. Blend until thoroughly combined, drizzling in the remaining 2 tablespoons of extra-virgin olive oil until desired consistency is achieved.

5. Spread ½ of spicy chickpea sauce over each tortilla, top with roasted red peppers and onions, and fold to close.

PER SERVING Calories: 452 | Fat: 29 g | Protein: 8 g | Sodium: 1,280 mg | Fiber: 7.5 g | Carbohydrates: 38 g | Sugar: 9 g

Sweet and Spicy Avocado Burger

Vibrant avocados lend their healthy fat creaminess to the crunchy celery and bell pepper, while the sweet mango and agave perfectly complement the spicy red pepper flakes in this burger.

INGREDIENTS | SERVES 4

1 Hass avocado, peel and pit removed
1 teaspoon lemon juice
½ red onion, minced
½ yellow pepper, minced
½ cup celery, minced
½ cup mango, minced
1 tablespoon agave nectar
½ teaspoon red pepper flakes
1 teaspoon all-natural sea salt
1 cup crumbled sprouted grain or whole-wheat bread
4 100% whole-wheat hamburger buns

1. In a large bowl, mash avocado with lemon juice, and add onion, pepper, celery, mango, agave nectar, red pepper flakes, and salt. Combine well.

2. Add bread crumbs to wet ingredients and blend thoroughly until thick.

3. Form into 4 even patties, and place on toasted buns.

PER SERVING Calories: 237 | Fat: 9 g | Protein: 5 g | Sodium: 713 mg | Fiber: 6.5 g | Carbohydrates: 30 g | Sugar: 10 g

Italian Eggplant Sandwiches

Italian-inspired, this is a wonderful meal option that combines tasty ingredients for a vegetarian "burger" alternative.

INGREDIENTS | SERVES 4

4 ½"-thick slices of eggplant

1 tablespoon dried Italian seasoning

2 teaspoons garlic powder

1 teaspoon all-natural sea salt

4 slices buffalo mozzarella, or vegan mozzarella

1 teaspoon cracked black pepper

4 whole-wheat, whole-grain hamburger buns

½ cup Tasty Tomato Sauce (see Chapter 5)

1. Prepare a grill with olive oil spray over medium heat.

2. Sprinkle eggplant slices with half of the Italian seasoning, garlic powder, and sea salt, and place seasoned-side down on grill. Grill for 6–9 minutes or until tender.

3. Sprinkle unseasoned sides with remaining Italian seasoning, garlic powder, and sea salt, and flip. Continue grilling for 5–7 minutes, or until cooked through.

4. Flip slices and immediately top with mozzarella slices. Cook for about 1 minute, or until cheese is melted, and sprinkle cracked black pepper over cheese.

5. Remove from heat, set on bun bottoms, and top with equal amounts of Tasty Tomato Sauce.

PER SERVING Calories: 201 | Fat: 7 g | Protein: 11 g | Sodium: 897 mg | Fiber: 6 g | Carbohydrates: 24 g | Sugar: 4 g

Chick Patties

Deep-fried chicken patties provide nothing of nutritional value, unlike this clean vegetarian chickpea patty that loads up on rich, satisfying flavors and clean carbohydrates, protein, and fiber.

INGREDIENTS | SERVES 4

1 tablespoon plus 1 teaspoon extra-virgin olive oil

1 cup mushrooms, diced

1 yellow onion, diced

1 teaspoon minced garlic

2 slices sprouted grain bread

1 pound garbanzo beans (soaked and drained)

2 eggs, or ½ cup vegan egg substitute

1 teaspoon all-natural sea salt

1 teaspoon cracked black pepper

1 teaspoon cumin

1 teaspoon curry powder

Skip the Fryer

With healthy cooking methods that can mimic the taste and texture that results from frying, why choose the unhealthier option? Quickly, easily, inexpensively, and with less mess, you can bake, sauté, grill, or broil any "fried" ingredient with the same great taste by simply choosing the right batter or coating that achieves the same taste and texture . . . without using large amounts of unhealthy oils.

1. In a large sauté pan, sauté the teaspoon of olive oil, mushrooms, onions, and minced garlic until soft and cooked through, about 5–7 minutes. Move from the skillet to a mixing bowl, and save skillet for cooking the completed patties.

2. In a food processor, reduce the bread slices to fine crumbs and move to the mixing bowl.

3. Add the tablespoon of olive oil, garbanzo beans, and eggs to the food processor and blend well. Move to the mixing bowl.

4. Add the sautéed vegetables to the crumbs and bean mix, and thoroughly combine all ingredients with the seasonings.

5. Bring the skillet back to medium heat, and spray with olive oil spray.

6. Form the mix into 4 patties, and set into the preheated skillet. Cook for 4–6 minutes on each side, until cooked through.

PER SERVING Calories: 548 | Fat: 14 g | Protein: 28 g | Sodium: 759 mg | Fiber: 21 g | Carbohydrates: 81 g | Sugar: 14 g

CHAPTER 7

Soups

Simple Stock
110

Spicy Sweet Potato Soup
111

Lentil-Vegetable Soup
112

Refreshing Red Lentil Soup
113

Best-Ever Vegetable-Barley
Soup
114

Simple Sweet and Spicy
Carrot Soup
114

Clean Creamy Corn Chowder
115

Cream of Broccoli Soup
115

Saucy Southwestern Soup
116

Creamy Onion-Fennel Soup
117

Clean French Onion Soup
118

Lemon, Leek, and Fennel Soup
119

Sweet Green Chickpea Soup
119

Gazpacho
120

Creamy Tomato-Basil Soup
121

Squash and Sage Soup
121

Curried Pumpkin Bisque
122

Potato-Broccolini Soup
123

Creamy Asparagus Soup
124

Clean Creamy Zucchini Soup
125

Miso Soup
126

Simple Stock

With vegetable stock acting as the main ingredient in a variety of vegetable-based soups, this clean homemade version is a great prepare-ahead stock to have on hand. Able to be stored for 1 week in the fridge, and up to 2 months in the freezer, this is an easy to make vegetable stock that's clean, quick, and inexpensive.

INGREDIENTS | MAKES 10 CUPS

1 tablespoon extra-virgin olive oil

1 pound carrots, washed and roughly chopped

1 pound celery, rinsed thoroughly and roughly chopped

1 large yellow onion, skins removed and roughly chopped

5 cloves garlic, smashed

10 whole black peppercorns

1 bay leaf

1 gallon purified water

¼ cup Tasty Tomato Sauce (see Chapter 5)

3 teaspoons all-natural sea salt

Bigger Batches Save Time

Rather than having to pick and choose meals according to what ingredients you have (or don't have!) on hand, you can simplify your clean meal prep by having large batches of certain staples ready to go in your freezer. Stocks and sauces that save well can be made in large quantities, stored in glass containers, and frozen for weeks, making meal prep as simple as defrosting while at work or play.

1. In a large stockpot over medium heat, heat olive oil until it runs smoothly. Add carrots, celery, onions, and garlic, and sauté until aromatic and slightly softened, about 4–5 minutes.

2. Add peppercorns and bay leaf; stir gently for about 1 minute to heat through. Add the water and tomato sauce. Bring to a boil, reduce heat to low, and cover. Cook for about 1 hour.

3. Remove lid, stir, add salt, and continue cooking (without cover) for another 30–45 minutes.

4. Set a strainer over a large pot and strain the vegetables from the stock.

5. If you prefer to strain more, you can pour the stock back into the pot through cheesecloth. This would ensure no bits of the vegetables remain.

PER SERVING (1 CUP) Calories: 47 | Fat: 1 g | Protein: 1 g | Sodium: 718 mg | Fiber: 1 g | Carbohydrates: 3 g | Sugar: 3 g

Spicy Sweet Potato Soup

Succulent sweet potatoes provide a vibrant flavor and color to this delectably sweet and spicy soup.

INGREDIENTS | SERVES 4

3 cups water
2 medium sweet potatoes
½ teaspoon cayenne pepper
½ teaspoon all-natural sea salt

Boil or Bake Sweet Potatoes for Better Nutrition

With a number of studies focusing on determining which foods provide the best nutritional values, more studies are focusing on the benefits of the *manner* in which those foods are prepared. By testing the nutrition content of foods in their natural state (raw), and then again after cooking them by a variety of methods, researchers have been able to identify which cooking methods maintain, promote, or deteriorate the nutrients of those foods. Sweet potatoes, for example, have been found to hold most of their nutritional value through the process of baking or boiling, while steaming has been determined to undermine the vitamin A levels.

1. In a medium pot over medium-high heat, add water.

2. Peel sweet potatoes, rinse thoroughly, and cut into ¼" slices.

3. Add sweet potato slices to pot and bring to a boil. Reduce heat to simmer and cook until sweet potatoes are fork tender, about 15–20 minutes. Remove from heat and reserve water from pot in a separate measuring cup.

4. Sprinkle sweet potatoes with ¼ teaspoon of the cayenne, and add ¼ cup of removed water back to pot.

5. Using an immersion blender, emulsify potatoes, adding removed water as needed until desired thickness is achieved.

6. While emulsifying, add remaining cayenne and salt.

PER SERVING Calories: 56 | Fat: 0 g | Protein: 1 g | Sodium: 335 mg | Fiber: 2 g | Carbohydrates: 13 g | Sugar: 2 g

Lentil-Vegetable Soup

Combining sweet and savory vegetables and spices with the lovely lentils,
this is a "souped" up version of lentil soup you're sure to enjoy!

INGREDIENTS | SERVES 8

1 tablespoon extra-virgin olive oil

½ cup yellow onion, chopped

½ cup carrot, diced

½ cup celery, diced

2 cloves garlic, minced

2 teaspoons dried Italian seasoning

1 bay leaf

2 cups dry lentils

4 cups Simple Stock (see recipe in this chapter)

4 cups water

2 large tomatoes, peeled, cored, and chopped

½ cup baby spinach leaves, rinsed

1 teaspoon all-natural sea salt

½ teaspoon cracked black pepper

1. Pour olive oil into a large pot over medium heat. After oil runs thin, add the onion, carrot, and celery, and sauté for 5 minutes, or until tender but not burned. Add the garlic, Italian seasoning, and bay leaf, and sauté for about 1 minute before adding the lentils, Simple Stock, water, and tomatoes.

2. Bring pot to a boil, reduce heat, and simmer soup uncovered for about 1 hour.

3. Before removing from heat, add spinach, salt, and pepper. Stir until spinach is wilted. Remove bay leaf before serving.

PER SERVING Calories: 198 | Fat: 3 g | Protein: 12 g | Sodium: 416 mg | Fiber: 6 g | Carbohydrates: 32 g | Sugar: 2 g

Refreshing Red Lentil Soup

Bright red lentils get paired perfectly with aromatic vegetables that create a light, luscious soup that provides amazing nutrition in a simple meal that will help you feel full and satisfied.

INGREDIENTS | SERVES 4

1 cup yellow onion, chopped

1 cup celery, chopped

1 cup carrot, chopped

4 cups Simple Stock (see recipe in this chapter)

2 cups red lentils

2 cloves garlic, minced

1 bay leaf

1 teaspoon all-natural sea salt

½ teaspoon cracked black pepper

2 large tomatoes, peeled, cored, and chopped

Lentils: Providing a One-Two Punch of Fiber

Fibrous foods can be classified into two groups: those containing *soluble fiber*, which can be absorbed by the body during digestion, and those containing *insoluble fiber*, which cannot be absorbed by the body and is flushed out with waste. Many beans and legumes are lucky enough to cross the fiber threshold and contribute both types of essential fiber to a healthy diet. Lentils, split peas, garbanzos, navy beans, and kidney beans are just a few examples of the luscious legumes that pack a one-two punch of fiber.

1. In a large pot over medium heat, add the onion, celery, carrot, and 2 tablespoons of the stock, and sauté for 5 minutes, or until vegetables are tender but not burned. Add the lentils, garlic, bay leaf, salt, and pepper, and sauté for about 1 minute before adding the remaining stock, and tomatoes.

2. Bring pot to a boil, reduce heat, and simmer soup uncovered for about 30 minutes, or until lentils are tender. Remove from heat and allow to cool for 10–15 minutes. Remove bay leaf.

3. Using an immersion blender, emulsify the lentils and vegetables until desired thickness and/or chunkiness is achieved.

PER SERVING Calories: 381 | Fat: 2 g | Protein: 22 g | Sodium: 645 mg | Fiber: 13 g | Carbohydrates: 67 g | Sugar: 6 g

Best-Ever Vegetable-Barley Soup

This rich vegetable soup gets beefed up with barley for a thick and delicious meal or snack that's packed with healthy, protective nutrients. Providing protein, complex carbohydrates, fiber, vitamins, and minerals, this soup has got all you need with the taste you want.

INGREDIENTS | SERVES 4

1 medium yellow onion, chopped

1 cup carrots, chopped

1 cup celery, chopped

4 cups Simple Stock (see recipe in this chapter)

1 cup Tasty Tomato Sauce (see Chapter 5)

1 cup quick-cooking barley

1 teaspoon all-natural sea salt

½ teaspoon cracked black pepper

1 cup green beans, cut

1. In a large pot, combine the onion, carrots, celery, and 3 tablespoons of the stock. Sauté for about 4 minutes, or until vegetables are tender but not burned.

2. Add the remaining stock, tomato sauce, barley, salt, and pepper. Cover and reduce heat to allow soup to simmer for 10 minutes.

3. Add green beans, replace cover, and continue to simmer for 10 more minutes, or until green beans are tender and barley is cooked.

PER SERVING Calories: 226 | Fat: 1 g | Protein: 7 g | Sodium: 850 mg | Fiber: 11 g | Carbohydrates: 47 g | Sugar: 6 g

Simple Sweet and Spicy Carrot Soup

Sweet carrots get even sweeter as they simmer in their own juices. Spiced up with delicious ginger and subtle shallots, the carrots take on a depth of flavor that makes this soup perfect for any occasion.

INGREDIENTS | SERVES 4

2 tablespoons ginger, grated

2 shallots, minced

4 cups purified water

1 pound baby carrots

¼ teaspoon cayenne pepper

1. In a pot over medium heat, combine the ginger and shallots with ¼ cup of the water. Sauté for 4–5 minutes, or until shallots are soft and translucent.

2. Add remaining water, carrots, and cayenne pepper to pot, and bring to a boil. Cover and reduce heat to low.

3. Simmer for 30–45 minutes or until carrots are fork tender. Remove from heat.

4. Using an immersion blender, emulsify until desired thickness is achieved.

PER SERVING Calories: 48 | Fat: 1.5 g | Protein: 1 g | Sodium: 88 mg | Fiber: 3.5 g | Carbohydrates: 11 g | Sugar: 5 g

Clean Creamy Corn Chowder

Traditional recipes for corn chowder are loaded with fattening, calorie-laden creams and preservative-packed canned ingredients that can result in a diet debacle. This clean recipe uses fresh ingredients in a creamy corn chowder you'll enjoy time and time again.

INGREDIENTS | SERVES 6

6 cups almond milk, divided

1 cup potatoes, peeled and chopped

1 cup carrots, chopped

4 cups kernel corn

1 teaspoon all-natural sea salt

1 cup low-fat plain Greek-style yogurt, or soy yogurt

1. In a large pot over medium heat, bring 3 cups of the almond milk, potatoes, and carrots to a boil. Reduce heat to low and simmer for 10 minutes.

2. Add remaining 3 cups almond milk, kernel corn, and salt. Simmer for another 5–8 minutes.

3. Remove the soup from the heat and allow to cool about 5 minutes.

4. Slowly mix in ¼ cup of the Greek-style yogurt at a time until well blended.

PER SERVING Calories: 116 | Fat: 0.5 g | Protein: 7 g | Sodium: 608 mg | Fiber: 3 g | Carbohydrates: 14 g | Sugar: 4 g

Cream of Broccoli Soup

The delicious texture of this creamy soup doesn't come from loads of heavy creams and milks, but from heart- and muscle-healthy, protein-rich yogurt. Loaded with flavor and valuable nutrients, this is a scrumptious save of the fat-laden classic.

INGREDIENTS | SERVES 4

3 cups unsweetened almond milk

2 teaspoons all-natural sea salt

2 teaspoons garlic powder

1 teaspoon cracked black pepper

2 pounds broccoli florets

1 cup plain low-fat Greek-style yogurt, or soy yogurt

1. In a large pot over medium heat, bring the almond milk, salt, garlic powder, pepper, and broccoli to a boil. Reduce heat to low and simmer about 10–12 minutes.

2. Remove from heat, and chill for 5 minutes. Using an immersion blender, emulsify the broccoli mixture until no bits remain.

3. Add yogurt, ¼ cup at a time, and continue blending with the immersion blender until well blended. Serve hot or cold.

PER SERVING Calories: 149 | Fat: 1 g | Protein: 14 g | Sodium: 1,418 mg | Fiber: 7 g | Carbohydrates: 19 g | Sugar: 6 g

Saucy Southwestern Soup

Using natural ingredients that turn a sodium-packed classic into a clean and delicious healthy alternative, this soup packs a punch of flavor, beauty, and nutrients into every bowlful.

INGREDIENTS | SERVES 6

1 yellow onion, chopped

1 cup chopped celery

1 teaspoon garlic powder

1 tablespoon fresh jalapeño, minced (optional)

½ teaspoon cayenne pepper

1 teaspoon cilantro, chopped

6 cups Simple Stock (see recipe in this chapter)

2 cups Spicy Clean Refried Beans (see Chapter 9)

1 cup tomatoes, chopped

1 cup fresh or frozen corn kernels

1 teaspoon all-natural sea salt

½ teaspoon cracked black pepper

1. In a large pot, combine the onion, celery, garlic powder, jalapeño, cayenne, and cilantro, plus ¼ cup of the stock. Sauté for about 2 minutes, or until vegetables are only slightly tender.

2. Add the remaining stock, refried beans, tomatoes, corn, salt, and pepper. Bring to a boil. Reduce heat to low and allow soup to simmer for 10–15 minutes, or until corn is cooked through and flavors are married.

PER SERVING Calories: 112 | Fat: 1 g | Protein: 6 g | Sodium: 556 mg | Fiber: 5.5 g | Carbohydrates: 21 g | Sugar: 2 g

Creamy Onion-Fennel Soup

If you like onions and fennel, you'll love this soup! The bright flavors of its tangy ingredients get heightened with roasting, then cooled with creamy yogurt for a refreshing soup that's soon to be one of your favorites!

INGREDIENTS | SERVES 2

2 fennel bulbs

2 large Vidalia onions

1 tablespoon extra-virgin olive oil

1 teaspoon all-natural sea salt

1 cup Simple Stock (see recipe in this chapter)

2 cups Greek-style nonfat yogurt, or soy yogurt

1. Preheat oven to 400°F and prepare a roasting pan with olive oil spray.

2. Roughly chop the fennel bulbs and onions into ¼" pieces, and scatter over pan. Drizzle fennel and onion with olive oil and sprinkle with salt. Roast for 30 minutes, turning every 10–15 minutes to prevent burning.

3. Remove the roasting pan from the heat, pour the stock over the vegetables, and allow to sit for about 5 minutes. Pour the vegetables, stock, and any bits from roasting pan into a mixing bowl and allow to cool for 10–15 minutes.

4. Using an immersion blender, emulsify vegetables to desired chunkiness. Gradually stir in the yogurt until desired thickness is achieved.

PER SERVING Calories: 288 | Fat: 7 g | Protein: 13 g | Sodium: 1,290 mg | Fiber: 10 g | Carbohydrates: 37 g | Sugar: 12 g

Clean French Onion Soup

Topped with croutons and heavy Gruyère cheese, the classic calorie-, sodium-, and preservative-stocked French onion soup is nothing shy of a clean diet nightmare. With a few ingenious swaps and natural substitutions, you can create your old favorite without the guilt.

INGREDIENTS | SERVES 4

¼ cup olive oil

4 Vidalia onions, sliced

4 cloves garlic, minced

1 tablespoon dried thyme

½ cup vegan Worcestershire sauce

4½ cups Simple Stock (see recipe in this chapter)

1 teaspoon all-natural sea salt

1 teaspoon cracked black pepper

4 slices 100% whole-wheat French bread

4 ounces buffalo mozzarella, or vegan mozzarella

1. In a sauté pan, heat the olive oil over medium-high heat and cook the onions until golden brown, about 3 minutes. Add the garlic and sauté for 1 minute.

2. In a 4-quart slow cooker, pour the sautéed vegetables, thyme, Worcestershire sauce, stock, salt, and pepper. Cover and cook on low heat for 4 hours.

3. While the soup is cooking, preheat the oven to the broiler setting. Lightly toast the slices of French bread.

4. To serve, ladle the soup into 4 broiler-safe bowls, place a slice of the toasted French bread on top of the soup in each bowl, followed by a slice of the mozzarella cheese on top of the bread. Place the soup under the broiler until the cheese has melted.

PER SERVING Calories: 375 | Fat: 19 g | Protein: 12 g | Sodium: 1,197 mg | Fiber: 3 g | Carbohydrates: 37 g | Sugar: 8 g

Lemon, Leek, and Fennel Soup

With the lightly licorice flavors of fennel, heightened by the zing of lemon and the slight spice of leeks, this soup is brimming with powerful, fragrant flavors that are just the right combination.

INGREDIENTS | SERVES 4

1 tablespoon extra-virgin olive oil

4 cups Simple Stock (see recipe in this chapter)

2 fennel bulbs, roughly chopped into ¼" chunks

4 large leeks, trimmed, rinsed, and chopped into ¼" pieces

2 lemons, rinsed, quartered, and deseeded

1 teaspoon all-natural sea salt

1. In a pot over medium heat, combine olive oil, 4 tablespoons of the stock, fennel, and leeks. Juice the lemons into the pot, and add lemon quarters. Sauté for 3–5 minutes, stirring frequently until leeks and fennel are soft. Remove lemon quarters and discard.

2. Add remaining stock to pot, bring to a boil, reduce heat, and simmer uncovered for 10–15 minutes. Add salt.

PER SERVING Calories: 128 | Fat: 4 g | Protein: 3 g | Sodium: 668 mg | Fiber: 6 g | Carbohydrates: 23 g | Sugar: 4 g

Sweet Green Chickpea Soup

The delightful sweetness of perfect petite peas explodes in every sip of this thick chickpea creation. With vibrant, clean ingredients that provide tons of essential nutrition, this recipe is a flavor-packed meal or snack that's as delicious and nutritious as it is beautiful.

INGREDIENTS | SERVES 4

4 cups water

1 cup broccoli spears, chopped

1 leek, cleaned and chopped

2 cups soaked chickpeas (24 hours or more of soaking is best)

4 garlic cloves, finely minced

2 cups spinach leaves, chopped

1 cup petite peas, fresh or frozen

1 teaspoon cracked black pepper

1. In a large pot over medium heat, bring the water, broccoli, leek, chickpeas, and garlic to a boil. Reduce heat to low and simmer 15–20 minutes.

2. Add the spinach leaves, peas, and black pepper, and continue to cook for about 5 minutes. Remove from heat.

3. With an immersion blender, emulsify the ingredients until well blended and no bits remain.

PER SERVING Calories: 395 | Fat: 6 g | Protein: 21 g | Sodium: 56 mg | Fiber: 19 g | Carbohydrates: 67 g | Sugar: 12 g

Gazpacho

This recipe takes an old favorite and cleans it up with all-natural ingredients that combine for healthy nutrition and none of the undesirable sodium, fat, and calories found in the not-so-clean classic.

INGREDIENTS | SERVES 4

2 cups Tasty Tomato Sauce (see Chapter 5)

2 cups water

2 tomatoes, chopped

1 yellow onion, chopped

1 green pepper, chopped

½ cup scallions, chopped

1 English cucumber, chopped

2 cloves garlic, finely minced

2 tablespoons freshly squeezed lemon juice

2 tablespoons red wine vinegar

1 teaspoon dried basil

1 teaspoon dried thyme

1 teaspoon all-natural sea salt

1 teaspoon cracked black pepper

1. In a food processor, combine all ingredients and pulse until thoroughly blended and still slightly chunky.

2. Chill at least 2–4 hours, but overnight is best.

PER SERVING Calories: 79 | Fat: 1 g | Protein: 3.5 g | Sodium: 1,246 mg | Fiber: 4 g | Carbohydrates: 18 g | Sugar: 11 g

Creamy Tomato-Basil Soup

Packed with vitamins like vitamin A that do double duty as antioxidants and powerful phytochemicals like lutein, this soup loads up any body with powerful nutrition to guard and protect health.

INGREDIENTS | SERVES 4

1 cup water

10 tomatoes, peeled and chopped

1 cup chopped basil

1 tablespoon minced garlic

2 teaspoons all-natural sea salt

2 cups Tasty Tomato Sauce (see Chapter 5)

1 cup plain Greek-style low-fat yogurt, or soy yogurt

1. In a large pot, bring the water, tomatoes, basil, and garlic to a boil. Reduce heat to low and simmer for about 15–20 minutes. Allow to cool.

2. With an immersion blender, emulsify the tomatoes and spices completely until no bits remain.

3. Add the sea salt and tomato sauce. Add the yogurt, ¼ cup at a time, and use the immersion blender to fully combine. Serve hot or cold.

PER SERVING Calories: 127 | Fat: 1 g | Protein: 11 g | Sodium: 1,868 mg | Fiber: 6 g | Carbohydrates: 22 g | Sugar: 16 g

Squash and Sage Soup

The unique essence of dried sage swirls throughout every delightful sip of this scrumptious soup, adding a delightful hint of spice to the sweetness of the acorn squash.

INGREDIENTS | SERVES 4

4 cups water

3 cups cubed summer squash, peeled and seeds removed

2 teaspoons all-natural sea salt

½ cup dried sage leaves

½ cup plain nonfat Greek yogurt

1. Bring the water to a boil in a large pot over medium heat.

2. Reduce heat to low, add the squash, salt, and sage, and simmer for about 20–25 minutes, or until fork tender.

3. Using an immersion blender, emulsify the squash and sage until no bits remain.

4. Serve hot or cold, and garnish with a dollop of nonfat yogurt or crumbled sage leaves.

PER SERVING Calories: 26 | Fat: 1 g | Protein: 1.5 g | Sodium: 1,188 mg | Fiber: 2.5 g | Carbohydrates: 5 g | Sugar: 2 g

Curried Pumpkin Bisque

Pumpkin purée isn't just for pumpkin pie anymore! The warm spice of curry packs a punch of flavor into this rich soup of vibrant pumpkin and cool coconut milk.

INGREDIENTS | SERVES 4

4 cups pumpkin purée

2½ cups coconut milk

3 teaspoons curry

1 teaspoon all-natural sea salt

1 teaspoon cracked black pepper

The "Good-for-You" Starch in Pumpkin

When most people think of starchy carbohydrates, their minds turn to a list of foods they've been told to avoid. While early researchers who studied carbohydrates like breads, potatoes, and pastas warned consumers to beware of foods high in starch because of their effects on blood sugar and the waistline, recent research has shown that the *source* of starch is far more important than the starch itself. Pumpkin and other winter squashes have actually been deemed as beneficial starches because they produce phytochemicals called *pectins* that contain a specific acid called *homogalacturonan* that acts as a triple-threat to fending off disease by promoting the health of cells as an antioxidant, preventing cell damage as an anti-inflammatory agent, and stabilizing blood sugar with its ability to regulate blood insulin.

1. In a large pot over medium heat, whisk together the pumpkin purée and coconut milk. Add curry and combine thoroughly.

2. Heat through, about 5–7 minutes, and remove from heat.

3. Add sea salt and black pepper.

PER SERVING Calories: 313 | Fat: 30 g | Protein: 4 g | Sodium: 608 mg | Fiber: 1 g | Carbohydrates: 12 g | Sugar: 1.5 g

Potato-Broccolini Soup

Thick and hearty, this soup pairs the starchy potato with spicy Broccolini for a texture and flavor sensation that's hard to beat. Naturally packed with essential vitamins and minerals, these ingredients boast complex carbohydrates that provide long-lasting energy in a soup that will fill you up but won't weigh you down.

INGREDIENTS | SERVES 4

3 cups unsweetened almond milk

2 Idaho potatoes, peeled

1 pound Broccolini

1 cup plain low-fat Greek-style yogurt, or soy yogurt

2 teaspoons all-natural sea salt

Broaden Your Definition of "Hearty"

Hearty bowls of soup don't have to be thick stews made of meat and thickly cut vegetables. By puréeing a blend of yogurt or milk with a combination of your favorite vegetables and ingredients, you can end up with a filling meal. Thick and hearty, or thinned and hearty, it's the vegetables and ingredients that make up your delicious soup that make it a "hearty" helping.

1. In a large pot over medium heat, bring the almond milk and potatoes to a boil. Reduce heat to low and simmer about 8–10 minutes.

2. Add Broccolini, and continue to simmer for 8–10 minutes.

3. Remove from heat, and chill for 5 minutes.

4. Using an immersion blender, emulsify ingredients.

5. Add yogurt, ¼ cup at a time, and continue blending with the immersion blender.

6. Add salt, blend well, and serve.

PER SERVING Calories: 178 | Fat: 0.5 g | Protein: 12 g | Sodium: 1,386 mg | Fiber: 6 g | Carbohydrates: 27 g | Sugar: 6 g

Creamy Asparagus Soup

The sweetness of asparagus spears brightens this soup to make for a palate-pleasing and aesthetically pleasing soup with a shade of green that is indicative of its high concentration of vitamin K. Combined with the protein from the yogurt, this soup's ingredients provide top-notch nutrition.

INGREDIENTS | SERVES 4

1 tablespoon extra-virgin olive oil

1 yellow onion, chopped

2 pounds asparagus

2 cups Simple Stock (see recipe in this chapter), divided

1 teaspoon all-natural sea salt

1 teaspoon cracked black pepper

1 cup coconut milk

½ cup Greek-style low-fat yogurt, or soy yogurt

1. In a large pot over medium heat, combine the olive oil and onions, and sauté until onions are translucent, about 5 minutes.

2. Trim the asparagus spears and add to the pot with 3 tablespoons stock. Season with salt and pepper, and sauté for 5 minutes or until fork tender.

3. Add the remaining stock, bring to a boil, and reduce heat to low. Stir in coconut milk and simmer for about 15–20 minutes.

4. Remove from heat and allow to cool for about 10–15 minutes.

5. Using an immersion blender, emulsify ingredients until smooth. Add the yogurt, and mix until completely blended.

PER SERVING Calories: 217 | Fat: 16 g | Protein: 8 g | Sodium: 624 mg | Fiber: 5 g | Carbohydrates: 15 g | Sugar: 7 g

Clean Creamy Zucchini Soup

A creamy soup packed with rich colors, flavors, and textures from the zucchini, sweet onion, spicy garlic, and creamy yogurt, this is a one-pot creation that is delicious and amazingly nutritious.

INGREDIENTS | SERVES 6

1 tablespoon extra-virgin olive oil

1 large Vidalia onion, sliced

2 cups Simple Stock (see recipe in this chapter)

2 pounds zucchini, rinsed and sliced

2 cloves garlic, minced

1 teaspoon all-natural sea salt

1 teaspoon cracked black pepper

1 teaspoon Italian seasoning

2 cups nonfat Greek-style yogurt or soy yogurt

Zucchini: A Blank Canvas

Aside from all of the valuable nutrients like vitamins B_6 and C, minerals like magnesium and folate, and amazing antioxidants that all combine to protect and improve your health, zucchini has the added benefit of being able to absorb the flavors of any dish. Much like a blank canvas, zucchini can be painted with flavors from foods or spices to provide a unique crunch or softness to any dish but with the flavors of other powerful ingredients.

1. In a large pot over medium heat, warm the olive oil and add the sliced onions. Sauté for about 4–5 minutes, or until onions are soft and translucent.

2. Add 3 tablespoons of the stock to the pot, and the zucchini, garlic, salt, pepper, and Italian seasoning. Sauté for 10–12 minutes, or until zucchini is soft.

3. Add the remaining stock, bring to a boil, reduce heat to low, and simmer for 25–30 minutes.

4. Remove the pot from heat, and allow soup to cool for about 15–20 minutes. Using an immersion blender, emulsify the ingredients to desired chunkiness. Gradually stir in the yogurt, ½ cup at a time, until desired thickness and texture is achieved.

PER SERVING Calories: 98 | Fat: 3 g | Protein: 9 g | Sodium: 450 mg | Fiber: 2 g | Carbohydrates: 13 g | Sugar: 10 g

Miso Soup

This classic Asian favorite can be made at home, allowing you to control the quality of each ingredient. Now you don't have to visit your favorite restaurant to indulge in miso soup, you can enjoy a clean version any time you like!

INGREDIENTS | SERVES 4

4 cups water

3 teaspoons dashi granules

2 tablespoons red miso paste

1 (8-ounce) package of silken tofu, cubed

4 scallions, diced

Miso's Main Ingredients

If you love miso, you may wonder what it is that makes the soup such a unique flavor combination that stands out. In the traditional miso soup, seaweed and dried fish are simmered in order to brighten the stock with their intense flavors; dashi is the condensed version of these ingredients that is available in granules, pastes, or powders. The miso is the other flavor element, and it can be purchased in a variety of textures, flavors, and intensities; sweeter miso pastes are normally yellow and creamy, while the red version is saltier. Making the miso soup-making easy to do at home, these essential elements are now readily available at most local grocery stores.

1. In a large pot over medium heat, combine the water and dashi granules and bring to a boil. Reduce heat to low and add the miso paste, stirring or whisking to combine thoroughly. Allow to simmer for about 5 minutes.

2. Add the tofu and scallions, and gently simmer for 5 minutes.

3. Remove from heat and serve.

PER SERVING Calories: 56 | Fat: 2 g | Protein: 4 g | Sodium: 334 mg | Fiber: 1 g | Carbohydrates: 5 g | Sugar: 1 g

CHAPTER 8

Salads

Cucumber-Tabbouleh Salad
128

Citrus, Fennel, and
Spinach Salad
128

Ginger-Citrus-Apple Salad
129

Crisp Romaine Salad with
Balsamic Tomatoes
129

Antipasto Salad
130

Colorful Vegetable-Pasta Salad
130

Cucumber-Melon Salad
131

Tropical Island Salad
131

Avocados and Greens
132

Spicy Cilantro-Tomato Salad
132

Baked Apples and Pears with
Leafy Greens
133

Sweet and Spicy Cabbage with
Cranberries and Walnuts
134

Strawberry-Walnut-Flaxseed
Salad
135

Tomato, Mozzarella, and
Spinach Salad
136

Asian Almond-Mandarin Salad
136

Tex-Mex Salad
137

Roasted Fennel, Tomato, and
Chickpea Toss
138

Lighter Waldorf Salad
139

Tangy Three-Bean Salad
139

Bean and Couscous Salad
140

Lemon-Scented Rice with
Fruit Salsa Salad
140

Cucumber-Tabbouleh Salad

This delightful blend of cucumbers and bulgur makes a versatile salad that can be enjoyed as a refreshing snack on its own or as a delicious side to your favorite tofu recipe.

INGREDIENTS | SERVES 2

2 large cucumbers, peeled and chopped
2 tablespoons extra-virgin olive oil
2 tablespoons red wine vinegar
2 cups cooked bulgur

Cucumbers for . . . Everything

Not only are cucumbers heralded for their high water content, they are also packed with an amazing nutrient called silica, which may make your skin look and feel younger, your nails stronger, and your hair shinier. Cucumbers also produce lignans, which scientists believe might play a role in preventing certain estrogen-related cancers.

1. Combine the cucumbers, olive oil, and vinegar in a mixing bowl, and toss to combine.

2. Fold the bulgur into the cucumber mix, and combine thoroughly.

3. Refrigerate for 1 hour, and serve in 2 salad bowls.

PER SERVING Calories: 279 | Fat: 18 g | Protein: 5 g | Sodium: 44 mg | Fiber: 5 g | Carbohydrates: 28 g | Sugar: 5 g

Citrus, Fennel, and Spinach Salad

Tangy citrus and licorice-flavored fennel combine with rich spinach in this refreshing salad that will tantalize your taste buds and leave you feeling full but not weighed down.

INGREDIENTS | SERVES 2

1 tablespoon extra-virgin olive oil
1 lemon, juiced (about ¼ cup)
1 tablespoon agave nectar
1 red grapefruit, peeled and deseeded
1 white grapefruit, peeled and deseeded
2 oranges, peeled and deseeded
1 fennel bulb, cut into bite-sized chunks
2 cups baby spinach, washed

1. In a mixing bowl, combine the olive oil, lemon juice, and agave nectar. Whisk to combine thoroughly.

2. Slice the peeled grapefruits and oranges into bite-sized chunks; combine with the fennel in the mixing bowl of the olive oil, lemon juice, and agave nectar; and toss to coat.

3. Add the spinach and toss to coat. Serve immediately, or cover and refrigerate for 1 hour before serving.

PER SERVING Calories: 286 | Fat: 7 g | Protein: 6 g | Sodium: 85 mg | Fiber: 11 g | Carbohydrates: 57 g | Sugar: 36 g

Ginger-Citrus-Apple Salad

Spicy ginger is a perfect complement to the bright citrus flavors in this nutritious and delightful salad.

INGREDIENTS | SERVES 2

1 red grapefruit, peeled and deseeded

2 oranges, peeled and deseeded

1 pineapple, peeled and cored

2 Granny Smith apples, cored

3 tablespoons lemon juice

2 tablespoons freshly grated ginger

1. Cut the grapefruit, oranges, pineapple, and apples into bite-sized pieces. Place all fruit in a shallow glass bowl.

2. Sprinkle the fruit with the lemon juice and top with the grated ginger. Toss to coat evenly. Cover and marinate for 1 hour before serving, tossing every 15–20 minutes to prevent the apple from discoloring.

PER SERVING Calories: 402 | Fat: 1 g | Protein: 5 g | Sodium: 4.5 mg | Fiber: 12 g | Carbohydrates: 92 g | Sugar: 76 g

Crisp Romaine Salad with Balsamic Tomatoes

Sweetness from the balsamic vinegar and maple syrup soak the tomatoes through and through to brighten their natural flavors and create a delicious depth to this crisp romaine salad.

INGREDIENTS | SERVES 2

1 teaspoon maple syrup

1 cup balsamic vinegar

2 pints of grape tomatoes

2 large heads of romaine lettuce

1. In a mixing bowl, combine the maple syrup and balsamic vinegar. Prick grape tomatoes with a fork and toss in the balsamic mixture. Cover and marinate for 1 hour.

2. Remove the hard "spine" of the romaine leaves and discard. Rip or chop the leaves and combine with the balsamic tomatoes tossing to coat thoroughly.

3. Serve cold.

PER SERVING Calories: 282 | Fat: 2.5 g | Protein: 11 g | Sodium: 94 mg | Fiber: 16 g | Carbohydrates: 58 g | Sugar: 36 g

Antipasto Salad

Traditional antipasto salads load up on preservative-packed ingredients that provide way too much sodium and unnecessary chemicals. This truly amazing blend of delightful vegetables and vinegars combine for an all-natural, clean antipasto you can indulge in guilt-free and healthfully!

INGREDIENTS | SERVES 4

2 cups black olives
2 cups artichoke hearts
2 cups roasted red pepper strips
8 pepperoncinis
1 cup sliced banana peppers
4 tablespoons white vinegar
4 cups chopped romaine lettuce
2 tablespoons red wine vinegar
2 tablespoons extra-virgin olive oil
1 tablespoon dried oregano

1. In a large shallow dish, combine the olives, artichoke hearts, red peppers, pepperoncinis, and banana peppers in the white vinegar. Soak for 1 hour, tossing frequently.

2. In a large mixing bowl, combine the romaine, red wine vinegar, olive oil, and oregano. Toss to coat.

3. Drain the vegetables, and add them to the romaine. Toss to blend thoroughly.

PER SERVING Calories: 288 | Fat: 15 g | Protein: 10 g | Sodium: 1,277 mg | Fiber: 22 g | Carbohydrates: 44 g | Sugar: 7 g

Colorful Vegetable-Pasta Salad

This pasta salad's blend of fresh vegetables, whole-wheat pasta, and spicy vinegars make for a healthy alternative to the traditional mayo-based pasta salads . . . with the added benefit of packing health-promoting, cell-protecting antioxidants into every bite.

INGREDIENTS | SERVES 2

1 large yellow bell pepper, sliced
1 large red bell pepper, sliced
1 cup yellow onion, sliced
1 cup zucchini, sliced
1 tablespoon extra-virgin olive oil
1 teaspoon all-natural sea salt
2 cups cooked 100% whole-wheat rigatoni
2 tablespoons balsamic vinegar

1. In a large skillet over medium heat, sauté the sliced vegetables with the olive oil and sea salt until tender, about 5 minutes.

2. Remove the vegetables from the heat and allow to cool.

3. In a large mixing bowl, combine the sautéed vegetables, cooked pasta, and balsamic vinegar until thoroughly combined.

4. Serve immediately for a hot dish, or cover and refrigerate 2–4 hours for a chilled variation.

PER SERVING Calories: 473 | Fat: 15 g | Protein: 15 g | Sodium: 1,202 mg | Fiber: 17 g | Carbohydrates: 75 g | Sugar: 10 g

Cucumber-Melon Salad

Refreshingly replenishing every cell with their water and silica content, the cucumbers and melons in this light and delightful complex carbohydrate–rich salad will leave you feeling full and satisfied with quality energy that will last for hours!

INGREDIENTS | SERVES 2

2 large cucumbers, peeled
½ cantaloupe, peeled and deseeded
½ honeydew, peeled and deseeded
2 cups watermelon chunks
1 tablespoon agave nectar
1 tablespoon lemon juice

1. Slice cucumbers lengthwise and then into ¼"-thick pieces. Either use a melon baller to form melons into bite-sized balls, or cut the cantaloupe and honeydew into bite-sized chunks. Cut the watermelon into same size pieces.

2. In a large mixing bowl, whisk together the agave nectar and lemon juice until thoroughly combined.

3. Add the melon pieces to the mixing bowl and toss to coat completely. Serve immediately, or cover and marinate for 1 hour, tossing every 15–20 minutes.

PER SERVING Calories: 277 | Fat: 1 g | Protein: 4 g | Sodium: 70 mg | Fiber: 4 g | Carbohydrates: 52 g | Sugar: 49 g

Tropical Island Salad

This salad is a bright snack or meal that packs a punch of complex carbohydrates, protein, omega-3s, and omega-6s in every sweet, enjoyable bite.

INGREDIENTS | SERVES 2

1 cup coconut milk
1 tablespoon agave nectar
1 tablespoon ground flaxseed
2 tablespoons chia seeds
2 cups unsweetened shredded coconut
1 cup chopped walnuts
4 cups pineapple chunks

1. In a blender, combine the coconut milk, agave nectar, ground flaxseed, and chia seeds. Blend until thoroughly combined and thick. Pour mixture into a large mixing bowl.

2. Add the shredded coconut and walnuts to the coconut milk mixture, and toss to combine.

3. Add the pineapple chunks to the mixture, toss to combine, and plate equal amounts into 2 bowls.

PER SERVING Calories: 1,029 | Fat: 79 g | Protein: 17 g | Sodium: 29 mg | Fiber: 16 g | Carbohydrates: 70 g | Sugar: 39 g

Avocados and Greens

Filling, yet light, this salad is rich with healthy fats that will satisfy your hunger, calm your cravings, and make your meal a delicious one that's packed with a variety of nutrients that will boost your energy levels and benefit your body and your brain in a number of ways.

INGREDIENTS | SERVES 2

2 limes, juiced (about ½ cup)
1 tablespoon agave nectar
3 tablespoons red wine vinegar
1 teaspoon all-natural sea salt
1 large Hass avocado, peeled and pitted
¼ pound cherry tomatoes, halved
½ pound baby spinach leaves, washed

1. In a mixing bowl, combine the lime juice, agave nectar, red wine vinegar, and salt. Whisk well until combined.

2. Slice the avocados into ¼"-thick lengthwise strips, combine with the halved cherry tomatoes, and add to the lime juice and agave mixture. Toss to coat, cover, and refrigerate for 20 minutes.

3. Add baby spinach to the marinated avocados and tomatoes; toss to combine thoroughly. Serve immediately.

PER SERVING Calories: 253 | Fat: 14 g | Protein: 6 g | Sodium: 1,230 mg | Fiber: 11 g | Carbohydrates: 30 g | Sugar: 12 g

Spicy Cilantro-Tomato Salad

The richness of goat cheese and the bite of balsamic vinegar bring the cool romaine and spicy arugula to a new level of deliciousness. This salad is a satisfying snack or main course meal you're sure to enjoy.

INGREDIENTS | SERVES 2

½ cup chopped cilantro
¼ cup extra-virgin olive oil
¼ cup balsamic vinegar
2 large tomatoes, cored and quartered
1 cup romaine hearts, rinsed and torn into bite-sized pieces
1 cup spicy arugula, rinsed
1 teaspoon all-natural sea salt
1 teaspoon cracked black pepper
½ cup crumbled goat cheese

1. In a large salad bowl, add the cilantro, olive oil, and balsamic vinegar, and whisk until well blended.

2. Add the tomatoes to the cilantro mixture, cover, and marinate for 1 hour.

3. Toss the romaine heart pieces and arugula in the marinated tomatoes mixture, sprinkle with sea salt and pepper, and plate equal amounts on 2 salad plates.

4. Top with goat cheese and serve.

PER SERVING Calories: 459 | Fat: 39 g | Protein: 12 g | Sodium: 1,301 mg | Fiber: 3 g | Carbohydrates: 15 g | Sugar: 10 g

Baked Apples and Pears with Leafy Greens

Baking the apples and pears that top this sinfully sweet salad makes for brighter flavors that combine perfectly with a delightful mix of greens and creamy goat cheese. Perfect for a snack or meal, this salad calms your cravings in a healthful way.

INGREDIENTS | SERVES 2

1 yellow apple, cored and quartered

1 pear, cored and quartered

2 cups hot water

2 tablespoons maple syrup

1 tablespoon extra-virgin olive oil

1 cup baby spinach, rinsed

1 cup mixed greens, rinsed

½ cup crumbled low-fat goat cheese

A Super Fruit to Promote SOD Production

If you have no idea what "SOD" is, you're not alone. A specific enzyme called *superoxide dismutase* (SOD) is a "super-antioxidant" produced by the body to fend off dangerous free radicals, termed *superoxide radicals*. In order to eliminate the dangerous free radicals, *superoxide dismutase* depends on the body's availability of copper stores to act effectively against the superoxide radicals. Because of pears' copper content, these fruits are an excellent part of a daily diet that can prepare the body for super-protection by supplying essential copper the body needs.

1. Preheat the oven to 400°F, and place apple and pear quarters in a 13"×9" glass dish. Cover apples and pears with hot water, and drizzle with 1 tablespoon of the maple syrup. Bake for 30–45 minutes, or until fork tender. Remove pan from heat, transfer apples and pears to a salad bowl, and allow to cool for 15 minutes.

2. In a large mixing bowl, combine the remaining tablespoon of maple syrup and the olive oil by whisking. Add spinach and mixed greens to mixing bowl and toss to coat. Plate equal amounts of the salad on 2 salad plates or bowls.

3. Top the salads with 2 slices each of the apples and pears and ¼ cup each of the goat cheese.

PER SERVING Calories: 355 | Fat: 18 g | Protein: 12 g | Sodium: 232 mg | Fiber: 4 g | Carbohydrates: 36 g | Sugar: 26 g

Sweet and Spicy Cabbage with Cranberries and Walnuts

Vibrant red cabbage gets all sweet and spicy with the delightful additions of sweet maple syrup, tangy lemon, crunchy walnuts, cranberries, and ginger.

INGREDIENTS | SERVES 2

2 cups cranberries, cooked

2 tablespoons grated ginger

¼ cup lemon juice (about 1 lemon)

1 tablespoon maple syrup

1 teaspoon lemon zest

2 cups red cabbage, shredded

1 cup walnuts, crushed

Cranberries' Proanthrocyanadins

Cranberries have long been used to prevent urinary tract infections (UTIs) and alleviate the intensity of symptoms resulting from the infection, but few know what the active aid in cranberries is that helps this uncomfortable situation. Cranberries contain unique phytochemicals called *proanthrocyanadins* that act as a protective barrier in the urinary tract's lining to prevent bacteria from adhering to the walls and causing an infection.

1. Using a blender, food processor, or immersion blender, emulsify 1 cup of the cooked cranberries, grated ginger, lemon juice, and maple syrup until well blended. In a large mixing bowl, combine the emulsified mixture with the remaining whole cooked cranberries and lemon zest.

2. Add the shredded cabbage to the cranberry mixture, toss to coat well, cover, and refrigerate for a minimum of 1 hour, or as long as overnight.

3. Toss cabbage with walnuts, plate equal amounts onto 2 salad plates, and serve.

PER SERVING Calories: 487 | Fat: 38 g | Protein: 10 g | Sodium: 24 mg | Fiber: 11 g | Carbohydrates: 36 g | Sugar: 14 g

Strawberry-Walnut-Flaxseed Salad

Heightened and brightened by the addition of mint, this salad's ingredients pop with intense delicious flavor that makes for a salad so good it doesn't need greens!

INGREDIENTS | SERVES 2

4 cups strawberries, tops removed
1 cup walnuts, crushed
2 tablespoons ground flaxseed
1 tablespoon red wine vinegar
½ tablespoon agave nectar
2 sprigs mint leaves

Sneak Extra Nutrition Into Every Bite

Adding a beautiful appearance, a nutty flavor, and a delicious crunch to your salads, flaxseeds also contribute essential fats to your favorite foods. You can top salads, pastas, entrées, and even sandwiches with these delightful golden seeds of deliciously nutty tasting nutrition, and relish the flavor and benefits!

1. Quarter the strawberries and place in a mixing bowl.

2. Add the walnuts and ground flaxseed to the strawberries.

3. Drizzle the red wine vinegar and agave nectar over the salad, and toss to coat.

4. Split the salad between 2 salad bowls, garnish each with a mint sprig, and serve.

PER SERVING Calories: 516 | Fat: 41 g | Protein: 12.5 g | Sodium: 4 mg | Fiber: 12 g | Carbohydrates: 34 g | Sugar: 17 g

Tomato, Mozzarella, and Spinach Salad

This is a quick and easy salad that provides a solid foundation of complex carbohydrates, protein, and fat with an abundance of vitamins and minerals that come together in a mouthwatering combination.

INGREDIENTS | SERVES 2

2 cups baby spinach leaves, washed
1 cup tomatoes, chopped
½ cup fresh buffalo mozzarella, chopped
2 tablespoons extra-virgin olive oil
2 teaspoons dried basil leaves

1. Set out 2 salad bowls, and split the spinach evenly between them.

2. Top each salad with half of the tomatoes.

3. Top each salad with half of the mozzarella.

4. Drizzle the olive oil over the top of both salads and sprinkle with the dried basil.

PER SERVING Calories: 227 | Fat: 20 g | Protein: 8 g | Sodium: 205 mg | Fiber: 2 g | Carbohydrates: 5 g | Sugar: 3 g

Asian Almond-Mandarin Salad

The intense fragrances and flavors of sesame oil and rice wine vinegar give this salad's sweet ingredients the perfect background of sensational taste. This Asian-inspired salad is a light, healthy snack that will surprise your taste buds and satisfy your hunger.

INGREDIENTS | SERVES 2

1 tablespoon rice wine vinegar
1 tablespoon sesame oil
1 teaspoon agave nectar
1 tablespoon fresh ginger, minced
2 cups endive leaves, chopped
½ cup slivered almonds
1 cup mandarin orange slices

1. In a mixing bowl, whisk together the vinegar, sesame oil, agave nectar, and the minced ginger until well blended.

2. Toss the chopped endive leaves in the dressing to coat.

3. Split the salad between 2 salad bowls.

4. Top evenly with the slivered almonds and mandarin oranges.

PER SERVING Calories: 284 | Fat: 19 g | Protein: 7 g | Sodium: 5.5 mg | Fiber: 8 g | Carbohydrates: 26 g | Sugar: 14 g

Tex-Mex Salad

Feel a little spicy? With vibrantly colored ingredients that are loaded with a variety of nutrition, flavors, and textures, this is a healthy salad that will calm any spicy food craving.

INGREDIENTS | SERVES 2

1 tablespoon extra-virgin olive oil
1 cup black beans, soaked and drained
1 cup corn kernels
1 cup chopped tomatoes
1 teaspoon cayenne pepper
1 teaspoon cumin
2 cups romaine lettuce, chopped

Any Salad Can Be a Meal

If you start getting really creative with your salads, you can start converting your favorite dishes into healthier versions. Take any cuisine like Asian, Italian, Mediterranean, Southern, or Mexican, and you can twist any favorite recipe into a salad recipe. Start with a bed of lettuce, and start loading up the ingredients. Whether the spices are what make the cuisine unique, or the protein sources that make it great, throw them in a salad.

1. In a large mixing bowl, combine the olive oil, black beans, corn, and tomatoes with the cayenne and cumin, and toss to coat.

2. Add the chopped romaine lettuce, and toss to thoroughly combine.

3. Divide the salad evenly between 2 salad bowls, and serve.

PER SERVING Calories: 275.5 | Fat: 9 g | Protein: 11 g | Sodium: 393 mg | Fiber: 11 g | Carbohydrates: 43.5 g | Sugar: 8.5 g

Roasted Fennel, Tomato, and Chickpea Toss

Roasting tomatoes and fennel intensifies their delightful flavors and makes this salad a bright fusion of flavors.

INGREDIENTS | SERVES 2

2 large fennel bulbs, cut into ¼" chunks

2 pints cherry tomatoes

2 tablespoons extra-virgin olive oil

1 teaspoon all-natural sea salt

1 teaspoon cracked black pepper

2 cups chickpeas, cooked

1. Preheat the oven (on broiler setting) or broiler to 400°F. Line a baking sheet with tinfoil. Spread the fennel chunks and tomatoes in an even layer on the pan and drizzle with olive oil. Sprinkle with salt and pepper, and broil for 15–20 minutes, turning as needed to prevent burning.

2. Once the tomatoes have popped open and the fennel is soft, remove both from heat. Pour the tomatoes, fennel, and oil into a mixing bowl.

3. Add the chickpeas to the mixing bowl, toss to combine thoroughly, and plate equal amounts onto 2 serving dishes.

PER SERVING Calories: 517 | Fat: 17 g | Protein: 20 g | Sodium: 1,297 mg | Fiber: 19 g | Carbohydrates: 61 g | Sugar: 12 g

Lighter Waldorf Salad

From vitamin K to omega-6, antioxidants to polyphenols, this salad's combination of all-natural ingredients makes for a new and improved healthy version of an old favorite.

INGREDIENTS | SERVES 2

2 cups romaine lettuce, shredded
½ Granny Smith apple, cored and chopped
1 celery stalk, chopped
½ cup red grapes, halved
¼ cup nonfat Greek-style or soy yogurt
1 tablespoon maple syrup
1 teaspoon ground nutmeg
½ cup walnuts, crushed

1. In a large salad bowl, combine the romaine, apple, celery, and grapes, and toss to combine.

2. In a small bowl, combine the yogurt, maple syrup, and nutmeg, and blend well.

3. Plate equal amounts of the salad into 2 salad bowls, top with equal amounts of the sweetened yogurt mixture, and sprinkle with crushed walnuts.

PER SERVING Calories: 279 | Fat: 18 g | Protein: 7 g | Sodium: 39 mg | Fiber: 4.5 g | Carbohydrates: 25 g | Sugar: 18 g

Tangy Three-Bean Salad

Loaded with intense colors and flavors, this texture-rich salad is packed with a gorgeous variety of ingredients that are simple to combine and delicious to consume!

INGREDIENTS | SERVES 4

2 tablespoons extra-virgin olive oil
2 tablespoons red wine vinegar
2 tablespoons Italian seasoning
1 teaspoon all-natural sea salt
½ teaspoon cracked black pepper
1 cup artichoke hearts, quartered
½ red bell pepper, chopped
1 cup garbanzo beans, cooked
1 cup red kidney beans, cooked
1 cup pinto beans, cooked
2 cups endive leaves

1. In a large mixing bowl, add the olive oil, vinegar, Italian seasoning, salt, and pepper, and whisk to combine well.

2. Add artichoke hearts, bell pepper, and beans to mixture. Toss to coat, cover, and refrigerate minimum of 4–6 hours, or as long as overnight.

3. Toss endive leaves gently with bean mixture, and place equal amounts of salad on 4 serving dishes or salad bowls.

PER SERVING Calories: 268 | Fat: 8 g | Protein: 12 g | Sodium: 793 mg | Fiber: 12 g | Carbohydrates: 37 g | Sugar: 2 g

Bean and Couscous Salad

Couscous is the perfect backdrop for sweet peas, spicy scallions, and smooth white beans. Add the bite of balsamic vinegar to this crunchy carbohydrate-fueled salad, and you've got a full spectrum of flavors.

INGREDIENTS | SERVES 2

2 cups prepared couscous

1 cup white beans, soaked and drained (soaking 24 hours or more is best)

¼ cup scallions, chopped

¼ cup sweet peas

2 tablespoons balsamic vinegar

1 tablespoon extra-virgin olive oil

1. In a large mixing bowl, combine the couscous, beans, scallions, and peas, and blend thoroughly.

2. Add the balsamic vinegar and olive oil over the mix, and toss to coat, combining well.

3. Serve hot or cold.

PER SERVING Calories: 1,043 | Fat: 8.5 g | Protein: 42.5 g | Sodium: 40 mg | Fiber: 27 g | Carbohydrates: 196 g | Sugar: 11.5 g

Lemon-Scented Rice with Fruit Salsa Salad

Light and bright, the luscious lemon flavor of both juice and zest permeate through the wild rice of this sweet citrus salad.

INGREDIENTS | SERVES 2

2 cups wild rice, cooked

1 tablespoon freshly grated lemon zest

¼ cup lemon juice (about 1 lemon)

¼ cup champagne vinegar

1 tablespoon organic maple syrup

2 cups Fruit Salsa (see Chapter 5)

1. In a large mixing bowl, combine the cooked wild rice, lemon zest, and half of the lemon juice (about ⅛ cup). Allow flavors to marry for about 15 minutes.

2. In a small mixing bowl, whisk together the remaining ⅛ cup lemon juice, champagne vinegar, and maple syrup until thoroughly combined.

3. Add the Fruit Salsa to the wild rice, and toss to combine. Pour the lemon juice, vinegar, and maple syrup mixture over the fruit and rice, and toss to coat.

4. Serve immediately.

PER SERVING Calories: 288 | Fat: 1 g | Protein: 7.5 g | Sodium: 14 mg | Fiber: 5.5 g | Carbohydrates: 65 g | Sugar: 19 g

CHAPTER 9

Appetizers

Stuffed Pepper Poppers
142

Spicy Spinach and Artichoke Dip
143

Great Guacamole
143

Cool and Crunchy Spinach and
Artichoke Dip
144

Spicy Clean Refried Beans
144

Veggie-Packed Potato Skins
145

Roasted Veggie Dip with a Kick
146

Fantastic Falafel
147

Ginger-Vegetable Spring Rolls
148

Herbed Potato Patties
149

Balsamic Mushroom Skewers
150

Stuffed Baked Onions
151

Coconut Crusted Tofu Strips
152

Spicy Jalapeño Poppers
153

Yogurt-Veggie Dip
154

Veggie Dip Stuffed Tomatoes
155

Roasted Red Pepper and
Artichoke Dip
155

Layered Bean Dip
156

Delicious Deviled Eggs
157

Perfect Pinto Bean Pesto
158

Tomato-Basil Hummus
158

Stuffed Pepper Poppers

These sweet, vibrantly colored mini peppers are available in most grocers' produce aisles. Packed with tasty ingredients, these mini pepper poppers are the perfect hearty appetizer that's actually good for you!

INGREDIENTS | SERVES 16

20 mini bell peppers of assorted colors
1 cup cooked brown rice
1 cup Fresh Salsa (see Chapter 5)
1 cup kernel corn (fresh or thawed from frozen)
1 cup cooked black beans
1 teaspoon cumin
1 cup chopped romaine lettuce
⅛ teaspoon cayenne pepper (optional)

Amazing Apps That Go Above and Beyond Deliciousness

When it comes to great appetizers in a clean diet, foods that can deliver lots of great taste *and* lots of great nutrition are top-notch meal starters. Even better, if those healthy apps can provide a combination of complex carbohydrates, clean protein, and fats that provides a feeling of fullness that lasts and lasts, you've got an extraordinary appetizer that goes above and beyond the everyday variety.

1. To prepare peppers, remove tops and scoop out ribs and seeds. Set 16 aside, and chop 4 to use in stuffing mixture.

2. In a large mixing bowl, combine the chopped bell peppers, cooked rice, salsa, corn, beans, and cumin. Mix ingredients until well blended. Add romaine to the mixture and blend by tossing gently.

3. Set the mini peppers with top openings up. Pack filling into each of the peppers up to the top. Press gently to compact.

4. Sprinkle with cayenne as a spicy garnish, if desired.

PER SERVING Calories: 50 | Fat: 0 g | Protein: 2 g | Sodium: 156 mg | Fiber: 2.5 g | Carbohydrates: 10 g | Sugar: 1 g

Spicy Spinach and Artichoke Dip

The traditional spinach and artichoke dip gets kicked up a notch with the lovely addition of chipotle peppers.

INGREDIENTS | SERVES 6

2 cups fresh spinach leaves, torn

2 cups artichoke hearts, quartered and chopped

½ cup Vidalia onion, minced

½ cup chipotle peppers, minced

2 cups nonfat Greek-style yogurt, or soy yogurt

2 teaspoons dried mustard

1 teaspoon garlic powder

1 teaspoon all-natural sea salt

½ teaspoon cracked black pepper.

1. In a large mixing bowl, combine the torn spinach leaves, artichoke hearts, onion, chipotles, and yogurt. Mix well to thoroughly combine.

2. To the mixture, add mustard, garlic powder, sea salt, and pepper gradually, until desired flavor combination is achieved.

PER SERVING Calories: 67 | Fat: 0.5 g | Protein: 6 g | Sodium: 495 mg | Fiber: 3 g | Carbohydrates: 12 g | Sugar: 6.5 g

Great Guacamole

Guacamole is a beautiful dip that can be made quickly and easily, and using all-natural ingredients.

INGREDIENTS | SERVES 12

3 avocados, mashed to desired consistency

½ red onion, chopped

2 Roma tomatoes, chopped

2 tablespoons chopped cilantro

1 garlic clove, crushed

¼ cup freshly squeezed lime juice

1 teaspoon all-natural sea salt

1 teaspoon cracked black pepper

1. Combine all ingredients in a small mixing bowl and blend thoroughly.

2. Add salt and pepper.

3. Serve immediately.

PER SERVING Calories: 84 | Fat: 7.5 g | Protein: 1 g | Sodium: 200 mg | Fiber: 3.5 g | Carbohydrates: 5 g | Sugar: 1 g

Cool and Crunchy Spinach and Artichoke Dip

If you're tempted by the classic spinach and artichoke dip, but don't desire the loads of cheese and unhealthy additions, try this clean, cool, and crunchy version, instead.

INGREDIENTS | SERVES 12

2 cups torn spinach leaves
½ cup chopped water chestnuts
1 cup chopped artichoke hearts
2 cups nonfat yogurt, or vegan yogurt
2 teaspoons dried mustard
1 tablespoon white vinegar
1 teaspoon cracked black pepper
1 teaspoon garlic powder

1. Combine all ingredients thoroughly in a medium dish, cover, and refrigerate.

2. Allow flavors to marry, and dip to chill, 1–2 hours, and serve.

PER SERVING Calories: 39 | Fat: 1.5 g | Protein: 2 g | Sodium: 40 mg | Fiber: 1 g | Carbohydrates: 5 g | Sugar: 2 g

Spicy Clean Refried Beans

Refried beans from a can are a clean diet disaster! This recipe uses delicious natural ingredients that combine for the smooth, spicy taste of your favorite dish.

INGREDIENTS | SERVES 12

2½ cups dried pinto beans (soaked 12–24 hours)
4 tablespoons olive oil, divided
1 tablespoon chipotle powder
1 tablespoon cayenne pepper
2 teaspoons cumin
1 teaspoon onion powder
1 teaspoon garlic powder
½ teaspoon paprika
1 teaspoon all-natural sea salt
½ teaspoon cracked black pepper

1. Combine soaked beans, 2 tablespoons of the olive oil, chipotle powder, cayenne pepper, cumin, onion powder, garlic powder, and paprika in a food processor or blender and blend until thoroughly combined.

2. Gradually add remaining 2 tablespoons of olive oil until desired consistency is achieved.

3. Add salt and pepper.

PER SERVING Calories: 183 | Fat: 5 g | Protein: 9 g | Sodium: 6 mg | Fiber: 6.5 g | Carbohydrates: 26 g | Sugar: 1 g

Veggie-Packed Potato Skins

Packed with all-natural ingredients that will provide health benefits along with awesome flavors, this is the new and improved healthy version of potato skins that is sure to become your new favorite.

INGREDIENTS | SERVES 12

6 Idaho potatoes, baked
1 tablespoon extra-virgin olive oil
1 cup red onion, chopped
1 cup zucchini, chopped
1 cup mushrooms, sliced
2 tablespoons water
1 teaspoon all-natural sea salt
1 teaspoon cracked black pepper
1 teaspoon garlic powder
1 teaspoon cumin
1 cup nonfat Greek-style yogurt, or soy yogurt
2–3 medium Roma tomatoes, chopped

Make the Healthy Switch Here . . . and There

Many people dread the word "diet" because the stigma of dieting is wound tightly around deprivation and starvation. One of the greatest aspects of clean eating is that you *can* enjoy the foods you love. You just need to be creative and find ways to use natural, whole ingredients more often. Classic restaurant favorites like potato skins come packed with unhealthy ingredients and are topped with even more of the same; you can enjoy a healthier version of the same food that packs flavor, texture, and tons of nutrition . . . without the guilt and bloat of the restaurant-made alternative.

1. Allow potatoes to cool after baking, cut in half lengthwise, and scoop out the inside of the potatoes leaving about ⅛"–¼" of flesh. Reserve 1 cup of the scooped potatoes for stuffing mixture.

2. In a large skillet over medium heat, heat the olive oil until runny and smooth. Sauté the red onion for about 2 minutes, or until slightly tender. Add the zucchini, mushrooms, and 2 tablespoons of water to the onions. Sprinkle with ½ teaspoon of the salt, pepper, garlic powder, and cumin, and sauté for 5–6 minutes or until fork tender.

3. Move the sautéed vegetables to the mixing bowl, and combine thoroughly with the potatoes. Add the yogurt and remaining spices, and mix together until chunky and combined well.

4. Spoon the mixture into the potato skins, packing by pressing firmly. Garnish with chopped tomatoes.

PER SERVING Calories: 110 | Fat: 1 g | Protein: 4 g | Sodium: 211 mg | Fiber: 2 g | Carbohydrates: 21 g | Sugar: 3 g

Roasted Veggie Dip with a Kick

Delicious roasted vegetables get combined in a delicious dip that's great with tortilla chips, crisp vegetables, on crisp toast, or all by itself!

INGREDIENTS | SERVES 6

1 small eggplant
1 large zucchini
1 large yellow squash
1 red pepper
1 yellow onion
3 cloves garlic, peeled and crushed
1 tablespoon extra-virgin olive oil
¼ teaspoon cayenne pepper
1 teaspoon all-natural sea salt
1 teaspoon cracked black pepper
2 tablespoons lemon juice (optional)

1. Preheat the oven to 450°F and prepare a roasting pan with olive oil spray.

2. Cut the eggplant into cubes, the zucchini and yellow squash into quarters, and the red pepper and onion into ¼"–½" thick chunks. Scatter the vegetables and garlic on the roasting pan, drizzle with the olive oil, and sprinkle with the cayenne, salt, and pepper.

3. Roast for about 30–45 minutes, turning and basting with the oil drippings every 15–20 minutes. Once all vegetables are soft and cooked through, remove from heat and allow to cool for about 10 minutes.

4. Combine all vegetables in a food processor, and purée until desired chunkiness is achieved.

5. If including, gradually drizzle in the 2 tablespoons of lemon juice until desired taste and texture is achieved.

PER SERVING Calories: 47 | Fat: 2.5 g | Protein: 1.5 g | Sodium: 389 mg | Fiber: 2 g | Carbohydrates: 5 g | Sugar: 2.5 g

Fantastic Falafel

Delicious chickpea patties get all fried up . . . healthfully! Filled with tasty, vibrant vegetables that deliver flavor and nutrition, these falafels are little bites of heaven!

INGREDIENTS | SERVES 6

2 cups chickpeas (cooked)

1 large carrot, peeled

¼ red bell pepper

¼ cup yellow onion, diced

1 celery stalk, trimmed

2 garlic cloves, peeled

1 teaspoon coriander, ground

1 teaspoon cumin

1½ tablespoons extra-virgin olive oil

1½ tablespoons canola oil

1 teaspoon all-natural sea salt

1 teaspoon cracked black pepper

Don't Eliminate "Good" Fat Dishes

Health benefits that result from diets rich in healthy fats are impressive enough that more people should focus on consuming foods that include these healthy fats more regularly. From avocados to olive oil, "fatty" foods have been wrongly given a bad reputation by being included in the same group as "bad" fats like trans fats and saturated fats. While many consumers are catching on to the truth about different fats, there are still many eaters who shy away from dishes that include fat . . . even the healthy varieties. Don't do yourself this same disservice; strive to include a variety of foods and meals that contain healthy fats.

1. In a food processor, combine the chickpeas, carrot, bell pepper, onion, celery, garlic, coriander, and cumin. Process together while adding 1 tablespoon of olive oil until the mixture becomes thick and wet, adding remaining ½ tablespoon if needed.

2. Remove mixture from processor, and form into 6 even patties, about ¾" thick. Season with salt and pepper.

3. In a skillet over medium heat, heat the vegetable oil and place patties in skillet. Cook patties for about 5 minutes, or until golden brown. Flip patties and continue to cook for another 4–5 minutes, or until golden. Remove patties from heat and set on paper towels to drain excess oil.

4. Serve alone with a side sauce, atop a bed of rice or couscous, or on a simple salad.

PER SERVING Calories: 153 | Fat: 7 g | Protein: 5 g | Sodium: 411 mg | Fiber: 5 g | Carbohydrates: 17 g | Sugar: 3 g

Ginger-Vegetable Spring Rolls

Traditional spring rolls can be packed with preservatives, so creating these clean ones at home can be a simple way to enjoy what you love while still eating clean.

INGREDIENTS | SERVES 12

1 cup shredded red cabbage

½ cup shredded carrot

½ cup chopped green onion

½ cup chopped celery

½ cup extra-firm tofu, diced

1 tablespoon grated gingerroot

2 teaspoons garlic, minced

2 tablespoons sesame oil

2 tablespoons soy sauce

12 vegan spring roll wrappers

2 tablespoons water

1 tablespoon vegetable oil

Vegan Products Now Widely Available

You may be surprised to see that there are now vegan spring roll wrappers available, but it's true! Because the vegan lifestyle has become so strong throughout the world, many manufacturers have decided to dip into the popular industry of healthy vegan alternatives by providing their own products and adhering to vegan standards. The next time you think you have to skip a recipe just because it has an ingredient that you doubt is offered vegan-style, check your local grocer or health food store, and you may be pleasantly surprised.

1. Preheat the oven to 425°F and prepare an oven grate with olive oil spray.

2. In a large mixing bowl, combine the cabbage, carrots, onion, celery, tofu, gingerroot, and garlic. Add the sesame oil and soy sauce to the mixture and blend well until ingredients are wet and combined thoroughly.

3. In the center of each spring roll wrapper, place 2 tablespoons of vegetable mixture. Fold wrappers as if wrapping enchiladas: Wet the edges of the wrapper, fold in the right and left sides to cover edges of mixture, and roll to enclose completely.

4. Lay the spring rolls on the prepared grate; use fingers or a pastry brush to lightly coat the spring rolls with the vegetable oil.

5. Bake for 15 minutes, turn, and continue baking for an additional 5–10 minutes, or until spring rolls are brown and crispy.

PER SERVING Calories: 36 | Fat: 3 g | Protein: 0.5 g | Sodium: 155 mg | Fiber: 1 g | Carbohydrates: 1 g | Sugar: 0 g

Herbed Potato Patties

Hearty, nutrition-packed potatoes deliver amazing taste in these patties packed with delicious herbs and spices. Great with a cool or tangy dipping sauce, these delicious bites of potato perfection are amazing appetizers that are delicious and nutritious!

INGREDIENTS | SERVES 8

2 Idaho potatoes, shredded

1 egg, or ¼ cup vegan egg substitute

¼ cup scallions, chopped

2 teaspoons dried rosemary, chopped

1 teaspoon basil, chopped

1 teaspoon garlic powder

1 teaspoon all-natural sea salt

1 teaspoon cracked black pepper

1 tablespoon vegetable oil

1. In a large mixing bowl, combine the potatoes, egg, scallions, rosemary, basil, garlic, salt, and pepper. Combine all ingredients until wet and thoroughly combined, and form the mixture into 8 even patties.

2. Heat the vegetable oil in a large skillet over medium heat. Place 4 patties in the skillet at a time to avoid overcrowding and to allow enough room for even cooking. Cook patties for about 5 minutes, or until golden brown and crispy. Flip and continue cooking for 5 minutes, or until brown and crispy.

3. Remove patties from skillet and place on paper towels to drain excess oil and moisture.

PER SERVING Calories: 68 | Fat: 2 g | Protein: 2 g | Sodium: 306 mg | Fiber: 1 g | Carbohydrates: 10 g | Sugar: 0.5 g

Balsamic Mushroom Skewers

Marinated mushrooms become plump and perfect morsels of deliciousness that you can display skewered or in a simple setup of a bowl alongside handy toothpicks. However you choose to serve them up, these mushrooms are a great tangy treat you're sure to enjoy!

INGREDIENTS | SERVES 6

1 pound whole baby portobello mushrooms

1½ cups balsamic vinegar

½ cup organic apple juice, not from concentrate

2 teaspoons garlic, minced

2 teaspoons all-natural sea salt

1 teaspoon cracked black pepper

Simple, Subtle, Delicious, and Powerful!

While mushrooms are either loved or hated, there is no doubting the powerful effects these delicate vegetables can have on our health. Because of their rich content of vitamins, minerals, and antioxidants, mushrooms hold the natural powers of healing when it comes to certain illnesses and diseases. The vitamins and minerals help the body's production of healthy cells while also aiding in the ability to identify and eliminate unhealthy cells. The anti-inflammatory and antioxidant roles played by the mushroom allow this vegetable to help protect from cancerous invaders and changes in cells and organs while promoting their health and immunity functioning.

1. Wipe the portobello mushrooms clean of dirt and debris with a cloth or paper towel. Pierce the mushrooms' skin with a fork about 4 times per cap.

2. In a shallow mixing dish, combine the balsamic vinegar, apple juice, garlic, and 1 teaspoon of salt, and mix well. Submerge the mushrooms in the balsamic mixture, and cover with a piece of plastic wrap. Refrigerate for about 2–4 hours, removing every 30 minutes to shake the bowl and turn the mushrooms.

3. Remove the mushrooms and skewer immediately. Sprinkle with back pepper.

4. Prepare a grill to medium heat and spray the grates with olive oil spray. Set the mushrooms on the grill and sprinkle lightly with the salt. Cook for about 5–7 minutes, or until cooked through. Turn, sprinkle with remaining salt, and continue to cook until browned all over. Remove from heat, serve on the skewers.

PER SERVING Calories: 53 | Fat: 0 g | Protein: 2 g | Sodium: 708 mg | Fiber: 1 g | Carbohydrates: 9 g | Sugar: 6 g

Stuffed Baked Onions

To some, onions come minced, chopped, raw, roasted, or stir-fried, but baked is a novel idea. Packed with a delicious blend of clean ingredients, this may be your new favorite way to enjoy red onions!

INGREDIENTS | SERVES 6

6 red onions, outer skin peeled

½ pound baby portobello mushrooms, sliced

1 tablespoon garlic, minced

1 teaspoon all-natural sea salt

1 teaspoon cracked black pepper

1 tablespoon water

½ cup crumbled goat cheese, or vegan soft cheese

1. Fill a large pot with water, bring to a boil, and place onions in the pot. Boil for 10 minutes, or until soft.

2. Preheat the oven to 350°F, prepare a shallow oven-safe dish with olive oil spray. Transfer the onions from the pot to the dish, and scoop out the centers of the onions, leaving about ½" of the outer rim to act as the outer wall that will contain the stuffing. Chop the removed onion centers.

3. In a large sauté pan over medium heat, combine the mushrooms, minced garlic, salt, and pepper, and sauté until mushrooms are softened. Add the chopped onion (and water as needed) and sauté until cooked through and mixture is soft.

4. Scoop the onion and mushroom mixture into the opening of the onions, and bake for 20 minutes. Remove from heat, top with equal amounts of goat cheese, return to oven, and continue cooking for 10 minutes, or until cheese is melted and golden.

PER SERVING Calories: 105 | Fat: 4 g | Protein: 5.5 g | Sodium: 469 mg | Fiber: 2.5 g | Carbohydrates: 12 g | Sugar: 5 g

Coconut Crusted Tofu Strips

You can enjoy this light, delicious tofu crusted in a crunchy coconut coating, simply and easily, any night of the week!

INGREDIENTS | SERVES 12

1 (12-ounce) package extra-firm tofu

1 cup pineapple juice

2 cups finely shredded organic, unsweetened coconut

1 teaspoon all-natural sea salt

1. Cut the block of tofu in half, and cut each halved block into 6 equal strips.

2. Place the pineapple juice and shredded coconut into 2 separate shallow dishes. Soak the tofu strips in the pineapple juice, and then roll each strip into the shredded coconut to coat completely.

3. Preheat the oven to 400°F and prepare a baking sheet with tinfoil and olive oil spray.

4. Set the tofu strips on the prepared baking sheet and bake for 15 minutes or until crispy. Flip and continue to bake until golden brown, between 8–12 additional minutes.

5. Remove the tofu strips from the oven and sprinkle with the sea salt.

PER SERVING Calories: 68 | Fat: 4.5 g | Protein: 2 g | Sodium: 211 mg | Fiber: 1.5 g | Carbohydrates: 5 g | Sugar: 3 g

Spicy Jalapeño Poppers

Jalapeños get all dolled up with all-natural ingredients to make for a clean appetizer that delivers amazing nutrition with the kick you crave!

INGREDIENTS | SERVES 12

1 cup low-fat plain Greek-style yogurt, or vegan yogurt
½ red onion, minced
½ cup tomatoes, minced
2 tablespoons garlic, minced
1 teaspoon all-natural sea salt
12 jalapeño peppers
1 cup almond milk
1 cup 100% whole-wheat flour
½ cup olive oil

1. In a mixing bowl, combine yogurt, onion, tomatoes, garlic, and salt.

2. Remove tops and seeds from jalapeños, and stuff with the yogurt mixture.

3. Pour almond milk into a shallow dish next to a shallow dish filled with the whole-wheat flour.

4. Dip each jalapeño into the almond milk and roll in the flour; set aside.

5. Heat the olive oil in a large skillet over medium heat. Add the jalapeños, turning regularly, and cook until golden brown all over, about 4–7 minutes.

6. Remove from oil and place onto paper towels to soak up excess oil.

PER SERVING Calories: 141 | Fat: 9.5 g | Protein: 3 g | Sodium: 218 mg | Fiber: 2 g | Carbohydrates: 12 g | Sugar: 3 g

Yogurt-Veggie Dip

Packed with intense flavor, crunch, and valuable vitamins and antioxidants, this dip has all of the amazing flavor you're looking for in a vegetable dip . . . without everything you're not.

INGREDIENTS | SERVES 12

1 cup nonfat Greek-style yogurt, or silken tofu

1 cup soy yogurt

2 tablespoons white vinegar

2 tablespoons dried dill

2 tablespoons chopped chives

1 teaspoon garlic powder

1 teaspoon cracked black pepper

¼ cup minced red or yellow bell pepper

¼ cup minced white onion

¼ cup finely shredded carrot

¼ cup chopped cucumber

¼ cup finely shredded celery

1. In a medium glass dish, combine the yogurts, vinegar, dill, and chives, and mix well. Add garlic powder and black pepper.

2. Stir the bell pepper, onion, carrot, cucumber, and celery into the yogurt to combine thoroughly.

3. Cover and refrigerate for at least 1 hour before serving.

PER SERVING Calories: 17 | Fat: 0.5 g | Protein: 1.5 g | Sodium: 14 mg | Fiber: 0.5 g | Carbohydrates: 2 g | Sugar: 0 g

The Versatility of Delicious Dips

When you're looking for a delicious ingredient that can offer up a variety of ways to enjoy it, look no further than your favorite dip recipes. Easy to create, simple to store, and versatile as the mind is imaginative, dips are the clean go-to when you're in need of flavor in the form of a spread, sauce, or coating. Packed full of vegetables, made from vegetables, or loaded with nutrient-rich ingredients that are as natural as they come, indulge in the dip and enjoy their versatility.

Veggie Dip Stuffed Tomatoes

This recipe packs clean protein, complex carbohydrates, vitamins, minerals, and powerful antioxidants into tasty little plum tomatoes that are as beautiful as they are delicious!

INGREDIENTS | SERVES 12

12 plum tomatoes

2 cups Yogurt-Veggie Dip (see recipe in this chapter)

1 cup crumbled goat cheese, or vegan soft cheese

¼ cup chopped chives

1. Remove the tops from the tomatoes, and scrape the insides clean.

2. Fill the tomatoes with equal amounts of the dip.

3. Top the tomatoes with crumbled goat cheese and garnish with the chopped chives.

PER SERVING Calories: 90 | Fat: 4.5 g | Protein: 6 g | Sodium: 90 mg | Fiber: 2 g | Carbohydrates: 7 g | Sugar: 4 g

Roasted Red Pepper and Artichoke Dip

The fiery taste of roasted red peppers gets all mixed up with creamy artichoke hearts in this delicious dip. This dip is a great appetizer that's sure to surprise and please.

INGREDIENTS | SERVES 6

2 cups roasted red peppers (about 3 large)

2 cups artichoke hearts

2 teaspoons garlic powder

2 tablespoons red wine vinegar

1 teaspoon all-natural sea salt

1 teaspoon cracked black pepper

1. In a food processor, combine the roasted red peppers, artichoke hearts, and 1 teaspoon of garlic powder. Combine until chopped and chunky.

2. Drizzle in vinegar until desired consistency is achieved.

3. Add remaining garlic powder, salt, and pepper.

PER SERVING Calories: 45 | Fat: 0.5 g | Protein: 2.5 g | Sodium: 424 mg | Fiber: 3.5 g | Carbohydrates: 9 g | Sugar: 2 g

Layered Bean Dip

Using all of the delightful, clean recipes for refried beans, guacamole, and salsa packed in this book, you can create a healthy version of the traditionally unhealthy classic.

INGREDIENTS | SERVES 12

1½ cups plain low-fat yogurt, or vegan yogurt

1½ cups plain low-fat Greek-style yogurt, or silken tofu

2 cups Spicy Clean Refried Beans (see recipe in this chapter)

2 cups Fresh Salsa (see Chapter 5)

1 cup green onions, chopped

1 large tomato, chopped

2½ cups shredded lettuce

1 cup natural black olives, sliced

1. In a mixing bowl, combine the yogurt and Greek-style yogurt.

2. In a glass pie plate, layer the refried beans evenly for the bottom of the dip.

3. Top beans with ½ of the yogurt mix, followed by all of the salsa.

4. Top the salsa layer with the green onions, then tomatoes, and finally lettuce.

5. Complete the dip with a layer of the remaining yogurt mix spread, and top with the sliced olives.

PER SERVING Calories: 97 | Fat: 2 g | Protein: 6 g | Sodium: 576 mg | Fiber: 3.5 g | Carbohydrates: 15 g | Sugar: 6.5 g

Delicious Deviled Eggs

Deviled eggs are a classic appetizer, but can be riddled with fat, calories, sodium, and preservatives. Using fresh ingredients and clean protein-packed yogurt, you can enjoy healthy deviled eggs.

INGREDIENTS | SERVES 12

6 eggs, hard-boiled, cooled, and peeled

½ cup low-fat plain yogurt, or soy yogurt

1 stalk of celery, finely minced

1 teaspoon garlic powder

1 teaspoon onion powder

1 teaspoon cracked black pepper

Paprika, for garnish

"Deviled Egg" Egg Alternative

If you're a vegan, but love deviled eggs, what can you do?! Well, the mixture of ingredients you choose to put into your "eggs" can include anything you desire that would whip up to taste great and fit inside that lovely scoop-sized portion. As for the "egg," a simple vegan trick is to use a large spoon to scoop out egg-half-shaped tofu scoops, and then use a smaller scoop to mimic the hole left by a real egg's hardened yolk. Season with spices or marinate for even more intense flavor, and your deviled tofu-"eggs" can be as divine as the original!

1. Halve the eggs lengthwise, and remove yolks to a mixing bowl.

2. Mash the yolks, and mix with the yogurt, celery, garlic powder, onion powder, and black pepper.

3. Spoon the mixture into each of the egg white halves until filled and slightly bulging.

4. Sprinkle the eggs with paprika, cover, and refrigerate until ready to serve.

PER SERVING Calories: 44 | Fat: 2.5 g | Protein: 5 g | Sodium: 45 mg | Fiber: 0 g | Carbohydrates: 1 g | Sugar: 1 g

Perfect Pinto Bean Pesto

*Whipped up quickly, easy to store, and beautiful alongside a variety of dishes,
this appetizer is a tasty way to enjoy wonderful pinto beans.*

INGREDIENTS | SERVES 6

2 cups spinach leaves

1 cup fresh basil leaves

½ cup toasted pine nuts

2 cloves garlic

2 tablespoons lemon juice

½ cup extra-virgin olive oil

2 cups cooked pinto beans

1 teaspoon all-natural sea salt

1 teaspoon cracked black pepper

1. In a food processor, combine the spinach, basil, pine nuts, garlic cloves, and lemon juice. While processing, drizzle in the olive oil until the desired consistency is achieved.

2. Transfer the pesto to a medium-sized glass dish, toss with the pinto beans to coat, and add salt and pepper.

3. If desired, drizzle additional olive oil to add wetness to the pesto and bean mixture.

PER SERVING Calories: 351 | Fat: 27 g | Protein: 7 g | Sodium: 251 mg | Fiber: 6 g | Carbohydrates: 17 g | Sugar: 0 g

Tomato-Basil Hummus

*Ordinary hummus gets all jazzed up with the tang of prepared tomato sauce, the sweetness of basil,
and the spiciness of garlic, and delivers an extraordinary dish of intense flavors.*

INGREDIENTS | SERVES 6

1 cup chickpeas, soaked for 24 hours

½ cup basil leaves

2 cloves garlic

1 cup Tasty Tomato Sauce (see Chapter 5)

1 teaspoon all-natural sea salt

1. In a food processor, combine the chickpeas, basil, and garlic cloves. While processing, gradually add ¼ cup of the tomato sauce.

2. Once the mixture is chopped to desired chunkiness, transfer the hummus to a large glass dish. Combine the remaining tomato sauce with the hummus until well blended.

3. Add salt.

PER SERVING Calories: 62 | Fat: 1 g | Protein: 3 g | Sodium: 668 mg | Fiber: 2.5 g | Carbohydrates: 9 g | Sugar: 2 g

CHAPTER 10

Vegetarian Entrées

Gardener's Pie
160

Rustic Roasted Root Vegetables
161

Over-Stuffed Bean Burritos
162

Terriffic Tortillas
163

Thai Vegetable Curry
163

Vegetarian Meat Loaf
164

Creamy Veggie Casserole
165

Mushroom and Asparagus Bake
166

Italian Tofu Bake
167

Garlic Tofu Stir-Fry
168

Vegan Chili
169

Sweet Tofu with Summer Squash
170

Clean Cashew Stir-Fry
171

Pesto-Painted Tofu Sauté
172

Lemon-Basil Tofu
172

Best-Ever Tofu Enchiladas
173

Five-Alarm Enchiladas
174

Spinach Enchiladas
175

Tasty Tomatillo Enchiladas
176

Good-For-You Gumbo
177

Creamy Curry Tempeh with Vegetables
178

Sweet and Spicy Veggie Stir-Fry
179

Tofu Piccata
179

Ratatouille
180

Sautéed Tofu with Balsamic Onions and Mushrooms
181

Ginger-Lime Tofu
182

Gardener's Pie

*The delightful vegetarian alternative to shepherd's pie, this baked combination
of fresh vegetables makes for a hearty meal that can be enjoyed fresh from the oven,
or frozen for a quick thaw to be baked and on the table in no time!*

INGREDIENTS | SERVES 12

2 cups Simple Stock (see Chapter 7)

½ cup ground flaxseed

1 cup green beans, trimmed and halved

1 yellow onion, diced

1 cup sweet peas

1 cup kernel corn

1 cup carrots, chopped

2 teaspoons all-natural sea salt

4 teaspoons garlic powder

2 teaspoons cracked black pepper

4 cups Mashed Potatoes and Cauliflower
(see Chapter 15)

Tempting Textures

When you find yourself feeling like you're in a recipe rut, think outside of the box and aim to create new dishes that combine textures. While flavor is important, the texture of our foods is sometimes what satisfies those hunger pains. For the same reason why crunchy chips or creamy ice creams seem to "hit the spot" when those cravings strike, you can combine clean, natural foods like onions or peppers for spicy crunch, or yogurt or baked fruit for sweet creaminess.

1. In a large mixing bowl, combine stock and flaxseed, and set aside.

2. Preheat the oven to 350°F and prepare a 13" × 9" baking dish with olive oil spray.

3. To the stock mixture, add the green beans, onion, peas, corn, carrots, salt, garlic powder, and pepper. Toss to combine thoroughly.

4. Layer half of the Mashed Potatoes and Cauliflower in the bottom of the prepared pan. Pour the vegetable mixture as the second layer, and top with the remaining half of the Mashed Potatoes and Cauliflower.

5. Bake at 350°F for 35 minutes, or until top is browned.

PER SERVING Calories: 97 | Fat: 2.5 g | Protein: 4 g | Sodium: 498 mg | Fiber: 4 g | Carbohydrates: 17 g | Sugar: 2 g

Rustic Roasted Root Vegetables

Rustic root vegetables get crispy outside and creamy inside when they're tossed in light oil and baked at a high temp. With seasonings that flavor every bite, this one-pan meal is filling but healthfully light.

INGREDIENTS | SERVES 2

2 Idaho potatoes

1 large red onion

3 large carrots, peeled

1 turnip

2 parsnips

2 cloves garlic, smashed

1 tablespoon extra-virgin olive oil

1 tablespoon Italian seasonings

1 teaspoon all-natural sea salt

1 teaspoon cracked black pepper

1 teaspoon turmeric

Foolproof Fare

For even the most novice chef, potatoes and other root vegetables can make for delicious foods that are easy to prepare . . . and almost impossible to mess up. Root vegetables like potatoes, onions, carrots, garlic, turnips, and many more are a sure thing when it comes to steaming, baking, roasting, or boiling them to create a meal. Crunchy, creamy, or both, these vegetables make for foolproof fare that's not only easy but delicious and healthy, too!

1. Preheat the oven to 400°F and prepare a 13" × 9" baking dish with olive oil spray.

2. Cut the potatoes, onion, carrots, turnip, and parsnips into similarly sized chunks or rounds. Scatter the vegetables and smashed garlic in an even layer in the prepared dish.

3. Drizzle the vegetables with the olive oil, sprinkle with the seasonings, and bake for 20–25 minutes, or until golden. Toss and continue to bake for another 10 minutes until lightly browned and cooked through.

PER SERVING Calories: 428 | Fat: 7 g | Protein: 9 g | Sodium: 1,297 mg | Fiber: 15 g | Carbohydrates: 75 g | Sugar: 16 g

Over-Stuffed Bean Burritos

Forget the taco take-out and roll up some amazingly fresh and delicious bean burritos right in your own kitchen. Clean, quick, and easy, this recipe is a great option to use up leftover Vegan Chili and Spicy Clean Refried Beans.

INGREDIENTS | SERVES 2

2 (12") whole-wheat tortillas, or larger

1 cup Spicy Clean Refried Beans (see Chapter 9)

1 cup nonfat Greek-style yogurt, or soy yogurt

2 cups Vegan Chili (see recipe in this chapter)

1. Lay tortillas on a flat surface, and spread ½ cup of the refried beans on each in an even layer that reaches to the outer edge of the tortilla.

2. Spoon ½ cup of the yogurt onto each tortilla and repeat the same layering action that reaches to the outer edge.

3. Spoon 1 cup of the chili in a line down the center of each tortilla. Fold the sides in slightly and roll, allowing the bean and yogurt layers to act as a glue.

PER SERVING Calories: 687 | Fat: 21 g | Protein: 27 g | Sodium: 887 mg | Fiber: 15 g | Carbohydrates: 62 g | Sugar: 11 g

Loving Leftovers

With large batches of certain foods like chili, it's pretty common to have leftovers. But having loads of leftovers doesn't mean you have to eat chili every night for the next week; by getting creative with recipes that include your leftovers in a way that they become completely different taste experiences, you can max out your leftovers and save time by having half of the prep already done!

Terrific Tortillas

Slightly spicy for an added kick, these tostadas combine the fresh recipes for salsa, guacamole, and refried beans to make for an enjoyable treat.

INGREDIENTS | SERVES 2

2 whole-wheat tortillas

1 cup Spicy Clean Refried Beans
(see Chapter 9)

1 cup nonfat Greek-style yogurt, or
soy yogurt

1 cup Great Guacamole (see Chapter 9)

1 cup Fresh Salsa (see Chapter 5)

1 cup shredded romaine lettuce

1. Preheat the oven to 425°F and prepare a baking sheet with tinfoil. Place the tortillas on the baking sheet and mist with olive oil spray. Bake tortillas for 8–10 minutes, or until golden brown. Flip tortillas and cook for additional 5–8 minutes or until golden brown.

2. Spread ½ cup of the refried beans on each tortilla, and allow to warm from the heat of the tortillas, about 5 minutes. Top with ½ cup each of the nonfat yogurt, guacamole, salsa, and lettuce.

PER SERVING Calories: 426 | Fat: 16 g | Protein: 16 g | Sodium: 628 mg | Fiber: 16 g | Carbohydrates: 54 g | Sugar: 11 g

Thai Vegetable Curry

The warm uniqueness of curry swirls throughout every delicious bite of this dish while brightening your home with its amazing aroma, too!

INGREDIENTS | SERVES 2

1 eggplant, chopped

1 zucchini, chopped

1 tablespoon extra-virgin olive oil

1 cup coconut milk, divided

3 tablespoons almond butter

1 teaspoon minced garlic

1 yellow onion, minced

2 celery stalks, minced

2 teaspoons curry powder

1. In a large skillet, sauté the eggplant and zucchini in the olive oil over medium heat until softened, about 8–10 minutes.

2. Add half of the coconut milk, and all of the almond butter, minced garlic, onion, celery, and curry powder. Simmer for 5–10 minutes, or until veggies are fork tender and mixture is well-combined.

3. Add remaining coconut milk as a thinner if needed; remove from heat and serve hot.

PER SERVING Calories: 499.5 | Fat: 38 g | Protein: 9.5 g | Sodium: 65.5 mg | Fiber: 13.5 g | Carbohydrates: 40 g | Sugar: 20 g

Vegetarian Meat Loaf

This great recipe makes a delicious dinner that can be enjoyed by vegetarians and meat eaters, alike. Even though it's meat-free, this vegetarian "meat loaf" still pairs perfectly with the traditional sidekicks of mashed potatoes and greens.

INGREDIENTS | SERVES 4

1 cup cooked brown rice

1 pound portobello mushrooms, minced and sautéed

1 small yellow onion, minced

1 red pepper, minced

1 cup spinach, chopped

1 cup wheat germ, plain

2 eggs, beaten, or ½ cup vegan egg substitute

1 tablespoon vegan Worcestershire sauce

2 teaspoons garlic powder

2 teaspoons onion powder

2 teaspoons all-natural sea salt

2 teaspoons cracked black pepper

1. Preheat the oven to 350°F and prepare a 9" × 9" baking dish with olive oil spray.

2. Combine all ingredients in a mixing bowl, and refrigerate for 1 hour.

3. Pour mix into the center of the baking dish and form into a loaf.

4. Bake at 350°F for 30–45 minutes or until cooked through.

PER SERVING Calories: 252 | Fat: 6 g | Protein: 14.5 g | Sodium: 1,280 mg | Fiber: 8 g | Carbohydrates: 38.5 g | Sugar: 5.5 g

Hearty Ingredients for Filling Substance

If you need to thicken up any dishes, you can easily choose from a couple of clean ingredients. Brown rice is a great filler that you can add to vegetarian meat-like recipes to give a similar texture. Beans are another great thickening agent that can be added to soups, and thick yogurts like Greek-style varieties can be very helpful in thickening up smoothies, soups, sauces, and such.

Creamy Veggie Casserole

The perfect answer for dinner when you need something quick and easy, this one-pot dish can be frozen for later enjoyment, or put in the oven on-the-spot for a "set it and forget it" kind of meal.

INGREDIENTS | SERVES 4

1 cup sweet peas

1 cup kernel corn

1 cup sautéed sliced mushrooms

1 cup carrot, cut into matchsticks

½ cup yellow onion, minced

1 cup plain nonfat yogurt

1 cup plain nonfat Greek-style yogurt, or soy yogurt

1 tablespoon garlic powder

1 tablespoon onion powder

2 teaspoons cracked black pepper

4 cups cooked 100% whole-wheat farfalle pasta

½ cup crumbled goat cheese, or vegan soft cheese

1. Preheat the oven to 350°F and prepare a 9" × 13" baking dish with olive oil spray.

2. In a mixing bowl, combine the vegetables and yogurts with the seasonings.

3. Fold in the cooked pasta and pour into the prepared baking dish, and top with the crumbled goat cheese.

4. Bake for 30 minutes, or until cooked through and bubbly.

PER SERVING Calories: 588 | Fat: 16 g | Protein: 29 g | Sodium: 187 mg | Fiber: 14.5 g | Carbohydrates: 89 g | Sugar: 15 g

Veggies at Every Meal

When it comes to satisfying those essential daily recommended servings of fruits and vegetables, enjoying five daily meals that each pack a serving or two can get you to that daily quota every time. Sneaking spinach in a smoothie, packing a wrap full of vibrant vegetables, or diving into a delicious dinner that includes a variety of the nutritious foods can make vegetable serving success the easiest thing you accomplished all day.

Mushroom and Asparagus Bake

This fresh combination of mushrooms and asparagus makes for a light and bright meal that's packed with complex carbohydrates, clean protein, powerful antioxidants, and absolute deliciousness!

INGREDIENTS | SERVES 8

2 cups chopped asparagus spears

1 cup portobello mushrooms, sliced

1 cup oyster mushrooms, sliced

1 cup cremini mushrooms, sliced

1 tablespoon olive oil

1 tablespoon water

4 cups cooked 100% whole-wheat farfalle pasta

2 teaspoons garlic powder

1 teaspoon cracked black pepper

1 cup plain nonfat yogurt, or soy yogurt

1 cup plain nonfat Greek-style yogurt, or silken tofu

1 cup crumbled goat cheese, or vegan soft cheese

Bodybuilders' Secret to Beat the Bloat

Before bodybuilders go on stage for a competition, they go on strict diets to lose body fat and increase lean muscle mass. In the days leading up to a show, their diets get restricted even further to focus on foods that will reduce water retention in order to make muscles more pronounced. Two foods that many competing body-builders include in their diets during those important hours prior to show time are asparagus and mushrooms because they're well known foods for beating bloat. So take it from the pros, literally, and fight fluid retention with clean bloat-busting foods.

1. Preheat the oven to 350°F and prepare a 9" × 13" baking dish with olive oil spray.

2. Prepare a skillet with olive oil spray and place over medium heat. Sauté the asparagus and mushrooms in the olive oil until slightly softened, about 4–6 minutes, adding water as needed to prevent sticking and promote steaming.

3. Remove vegetables from heat and toss with the pasta in a mixing bowl. Add the seasonings, yogurts, and goat cheese. Blend thoroughly.

4. Pour the mix into the baking dish and bake for 30 minutes, or until cooked through and bubbly.

PER SERVING Calories: 336 | Fat: 14 g | Protein: 18.5 g | Sodium: 140 mg | Fiber: 6 g | Carbohydrates: 37 g | Sugar: 6 g

Italian Tofu Bake

With its versatility making it a perfect main ingredient in dishes with tons of flavor, tofu takes center stage in this delicious one-pan meal.

Tofu Instead of White Meat . . . or the Other White Meat . . . or the Other White Meat

Being a vegetarian or vegan doesn't mean you can't enjoy the same flavors found in delicious dishes that include chicken, turkey, fish, etc. Just replace the meat components of your favorite meal with tofu, and prepare it in the same manner. You can enjoy that chicken Parmesan, turkey tetrazzini, beefy burger, or whatever your heart desires.

1. In a food processor, reduce the bread slices to fine crumbs, then move the crumbs to a shallow dish and combine with 1 tablespoon of the Italian seasoning.

2. In a shallow bowl, beat the 2 eggs until frothy.

3. Slice the tofu into 8 equal slices.

4. Preheat the oven to 400°F and cover a baking sheet with foil and olive oil spray.

5. Dip the tofu slices into the egg, dredge through the bread crumbs, and place on the baking sheet. Repeat process with all of the tofu slices.

6. Bake the tofu slices for 10–15 minutes, or until golden brown and slightly crispy. Flip, and continue to bake for 8–10 minutes.

7. Remove the tofu from the oven, spoon ¼ cup of the tomato sauce on each, and top with half of a mozzarella slice and remaining Italian seasoning.

8. Return the tofu to the oven and continue baking until cheese is melted.

PER SERVING Calories: 242.5 | Fat: 11 g | Protein: 19 g | Sodium: 1,011 mg | Fiber: 2 g | Carbohydrates: 18 g | Sugar: 7 g

Garlic Tofu Stir-Fry

Spicy garlic infuses the clean tofu and vegetables that colorfully add tons of quality nutrition and taste to this delightful dish. Fragrant, flavorful, and delicious, this is a must-have stir-fry recipe that's sure to be loved by all!

INGREDIENTS | SERVES 2

1 (14-ounce) package of extra-firm tofu
2 tablespoons sesame oil
2 tablespoons minced garlic
1 cup shredded carrots
1 cup red pepper strips
1 yellow onion, cut into ½" chunks
1 cup broccoli florets
½ cup water chestnuts
½ cup bamboo shoots
½ cup water
¼ cup low-sodium soy sauce

1. Place a large skillet over medium heat, and cut the tofu into ½"–1" pieces. Combine the tofu with 1 tablespoon of the sesame oil in the pan and sauté until the tofu is golden brown and crispy, about 5–7 minutes. Remove from pan and set aside.

2. Return skillet to heat and combine remaining sesame oil with the minced garlic and all of the vegetables. Sauté for 2–3 minutes.

3. Add the water and soy sauce, and allow to steam while sautéing for about 10–12 minutes, or until broccoli is slightly softened but still crisp.

PER SERVING Calories: 492 | Fat: 24 g | Protein: 25 g | Sodium: 1,997 mg | Fiber: 9 g | Carbohydrates: 39 g | Sugar: 12 g

Sesame Seeds to the Rescue!

A little known benefit of indulging in the delightful little sesame seed is improved respiratory system functioning . . . especially for those who experience asthmatic symptoms. In recent studies, sesame seeds' mineral, magnesium, has been shown to reduce the occurrence and severity of spasms in the respiratory system.

Vegan Chili

Delicious chili doesn't have to include fat-laden meat to taste great. This wonderful chili recipe uses all-natural vegetables, beans, and spices that load up on nutrition and flavor, and come together perfectly for an out-of-this-world chili!

INGREDIENTS | SERVES 8

15 ounces dried black beans

15 ounces dried kidney beans

15 ounces dried garbanzo beans

15 ounces dried white beans

2 (14-ounce) packages extra-firm tofu, crumbled

1 tablespoon extra-virgin olive oil

2 cups Tasty Tomato Sauce (see Chapter 5)

2 cups chopped Roma tomatoes

2 cups fresh or frozen corn kernels

1 yellow onion, chopped

1 celery stalk, chopped

1 green pepper, chopped

4 tablespoons Italian seasoning

1 tablespoon cayenne pepper

1. Soak all bean for 24 hours, rinse, and drain.

2. In a large skillet over medium heat, sauté the crumbled tofu and olive oil until golden brown and slightly crispy, about 7–10 minutes.

3. In a cold slow cooker, combine all ingredients.

4. Set slow cooker to low.

5. Cook for 8–10 hours, or until ingredients are soft and flavors well blended.

PER SERVING Calories: 708 | Fat: 7 g | Protein: 45 g | Sodium: 550 mg | Fiber: 38 g | Carbohydrates: 122 g | Sugar: 19 g

Say "Yes!" to Freshness

Just because something's easy doesn't mean its better. When it comes to canned goods, this is exactly the case. It may be faster, easier, or more inexpensive to use canned varieties of tomatoes, vegetables, and beans in your meals, but those cans can hold far more than just your favorite foods. The corner-cutting of canned ingredients can come at the cost of lower-quality foods, additives used in manufacturing, and preservatives that push expiration dates to the extreme. The simplicity of preparing your own foods, like rehydrating beans, cutting your own artichoke hearts, and making your own tomato sauces, may entail a few more steps, but it comes with far more benefits and far fewer consequences.

Sweet Tofu with Summer Squash

Packed with clean protein and complex carbohydrates, this vitamin A–rich dish packs a punch with ingredients that not only taste great but promote health, too!

INGREDIENTS | SERVES 2

1 tablespoon extra-virgin olive oil

1 pound summer squash, peeled and cut into ½" squares

3 tablespoons pure maple syrup, divided

1 container of extra-firm tofu, cut into thin strips

½ teaspoon nutmeg

½ teaspoon ginger

½ teaspoon cinnamon

1 teaspoon all-natural sea salt

Pure Maple's Pure Sweetness

In studies that have researched the effects of certain sweeteners on blood sugar levels, maple syrup has held a surprising rating. When compared with natural sugars, honeys, agave nectars, and artificial sweeteners, all-natural maple syrup has been shown to provide a sweeter taste ounce for ounce, so less is required; contains fewer calories than its natural alternatives; and provides a higher concentration of essential minerals like manganese and zinc.

1. Prepare a large skillet with the olive oil and place over medium heat.

2. Add the squash to the pan with 1 tablespoon of the maple syrup, and sauté until tender, about 10 minutes.

3. Remove the squash from the skillet and place the tofu into the skillet with 1 tablespoon of maple syrup. Sauté until slightly browned.

4. Return the squash to the skillet and combine with the tofu. Add the spices and remaining tablespoon of maple syrup, and toss until squash and tofu are coated.

5. Remove from heat, plate, and serve immediately.

PER SERVING Calories: 266.5 | Fat: 11.5 g | Protein: 11.8 g | Sodium: 1,241 mg | Fiber: 0.5 g | Carbohydrates: 31 g | Sugar: 28 g

Clean Cashew Stir-Fry

Creamy, crunchy cashews add a depth of flavor to this dish that makes every bite pop with nutty goodness! With tons of amazing tastes and flavors from every natural ingredient, this stir-fry is a must-have for vegetable-lovers!

INGREDIENTS | SERVES 2

1 cup cashews, natural and unsalted

2 tablespoons sesame oil

1 cup chopped yellow onion, 1" pieces

1 cup chopped red onion, 1" pieces

1 cup thinly sliced carrot

1 cup sugar snap peas, trimmed

½ cup water chestnuts

1 cup broccoli florets

1 cup cauliflower florets

2 teaspoons garlic, minced

1 cup low-sodium soy sauce

1. In a large sauté pan over medium heat, toast the cashews for 3–5 minutes, turning constantly, until golden brown. Remove from heat and set aside.

2. In the same sauté pan, combine the sesame oil, onions, carrot, sugar snap peas, and water chestnuts, and sauté for about 2–3 minutes. Add the broccoli, cauliflower, minced garlic, and soy sauce. Sauté vegetables until slightly soft, but crisp, about 8–10 minutes.

3. Add the cashews to the sauté pan, combine thoroughly, and remove from heat.

PER SERVING Calories: 582 | Fat: 32 g | Protein: 21 g | Sodium: 2,132 mg | Fiber: 10 g | Carbohydrates: 56 g | Sugar: 16 g

"C" for Cauliflower

With its white color and broccoli-like composition, some would assume that cauliflower contains few vitamins and minerals compared to other vibrant vegetables in its class, but the truth is that every cup of the beautiful "blank" florets actually provides more than 80 percent of your daily recommended intake for vitamin C, along with other essential nutrients like vitamin K, folate, and the ever-popular fiber.

Pesto-Painted Tofu Sauté

Blasting this dish with vibrant green color and jazzy garlic spice, Peppy Pesto sauces up traditional tofu with amazing flavors that get brightened by deep basil and nutty pine nuts.

INGREDIENTS | SERVES 2

2 (14-ounce) packages extra-firm tofu, cut into 1" cubes
2 cups Peppy Pesto (see Chapter 5)
1 cup basil, chopped
1 cup pine nuts, toasted
1 teaspoon all-natural sea salt

1. In a large sauté pan over medium heat, combine the tofu and 2 tablespoons pesto. Sauté until tofu is cooked through and slightly crisp, about 10 minutes.

2. Add remaining pesto and sauté until tofu is completely covered and heated through, about 5 minutes.

3. Remove from heat and transfer to a serving dish. Toss with chopped basil and pine nuts, and season with salt.

PER SERVING Calories: 1,253 | Fat: 98 g | Protein: 48 g | Sodium: 1,301 mg | Fiber: 19 g | Carbohydrates: 42 g | Sugar: 3 g

Lemon-Basil Tofu

Simple and delicious, lemon and basil team up to take tofu to a new level of flavor-filled deliciousness!

INGREDIENTS | SERVES 2

1 tablespoon extra-virgin olive oil
1 (14-ounce) package extra-firm tofu, crumbled
½ cup freshly squeezed lemon juice
¼ cup basil, chopped
1 teaspoon maple syrup
1 cup nonfat Greek-style yogurt, or soy yogurt
1 teaspoon all-natural sea salt
1 teaspoon cracked black pepper

1. In a large sauté pan over medium heat, sauté the tofu in the extra-virgin olive oil until tofu is lightly browned and crispy, about 10–12 minutes.

2. Add the lemon juice, basil, and maple syrup to the sauté pan, and sauté for about 5–6 minutes, or until flavors are well blended. Remove from heat, and allow to cool for 5–10 minutes before whisking in the yogurt.

3. Add salt and pepper and serve immediately.

PER SERVING Calories: 225 | Fat: 10 g | Protein: 26 g | Sodium: 1,269 mg | Fiber: 0.5 g | Carbohydrates: 14 g | Sugar: 12 g

Best-Ever Tofu Enchiladas

Restaurant enchiladas are packed with preservatives and mystery ingredients that are definitely not intended to support a healthy lifestyle. Opt for these delicious enchiladas that max out the flavor of natural ingredients.

INGREDIENTS | SERVES 6

2 tablespoons extra-virgin olive oil

2 (14-ounce) packages of firm tofu, crumbled

1 yellow onion, minced

1 red pepper, minced

2 tablespoons water

1 cup plain nonfat yogurt

½ cup plain low-fat Greek-style yogurt, or soy yogurt

1 teaspoon all-natural sea salt

¼ cup chopped green chilies

6 100% whole-wheat tortillas

1 teaspoon cayenne pepper

1. Prepare a large skillet with 1 tablespoon of olive oil and place over medium heat.

2. Add crumbled tofu, and sauté until slightly browned, about 7–10 minutes. Remove the tofu from the skillet. Add the onion and red pepper to the skillet with the 2 tablespoons of water. Sauté until slightly softened, about 5–7 minutes. Remove from heat and let cool with the cooked tofu in a mixing bowl.

3. After tofu and vegetables have cooled, add yogurts, salt, and chopped green chilies, and toss well to combine.

4. Prepare a large baking dish with olive oil spray and preheat oven to 350°F.

5. Set all tortillas out in a row, and place even amounts of the tofu mixture in the center of each.

6. Roll each tortilla's ends in first, and then roll to result in a completely enclosed enchilada.

7. Place tortillas face-down in the baking dish, paint with remaining tablespoon of olive oil, and sprinkle with cayenne pepper.

8. Bake for 30 minutes.

PER SERVING Calories: 255 | Fat: 11.5 g | Protein: 13 g | Sodium: 659 mg | Fiber: 2 g | Carbohydrates: 25 g | Sugar: 7 g

Five-Alarm Enchiladas

If you like spicy, you'll love these enchiladas. With onions and three kinds of peppers, you'll be loving every bite of these five-alarm enchiladas that do a body good!

INGREDIENTS | SERVES 6

3 tablespoons extra-virgin olive oil, divided

2 packages (14-ounce) extra-firm tofu, crumbled

1 yellow onion, minced

2 chipotle peppers, minced

½ cup green chilies, puréed

2 tablespoons water

1 cup plain nonfat yogurt, or soy yogurt

½ cup nonfat Greek-style yogurt, or silken tofu

1 teaspoon all-natural sea salt

6 whole-wheat tortillas

½ teaspoon cayenne

Turn Up the Heat!

If you love spicy foods, can't get enough heat in your treats, and want to spice things up, you can always increase your dishes' level of fiery flavor by adding the right ingredients in just the right way to get the job done. Jalapeños pack a punch when it comes to adding spiciness to your foods, and by keeping the seeds and ribs intact when adding them to your favorite recipes, you can boost the burn significantly! A little bit goes a long way, and the small amount rarely adjusts a recipe's intended outcome, so feel free to experiment with the level of heat you have in your culinary creations.

1. Heat 1 tablespoon olive oil in a large sauté pan over medium heat. Add crumbled tofu, and sauté until cooked through, about 5 minutes. Remove tofu from the pan and set aside.

2. Heat another tablespoon olive oil in the sauté pan. Add the onion, peppers, and half of the chilies, and water. Sauté until vegetables are slightly softened, about 4–6 minutes. Return the tofu to the pan, stir well, remove from heat, and allow to cool for 20 minutes.

3. Add the yogurts and/or silken tofu and salt to the vegetable mixture, and blend thoroughly.

4. Prepare a large baking dish with olive oil spray and preheat the oven to 400°F.

5. Set tortillas on a flat surface and place equal amounts of the vegetable and yogurt mixture down the center of each. Roll sides in slightly and then roll forward to enclose completely.

6. Place tortillas seam-side down in the baking dish, paint with remaining tablespoon of oil, and sprinkle with cayenne. Bake for 30 minutes, or until golden brown and crispy.

7. While enchiladas are cooking, place remaining half of chilis in a blender or food processor and purée.

8. Top tortillas with chili purée and return to oven to heat through, about 5 minutes. Remove from oven and serve immediately.

PER SERVING Calories: 195 | Fat: 9 g | Protein: 9.5 g | Sodium: 476 mg | Fiber: 2 g | Carbohydrates: 19 g | Sugar: 4 g

Spinach Enchiladas

Rich, creamy ingredients like yogurts and artichokes combine as the perfect backdrop for vibrant spinach in these delicious enchiladas.

INGREDIENTS | SERVES 6

3 tablespoons extra-virgin olive oil

2 (14-ounce) packages extra-firm tofu, crumbled

2 shallots, minced

1 clove garlic, minced

2 cups spinach

1 cup artichoke hearts, crushed

1 cup plain nonfat yogurt or soy yogurt

½ cup nonfat Greek-style yogurt, or silken tofu

1 teaspoon all-natural sea salt

6 whole-wheat tortillas

Cayenne pepper, ground

Using Shallots for a Mildly Sweet Spiciness

While shallots belong to the onion family and provide the tang that's found in the Vidalia or yellow onion to some extent, the taste is much milder than its larger onion alternatives. In addition to the subtle spice unique to the onion varieties, shallots lend a sweet undertone to dishes without sweetening the pot too much or overpowering other flavors.

1. Prepare a large sauté pan with 1 tablespoon of extra-virgin olive oil over medium heat. Add crumbled tofu, and sauté until cooked through; remove from pan and set aside.

2. Add 1 tablespoon of oil with the shallot and garlic to the pan, and sauté until slightly softened, about 3–5 minutes. Add spinach and artichoke hearts, and sauté until spinach is wilted, about 2–4 minutes. Combine with the tofu, remove from heat, and allow to cool for 20 minutes.

3. Add the yogurts and/or silken tofu and salt to the spinach mixture, and blend thoroughly.

4. Prepare a large baking dish with olive oil spray and preheat the oven to 400°F.

5. Set tortillas on a flat surface and place equal amounts of the spinach and yogurt mixture down the center of each. Roll sides in slightly and then roll forward to enclose completely.

6. Place tortillas seam-side down in the baking dish, paint with remaining tablespoon of oil, and sprinkle with cayenne. Bake for 30 minutes, or until golden brown and crispy.

PER SERVING Calories: 232 | Fat: 10 g | Protein: 15 g | Sodium: 543 mg | Fiber: 3.5 g | Carbohydrates: 22 g | Sugar: 5 g

Tasty Tomatillo Enchiladas

A great way to use any extra Tangy Tomatillo Salsa Verde, this quick and easy enchilada dish boosts the intense flavors of all-natural ingredients to create a creamy, spicy twist on enchiladas that's not too hot.

INGREDIENTS | SERVES 6

3 tablespoons extra-virgin olive oil, divided

2 (14-ounce) packages extra-firm tofu, crumbled

1 yellow pepper, chopped

1 clove garlic, minced

2 cups Tangy Tomatillo Salsa Verde (see Chapter 5)

½ cup nonfat Greek-style yogurt, or silken tofu

1 teaspoon all-natural sea salt

6 whole-wheat tortillas

Cayenne pepper, ground

1. Prepare a large sauté pan with 1 tablespoon of extra-virgin olive oil and place over medium heat. Add crumbled tofu, and sauté until cooked through, about 8–10 minutes; remove from pan and set aside.

2. Add 1 tablespoon of oil to the pan with the yellow pepper, and sauté until slightly softened, about 4 minutes. Add the garlic and ¼ cup salsa verde, and sauté 3 minutes. Combine with the tofu, remove from heat, and allow to cool for 20 minutes.

3. Add 1¼ cups of the salsa, the yogurt, and salt to the tofu mixture, and blend thoroughly.

4. Prepare a large baking dish with olive oil spray and preheat the oven to 400°F.

5. Set tortillas on a flat surface and place equal amounts of the salsa and yogurt mixture down the center of each. Roll sides in slightly and then roll forward to enclose completely.

6. Place tortillas seam-side down in the baking dish, paint with remaining tablespoon of oil, and sprinkle with cayenne. Bake for 30 minutes, or until golden brown and crispy.

7. Pour remaining ½ cup of the salsa verde over top of the tortillas and return to the oven to heat for about 5 minutes. Remove from heat and serve immediately.

PER SERVING Calories: 226 | Fat: 10 g | Protein: 13 g | Sodium: 997 mg | Fiber: 3.5 g | Carbohydrates: 21 g | Sugar: 4 g

Good-For-You Gumbo

Gumbo lovers rejoice! This delicious recipe for gumbo is not only delicious and aromatic, it's a hearty dish that packs a punch of nutrition, making a good dish even better.

INGREDIENTS | SERVES 6

½ cup vegetable oil

½ cup rice flour

1 white onion, diced

1 bell pepper, diced

4 cloves garlic, minced

4 cups water

2 cups Simple Stock (see Chapter 7)

1 tablespoon vegan Worcestershire sauce

1 (16-ounce) package frozen chopped okra

1 tablespoon Cajun seasoning

1 bay leaf

2 teaspoons salt

2 teaspoons pepper

1 (7-ounce) package Gardein Chick'n Strips, chopped

½ cup flat-leaf parsley, chopped

½ cup scallions, sliced

½ teaspoon filé powder

6 cups cooked brown rice

1. In a sauté pan, cook the oil and flour over medium heat, stirring continuously until the roux achieves a rich brown color, at least 10 minutes.

2. In a 4-quart slow cooker, add the roux and all remaining ingredients except the rice. Cover and cook on low heat for 6 hours.

3. Once done, remove the bay leaf. Pour each serving over 1 cup of cooked rice.

PER SERVING Calories: 491 | Fat: 21 g | Protein: 9 g | Sodium: 841 mg | Fiber: 7 g | Carbohydrates: 67 g | Sugar: 3 g

Filé Powder

Filé (pronounced FEE-lay) powder is made from ground sassafras leaves. It is an essential ingredient for authentic Cajun or Creole gumbo. Used to both thicken and flavor, filé powder is thought to have been first used by the Choctaw Indians from the Louisiana bayou region. It can be found in most well-stocked grocery stores.

Creamy Curry Tempeh with Vegetables

Beautiful, aromatic, and flavorful, this all-natural blend of creamy coconut milk, vibrant vegetables, and delightful spices makes for a delightful tempeh dish that's an amazingly healthy treat!

INGREDIENTS | SERVES 2

1 (8-ounce) package tempeh, cut into bite-sized pieces
2 tablespoons extra-virgin olive oil
1 green pepper, chopped
1 red pepper, chopped
1 yellow pepper, chopped
1 yellow onion, chopped
½ cup chopped celery
2 cloves garlic, minced
1 cup coconut milk
1½ teaspoons curry powder
⅛ cup ground flaxseed
1 teaspoon all-natural sea salt

1. In a large sauté pan over medium heat, sauté the tempeh and 1 tablespoon of the olive oil until cooked through and slightly browned, about 8–10 minutes. Remove from heat and set aside.

2. To the sauté pan, add the peppers, onion, celery, and garlic with remaining tablespoon of oil, and sauté until slightly softened.

3. Return tempeh to the sauté pan, and add the coconut milk, curry powder, and flaxseed. Mix well and simmer for 5–10 minutes.

4. Remove from heat, season with salt, and serve.

PER SERVING Calories: 649 | Fat: 53 g | Protein: 26 g | Sodium: 1,234 mg | Fiber: 6 g | Carbohydrates: 28 g | Sugar: 4.5 g

Sweet and Spicy Veggie Stir-Fry

Sweet maple syrup and spicy red pepper flakes add a full spectrum of amazing flavor to traditional stir-fry vegetables. This is a stir-fry free of preservatives and packed with goodness.

INGREDIENTS | SERVES 2

1 tablespoon sesame oil

1 tablespoon maple syrup

1 cup sugar snap peas, trimmed

1 cup pea pods, trimmed

1 cup yellow onion, cut into ½" pieces

1 cup broccoli florets

1 large red pepper, cut into strips

½ cup water chestnuts

1 clove garlic, minced

1 teaspoon red pepper flakes

¼ cup water

1 teaspoon all-natural sea salt

1. In a large skillet over medium heat, combine the sesame oil, maple syrup, sugar snap peas, pea pods, onion, broccoli, red pepper strips, water chestnuts, garlic, and red pepper flakes. Sauté until vegetables are softened but still crisp, about 10–12 minutes. Add water as needed to steam and prevent burning or sticking.

2. Remove from heat, add salt, and serve immediately.

PER SERVING Calories: 374 | Fat: 14 g | Protein: 13 g | Sodium: 1,221 mg | Fiber: 19 g | Carbohydrates: 62 g | Sugar: 21 g

Tofu Piccata

Lemon goodness flows from every savory bite of this slow cooker recipe. With deep flavors that marinate through tofu over hours in your slow cooker, you'll be amazed at how light and bright this meal tastes, and how simple it is to create.

INGREDIENTS | SERVES 4

1 (14-ounce) package extra-firm tofu, pressed and sliced into fourths

⅓ cup water

2 tablespoons lemon juice

1 teaspoon all-natural sea salt

3 thin slices fresh lemon

1 tablespoon nonpareil capers

½ teaspoon minced fresh rosemary

1. Place the tofu filets on the bottom of a 2-quart slow cooker. Pour the water, lemon juice, and salt over the tofu.

2. Arrange the lemon slices in a single layer on top of the tofu. Sprinkle with capers and rosemary.

3. Cover and cook on low for 2 hours. Discard lemon slices prior to serving.

PER SERVING Calories: 63 | Fat: 2.5 g | Protein: 7 g | Sodium: 689 mg | Fiber: 0.5 g | Carbohydrates: 3 g | Sugar: 1.5 g

Ratatouille

The traditional version of this recipe can pack a whopping amount of fat and calories, sodium and sugar, and dangerous preservatives. This clean variation makes for a one-pot meal that's simple, delicious, and good for your health.

INGREDIENTS | SERVES 4

1 tablespoon extra-virgin olive oil

1 large eggplant, cut into 1" cubes

2 tablespoons minced garlic

1 zucchini, cut in ½" pieces

1 yellow squash, cut in ½" pieces

2 Roma tomatoes, cut in slices

1 green pepper, cut in ½" pieces

1 red pepper, cut in ½" pieces

½ cup crumbled goat cheese, or vegan soft cheese (optional)

1. Preheat the oven to 350°F and coat a large casserole dish with olive oil spray.

2. In a large skillet, heat the tablespoon of olive oil over medium heat. Add the eggplant, and sauté until softened, about 10 minutes.

3. Place the eggplant on the bottom of the casserole dish for the first layer, and top with the minced garlic.

4. Layer the zucchini, followed by the squash, then the tomatoes, and the peppers last.

5. Cover the top layer with the goat cheese, and bake for 30–40 minutes.

PER SERVING Calories: 229 | Fat: 14 g | Protein: 12 g | Sodium: 108.5 mg | Fiber: 7 g | Carbohydrates: 17 g | Sugar: 8 g

Combining Vegetables for Flavor and Nutrition

When you're struggling to reach those daily vegetable servings, try whipping up a hearty dish that focuses on vegetables solely. Combining flavorful vegetables in a tomato sauce with garlic and cheese makes for a splendid dish that doesn't even taste like it consists of only vegetables. Adding extras like basil and spices only improves the flavor and nutritional content, so don't be shy.

Sautéed Tofu with Balsamic Onions and Mushrooms

*Beautiful Vidalia onions and portobello mushrooms blend perfectly in
a tart balsamic reduction that infuses amazing flavor through every bite.*

INGREDIENTS | SERVES 2

1 package (14-ounce) extra-firm tofu,
cubed to bite-sized pieces

1 tablespoon extra-virgin olive oil

1 Vidalia onion, peeled and chopped

1 cup balsamic vinegar

½ cup water

1 pound portobello mushrooms

1 teaspoon maple syrup

1 teaspoon all-natural sea salt

1. In a large skillet over medium heat, sauté the tofu cubes in the olive oil until lightly browned, about 6–8 minutes.

2. Add the Vidalia onion, ½ cup of the vinegar, and the water to the skillet, and sauté the tofu and onion together for 3–5 minutes before adding the mushrooms.

3. Drizzle the maple syrup over the tofu, onions, and mushrooms, and add the remaining ½ cup of vinegar to the skillet. Sauté all together for 5–7 minutes, or until mushrooms have started to decrease in volume. Sprinkle with salt, remove from heat, and serve.

PER SERVING Calories: 300 | Fat: 9 g | Protein: 13 g | Sodium: 1,302 mg | Fiber: 3 g | Carbohydrates: 37 g | Sugar: 29 g

Ginger-Lime Tofu

Spicy ginger and tart lime combine to delicately infuse tofu with their delicious flavors. Light and refreshing, yet enough of a meal to satisfy your dinner crowd, this healthy dinner option is nothing short of delightful!

INGREDIENTS | SERVES 8

2 (14-ounce) packages extra-firm tofu, pressed and sliced
¼ cup minced fresh ginger
¼ cup lime juice
1 lime, thinly sliced
1 onion, thinly sliced

All Cracked Up!

Before each use, check your slow cooker for cracks. Even small cracks in the glaze can allow bacteria to grow in the ceramic insert. If there are cracks, replace the insert or the entire slow cooker. To look for small cracks, you can fill your slow cooker to the top, and look for bubbles that would appear from even the slightest crevasse.

1. Place the tofu filets in a 6- to 7-quart slow cooker.

2. Pour the ginger and lime juice over the tofu, then arrange the lime and then the onion in a single layer over the top.

3. Cook on low for 3–4 hours.

PER SERVING Calories: 75 | Fat: 2 g | Protein: 8 g | Sodium: 63 mg | Fiber: 1 g | Carbohydrates: 6 g | Sugar: 2 g

CHAPTER 11

Grains and Pastas

Vegan Stroganoff
184

Red Pepper Rice with
Mushrooms and Sweet Peas
185

Balsamic Green Beans
with Quinoa
185

Asian Tofu Sauté with
Rice Noodles
186

Sweet Rice and Sweeter Peppers
186

Paella
187

Slow Cooker Red Beans and Rice
188

Vegetarian Lasagna
189

Baked Veggie Pasta
190

Pesto and Pine Nut Penne
190

Pasta Primavera
191

Summer Squash Casserole
192

Tofu Spaghetti
193

Linguine with Fire-Roasted
Tomatoes, Basil, and Mozzarella
193

Cheesy Spinach Shells
194

Great Greens Pasta Pot
195

Cheesy Mushroom and
Sweet Pea Pasta
196

Tomato-Basil Rigatoni
197

Linguine with Leeks, Artichokes,
and Garlic
197

Veggie-Stuffed Shells
198

Light and Creamy Green Linguine
199

Simple Spaghetti with Sautéed
Tofu and Onions
200

Sweet and Savory Pepper Penne
200

"Meat" Sauce Stuffed Shells
201

Wild Mushroom Risotto
202

Vegan Stroganoff

This clean vegetarian spin on the traditional beef stroganoff packs all the delicious flavors without the poor ingredients that pack fat, calories, sodium, and preservatives into the dish.

INGREDIENTS | SERVES 4

1 tablespoon extra-virgin olive oil

2 (14-ounce) packages extra-firm tofu, crumbled

1 yellow onion, minced

1 cup sliced mushrooms

1 teaspoon garlic powder

2 tablespoons low-sodium soy sauce

1 (12-ounce) container nonfat cottage cheese

2 tablespoons plain low-fat Greek-style yogurt, or soy yogurt

16 ounces 100% whole-wheat noodles, cooked

2 teaspoons cracked black pepper

1. Prepare a large skillet with olive oil and place over medium heat.

2. Sauté tofu crumbles and onion in the olive oil for 7 minutes, or until cooked through.

3. Add the mushrooms, garlic powder, and soy sauce, and combine well.

4. Stir in the cottage cheese and Greek-style yogurt, until the ingredients become a thick sauce. Remove from the heat.

5. In a large bowl, combine the cooked noodles, tofu mixture, and pepper. Blend well. Serve immediately.

PER SERVING Calories: 417.5 | Fat: 13 g | Protein: 29 g | Sodium: 374 mg | Fiber: 3 g | Carbohydrates: 46 g | Sugar: 7 g

The Clean Answer to Heavy Cream

Packed with fat and calories, heavily processed, and possibly containing hormones, antibiotics, and steroids, heavy dairy cream is a clean-eating nightmare! In recipes that include this classic creamy recipe staple, the clean-eating vegetarian knows that plain Greek-style yogurt, or vegan yogurt thickened with ground flaxseed, can serve as a perfect protein-packed substitute to the unhealthy alternative.

Red Pepper Rice with Mushrooms and Sweet Peas

Plain brown rice, though nutritious, can get a little bland. By adding bright red peppers, sweet green peas, and tasty mushrooms, this dish jazzes up a healthy staple to become a sweetened balsamic blast of flavorful nutrition that can serve as a main dish at any meal.

INGREDIENTS | SERVES 2

2 red bell peppers, chopped

2 cups baby portobello mushrooms, sliced

½ cup balsamic vinegar

2 teaspoons maple syrup

2 cups cooked brown rice

2 cups sweet peas

1. Heat a large skillet over medium heat and spray it with olive oil spray. Add the red peppers and mushrooms with ¼ cup of the balsamic vinegar and the maple syrup. Sauté until red peppers are cooked and mushrooms are softened.

2. Add cooked rice and remaining ¼ cup of balsamic vinegar, and sauté together until cooked through and combined, about 4–5 minutes.

3. Add peas and sauté until cooked thoroughly, about 2 minutes. Remove from heat and serve.

PER SERVING Calories: 465 | Fat: 2.5 g | Protein: 16 g | Sodium: 36 mg | Fiber: 14 g | Carbohydrates: 72 g | Sugar: 28 g

Balsamic Green Beans with Quinoa

Coming together for a simple dish with delicious flavors, balsamic vinegar and maple syrup complement one another while brightening the natural flavor of vibrant green beans all atop crunchy quinoa.

INGREDIENTS | SERVES 2

2 cups green beans, trimmed and cut in half

1 cup balsamic vinegar

2 teaspoons maple syrup

Several tablespoons of water

2 cups cooked quinoa

1 teaspoon all-natural sea salt

1 teaspoon cracked black pepper

1. In a large sauté pan over medium heat, combine the green beans, ½ cup of balsamic vinegar, and maple syrup, and sauté until green beans are cooked through. Add 1 tablespoon of water, as needed, to assist with cooking and prevent balsamic vinegar from evaporating.

2. Add the quinoa and remaining balsamic vinegar to the pan, and sauté until thoroughly combined.

3. Remove from heat and add salt and pepper.

PER SERVING Calories: 285 | Fat: 3 g | Protein: 11 g | Sodium: 1,128 mg | Fiber: 8 g | Carbohydrates: 53 g | Sugar: 10 g

Asian Tofu Sauté with Rice Noodles

Delicious, aromatic ingredients like garlic, green onions, and sesame oil take tofu to the extraordinary Asian-inspired side of flavors for an out-of-this world dish you can enjoy any night of the week!

INGREDIENTS | SERVES 2

1 package (14-ounce) extra-firm tofu, cubed

2 tablespoons sesame oil

1 cup green onions, chopped

1 clove garlic, minced

2 cups rice noodles, cooked

2 tablespoons rice wine vinegar

½ cup sesame seeds, toasted

1 teaspoon all-natural sea salt

1. In a large sauté pan over medium heat, sauté the tofu and 1 tablespoon of sesame oil until tofu is cooked through and slightly crunchy, about 6–8 minutes.

2. Add the green onions, garlic, and remaining tablespoon of sesame oil, and sauté 3–4 minutes more.

3. Add the cooked rice noodles and rice wine vinegar. Toss to combine thoroughly and heat noodles.

4. Remove from heat, plate, and sprinkle with toasted sesame seeds and salt.

PER SERVING Calories: 598 | Fat: 34 g | Protein: 17 g | Sodium: 1,295 mg | Fiber: 7 g | Carbohydrates: 57 g | Sugar: 3 g

Sweet Rice and Sweeter Peppers

Sweet peppers get all wrapped up in fluffy brown rice and creamy coconut milk for a vegetarian dish that's amazingly delicious! Sweetened with a hint of smooth maple syrup, this rice dish is anything but ordinary.

INGREDIENTS | SERVES 2

1 red pepper

1 yellow pepper

2 sweet peppers

1 cup coconut milk

2 teaspoons maple syrup

2 cups cooked brown rice

1 teaspoon all-natural sea salt

1. Prepare peppers by removing tops and cutting into bite-sized chunks, about ¼" squares.

2. In a large skillet over medium heat, sauté the pepper chunks in ¼ cup of the coconut milk and 1 teaspoon of the maple syrup until softened, but still crisp, about 4–6 minutes.

3. Add the cooked rice, remaining coconut milk, and remaining teaspoon of maple syrup. Stir together until well blended and heated through.

4. Remove from heat and add salt.

PER SERVING Calories: 512 | Fat: 26 g | Protein: 9 g | Sodium: 1,203 mg | Fiber: 8 g | Carbohydrates: 65 g | Sugar: 10 g

Paella

Simple and easy, this slow cooker creation takes the time-consuming, pot-watching element out of making paella. Now, your favorite paella dish can be waiting for your return home any night of the week!

INGREDIENTS | SERVES 6

1 tablespoon extra-virgin olive oil
½ onion, diced
1 cup diced tomato
½ teaspoon saffron or turmeric
1 teaspoon salt
2 tablespoons fresh parsley
1 cup long-grain white rice, uncooked
1 cup frozen peas
2 cups water
1 (12-ounce) package vegan chorizo, crumbled

1. Heat the olive oil in a sauté pan over medium heat. Add the onion and sauté for 3 minutes.

2. Add the tomato, saffron, salt, and parsley, and stir.

3. Pour the sautéed mixture into a 4-quart slow cooker. Add the white rice, then frozen peas and water.

4. Cover, and cook on low heat for 4 hours.

5. Pour the crumbled chorizo on top of the rice. Cover and cook for an additional 30 minutes. Stir before serving.

PER SERVING Calories: 421 | Fat: 24 g | Protein: 17 g | Sodium: 1,091 mg | Fiber: 2 g | Carbohydrates: 32 g | Sugar: 2.5 g

Slow Cooker Red Beans and Rice

Deliciously rich and creamy red beans get all wrapped up in fluffy rice for a simple-sounding, but amazing-tasting, recipe that's out of this world . . . and out of your slow cooker.

INGREDIENTS | SERVES 4

3 cups water

3½ cups vegetable stock

2 tablespoons butter, or vegan margarine

1 (15-ounce) can kidney beans, drained

2 cups white rice, uncooked

1 onion, chopped

1 green bell pepper, chopped

1 cup celery, chopped

1 teaspoon thyme

1 teaspoon paprika

1 teaspoon Cajun seasoning

½ teaspoon red pepper flakes

1 teaspoon salt

¼ teaspoon cracked black pepper

1. Combine all ingredients in a 4-quart slow cooker.

2. Cover and cook on low heat for 6 hours.

3. If the rice is tender, remove from heat. If the rice is not cooked through and tender, cook for an additional hour.

PER SERVING Calories: 340 | Fat: 7 g | Protein: 11 g | Sodium: 887 mg | Fiber: 8 g | Carbohydrates: 52 g | Sugar: 4.5 g

Recipe Variations for Completely Different Taste Sensations

For a heartier vegetarian meal, you can always add sliced vegetarian sausage or vegetarian beef crumbles during the last hour of cooking.

Vegetarian Lasagna

Lasagnas can be delicious, but packed with unhealthy ingredients that load up on poor nutrients and provide few good ones. This vegetarian lasagna explodes with flavor, texture, and immense quality nutrition all due to the fresh ingredients that come together perfectly in an Italian favorite that's classic and clean.

INGREDIENTS | SERVES 12

2 packages (8-ounce) 100% whole-wheat lasagna noodles

1 tablespoon extra-virgin olive oil

1 small zucchini, sliced thinly

1 green pepper, diced

3 teaspoons minced garlic

1 yellow onion, minced

1 pound portobello mushrooms, sliced

6 cups Tasty Tomato Sauce (see Chapter 5)

4 teaspoons Italian seasoning, divided

2 eggs or ½ cup egg substitute

1 cup cottage cheese

1 cup plain low-fat Greek-style yogurt, or soy yogurt

12 thin slices of fresh buffalo mozzarella, or vegan mozzarella

Ditch the Processed Cheese

The clean lifestyle makes a major point of still eating things you love but trying to use fresh ingredients and healthier alternatives whenever possible. Cheese is one thing that's common in the standard American diet that really shouldn't be. Heavily processed, fat-packed, and calorie-laden, dairy cheeses like deli slices and prepackaged singles are terribly unnatural. Fresh buffalo mozzarella and crumbled goat cheese are two natural alternatives that are very versatile, minimally processed, and taste great. These are two healthy options you can live with.

1. Preheat the oven to 350°F and prepare a 9" × 13" baking dish with olive oil spray.

2. Prepare a large pot with water over medium-high heat. Cook noodles until al dente. Remove, rinse, and cool.

3. Prepare the rinsed noodle pot with 1 tablespoon olive oil, and add the zucchini, pepper, minced garlic, and onion. Sauté for 2–3 minutes; add the mushrooms, tomato sauce, and half of the Italian seasoning. Reduce heat to medium and simmer for 15 minutes.

4. Combine the eggs, cottage cheese, and yogurt in a mixing bowl.

5. Pour 1 cup of the tomato sauce in the bottom of the dish to coat. Layer (for 2 layers) half of the noodles, followed by half of the tomato sauce, dollops of the yogurt mix spread, and half of the mozzarella cheese.

6. Layer, in the same order for a second time, and sprinkle the mozzarella topping with remaining Italian seasoning.

7. Bake for 30–45 minutes, or until bubbly and cooked through.

PER SERVING Calories: 397 | Fat: 6 g | Protein: 18 g | Sodium: 785 mg | Fiber: 5 g | Carbohydrates: 68 g | Sugar: 11 g

Baked Veggie Pasta

Seemingly simplistic, this dish has a wondrous depth of deliciousness from each vibrant vegetable. A delightful pasta dish that's packed with vibrant vegetables and baked for an even more intense marrying of flavors, this Baked Veggie Pasta is delicious and nutritious.

INGREDIENTS | SERVES 5

2 cups chopped spinach

3 roasted red peppers, sliced

2 cups portobello mushrooms, sliced

2 cups artichoke hearts, crushed

½ red onion, sliced

1 zucchini, sliced into ¼" rounds

2 cups black olives, sliced

2 cups crumbled goat cheese, or vegan soft cheese

4 cups cooked 100% whole-wheat penne pasta

1. Prepare a 9" × 13" baking dish with olive oil spray, and preheat the oven to 350°F.

2. In a mixing bowl, combine the spinach, red peppers, mushrooms, artichoke hearts, onion, zucchini, olives, and cheese. Fold in the pasta and combine well.

3. Pour the vegetable pasta mixture into the prepared baking dish and bake for 30–45 minutes.

PER SERVING Calories: 635 | Fat: 33 g | Protein: 35 g | Sodium: 738 mg | Fiber: 14 g | Carbohydrates: 57 g | Sugar: 6 g

Pesto and Pine Nut Penne

This penne is a sweet and savory dish that loads nutritious ingredients in a clean creation you'd never think was designed for better health.

INGREDIENTS | SERVES 2

2 cups Peppy Pesto (see Chapter 5)

1 cup toasted pine nuts

4 ounces crumbled goat cheese, or vegan soft cheese

3 cups cooked 100% whole-wheat penne pasta

¼ cup chopped basil

1. In a large bowl, combine the pesto, pine nuts, and goat cheese until well blended.

2. Add the penne to the pesto, pine nuts, and goat cheese and toss until evenly coated.

3. Plate 2 even servings, and garnish with the chopped basil.

PER SERVING Calories: 1,539 | Fat: 96 g | Protein: 42 g | Sodium: 329 mg | Fiber: 21 g | Carbohydrates: 87 g | Sugar: 1 g

Pasta Primavera

The clean version of this light and delightful vegetable pasta is similar to others but packs the beautiful dish full of whole, natural ingredients that take a potentially healthy meal to the limit of maxed out nutrition and taste!

INGREDIENTS | SERVES 4

4 tablespoons extra-virgin olive oil, divided

1 small zucchini, sliced

1 small yellow squash, sliced

1 yellow onion, sliced

1 large carrot, sliced

4 tablespoons water (as needed)

1 cup baby portobello mushrooms, sliced

½ red pepper

1 cup broccoli florets

4 cups cooked 100% whole-wheat rigatoni pasta

2 teaspoons garlic powder

2 teaspoons cracked black pepper

2 teaspoons all-natural sea salt

1 teaspoon onion powder

1. Prepare a skillet with 1 tablespoon of olive oil and place over medium heat. Sauté the zucchini, squash, onion, and carrots for about 7 minutes, adding water, as needed, to prevent sticking and promote steaming.

2. Add mushrooms, red pepper, and broccoli, and continue to sauté for another 7 minutes, or until all vegetables are slightly softened.

3. Pour the prepared pasta into a mixing bowl and add vegetables and seasonings. Drizzle remaining 2–3 tablespoons of olive oil (for desired taste) over the pasta and toss to coat.

PER SERVING Calories: 457 | Fat: 16 g | Protein: 14.5 g | Sodium: 1,216 mg | Fiber: 13 g | Carbohydrates: 72 g | Sugar: 7 g

Summer Squash Casserole

Packed with vitamin A, this dish is a feast for your eyes that also benefits your eyes.

INGREDIENTS | SERVES 8

1 large zucchini

1 large yellow squash

1 butternut squash

2 tablespoons extra-virgin olive oil

2 tablespoons Italian seasoning

1 tablespoon paprika

2 teaspoons all-natural sea salt

2 cups cooked brown rice

½ cup crumbled goat cheese, or vegan soft cheese

Versatile Deliciousness

If you're looking for a wonderful fresh vegetable that can be made creamy, crunchy, sweet, or salty, look no further than summer squash. Blended with fresh ingredients, natural nectars, or light and savory seasonings, you can create the most amazing-tasting dishes. Whether you'd like a sautéed dish, a hearty casserole, or a creamy soup, summer squash is an easy, inexpensive ingredient that makes for a delicious and nutritious meal any day or night of the week.

1. Cut the squashes into bite-sized pieces (strips or rounds) of comparable size.

2. Preheat the oven to 400°F and prepare a 9" × 13" baking dish with olive oil spray.

3. In a large mixing bowl, combine the squashes, olive oil, and seasonings, and mix well.

4. Fold in the rice and goat cheese, place into the prepared dish, and bake for 35–45 minutes or until cooked through and bubbly.

PER SERVING Calories: 154 | Fat: 9 g | Protein: 6 g | Sodium: 640 mg | Fiber: 1.5 g | Carbohydrates: 13 g | Sugar: 1 g

Tofu Spaghetti

Quick and easy, this vegetarian spaghetti is a delicious combination of natural ingredients that provides clean complex carbohydrates and protein for a good-for-you dish that's filling, nutritious, and terrifically tasty.

INGREDIENTS | SERVES 4

1 tablespoon extra-virgin olive oil

1 (14-ounce) package extra-firm tofu, crumbled

2 cups Tasty Tomato Sauce (see Chapter 5)

4 cups cooked 100% whole-wheat spaghetti

2 teaspoons all-natural sea salt

4 slices fresh buffalo mozzarella, or vegan mozzarella

¼ cup chopped basil

1. In a large skillet over medium heat, combine the olive oil and crumbled tofu and sauté until slightly browned.

2. Add the tomato sauce to the sautéed tofu and bring to a simmer.

3. Remove the tofu and sauce from the heat and move to a large serving bowl. Thoroughly combine with the pasta and salt.

4. Plate, and garnish with the mozzarella slices and chopped basil.

PER SERVING Calories: 375 | Fat: 10 g | Protein: 19 g | Sodium: 1,940 mg | Fiber: 4.5 g | Carbohydrates: 52 g | Sugar: 7 g

Linguine with Fire-Roasted Tomatoes, Basil, and Mozzarella

With vibrant green basil, brilliant red fire-roasted tomatoes, and bright white mozzarella, this pasta dish is packed with beautiful ingredients and powerful flavors.

INGREDIENTS | SERVES 2

2 cups fire-roasted tomatoes

1½ tablespoons extra-virgin olive oil

½ cup chopped basil

4 ounces buffalo mozzarella, or vegan mozzarella, cubed in ¼" cubes

2 cups cooked 100% whole-wheat linguine

1 teaspoon garlic powder

1 teaspoon all-natural sea salt

1 teaspoon cracked black pepper

1. In a large bowl, combine the fire-roasted tomatoes, 1 tablespoon of the olive oil, basil, and mozzarella. Toss well to combine and thoroughly coat with the olive oil.

2. Add the cooked linguine to the tomatoes, basil, and mozzarella, and fold gently to combine.

3. Add the garlic powder, salt, pepper, and remaining olive oil, as needed, to prevent spices from clumping. Mix well to distribute spices evenly throughout. Serve, or refrigerate to allow flavors to marry.

PER SERVING Calories: 526 | Fat: 24 g | Protein: 22 g | Sodium: 1,178 mg | Fiber: 5 g | Carbohydrates: 55 g | Sugar: 5 g

Cheesy Spinach Shells

*Traditionally stuffed shells use heavy cheeses, loads of sodium, and few natural ingredients.
This variation keeps the beloved flavors and textures of stuffed shells, but
cleans them up and makes them more nutritious.*

INGREDIENTS | SERVES 2

2 cups spinach

2 cups cottage cheese, or vegan cottage cheese

¼ cup ground flaxseed

4 ounces goat cheese, or vegan soft cheese, crumbled

1 garlic clove, chopped

1 teaspoon garlic powder

1 teaspoon all-natural sea salt

1 teaspoon cracked black pepper

6 cooked 100% whole-wheat pasta shells

Sneak Spinach in Any Dish

Green smoothies aren't the only place spinach can hide. Chopped or left in whole leaves, spinach can be scattered throughout almost any dish for a boost of essential vitamins and minerals without an overpowering taste that throws off a dish's design. Beautifully colored and one of the most nutritious leafy varieties, spinach is the perfect ingredient to top your list but to hide from taste buds.

1. Preheat the oven to 350°F and prepare a 9" × 9" dish with olive oil spray.

2. In a large bowl, mix the spinach, cottage cheese, ground flaxseed, goat cheese, and chopped garlic until thoroughly combined. Add garlic powder, sea salt, and pepper.

3. Place the shells into the prepared dish, seam-side up, and stuff each shell full of the spinach and cottage cheese mixture.

4. Cover the dish, and bake for 30–35 minutes. Remove cover, and continue to bake for 10–15 minutes, or until shells are firm and stuffing is bubbly.

PER SERVING Calories: 662 | Fat: 27 g | Protein: 46 g | Sodium: 1,895 mg | Fiber: 8 g | Carbohydrates: 58 g | Sugar: 7 g

Great Greens Pasta Pot

Vibrant green vegetables that add crisp, unique tastes all their own sprinkle through this dish in a variety of sizes so that every forkful holds a surprise of tastes.

INGREDIENTS | SERVES 2

2 cups broccoli florets

2 cups green beans

2 cups sweet peas

½ cup water

¼ cup lemon juice

2 cups cooked 100% whole-wheat penne pasta

¼ cup goat cheese, or vegan soft cheese

1 teaspoon all-natural sea salt

1 teaspoon cracked black pepper

1. In a large skillet over medium heat, combine the broccoli, green beans, and sweet peas with enough water to completely cover the bottom of the skillet. Sauté together until water evaporates and broccoli and green beans are slightly softened but still crisp, about 5–6 minutes.

2. Douse the vegetables with ¼ cup of the lemon juice and sauté for 1 minute more.

3. Add the cooked pasta to the skillet and sauté with the vegetables until heated through. Add the goat cheese and cook for 1–2 minutes or until the goat cheese has softened.

4. Remove from heat, stir well to combine, and season with salt and pepper.

PER SERVING Calories: 485 | Fat: 8 g | Protein: 25 g | Sodium: 1,235 | Fiber: 15 g | Carbohydrates: 80 g | Sugar: 15 g

Cheesy Mushroom and Sweet Pea Pasta

Woody mushrooms make for the perfect contrast to distinctly sweet petite peas in this light and refreshing dish of hearty rotini, portobellos, and peas enveloped in a yogurt and goat cheese cream.

INGREDIENTS | SERVES 2

1 tablespoon extra-virgin olive oil

2 cups baby portobello mushrooms, chopped

1 teaspoon all-natural sea salt

1 teaspoon cracked black pepper

2 cups petite sweet peas

¼ cup freshly squeezed lemon juice

1 cup goat cheese, crumbled

2 cups 100% whole-wheat rotini pasta, cooked

1 cup nonfat Greek-style yogurt, or soy yogurt

1 teaspoon garlic powder

1. Prepare a large skillet over medium heat with the tablespoon of olive oil. Sauté the mushrooms with ½ teaspoon each of the sea salt and black pepper. Cook for 3–5 minutes, or until cooked through and reduced.

2. Add the sweet peas, lemon juice, and goat cheese to the skillet and heat through for 1 minute or until a smooth sauce develops.

3. Add the cooked rotini, warm the pasta for 1 minute, and remove from heat.

4. Stir in the yogurt to combine thoroughly. Season with remaining salt and pepper, and the garlic powder.

PER SERVING Calories: 774 | Fat: 32 g | Protein: 43 g | Sodium: 1,580 mg | Fiber: 11 g | Carbohydrates: 79 g | Sugar: 19 g

Pasta Suggestions

If you prefer one type of pasta over another, you can always make substitutions to alter a recipe to better suit your tastes. Replacing a thin spaghetti with a thicker linguine, rotini for small shells, or any other variations are up to the creative consumer. The only things to bear in mind are the sauce and ingredients that accompany your pasta, and how well they will blend with the type of pasta of your choosing.

Tomato-Basil Rigatoni

Simple and quick to create, this tomato-basil concoction is the perfect blend of sweet and savory flavors to toss with pasta.

INGREDIENTS | SERVES 2

2 cups cooked 100% whole-wheat rigatoni pasta

2 cups Tasty Tomato Sauce (see Chapter 5)

1 teaspoon garlic powder

¼ cup chopped basil

2 tablespoons Italian seasoning

½ cup fresh buffalo mozzarella, or vegan mozzarella, crumbled

1. In a large mixing bowl, combine the hot cooked pasta with the tomato sauce, garlic powder, chopped basil, and Italian seasoning.

2. Plate pasta, and sprinkle the mozzarella crumbles over top.

PER SERVING Calories: 367 | Fat: 8 g | Protein: 18 g | Sodium: 1,462 mg | Fiber: 6 g | Carbohydrates: 58 g | Sugar: 11.5 g

Linguine with Leeks, Artichokes, and Garlic

Light and refreshing, this blend of subtle ingredients comes together for an amazingly simple dish that loads up on heart- and brain-healthy fats.

INGREDIENTS | SERVES 2

2 cups leeks, chopped (about 3 large)

2 cups artichoke hearts, chopped

2 cloves garlic, minced

3 tablespoons extra-virgin olive oil

2 cups 100% whole-wheat linguine, cooked

2 teaspoons all-natural sea salt

1 teaspoon cracked black pepper

1. In a large skillet over medium heat, sauté the leeks, artichokes, and garlic in 1 tablespoon of the olive oil until slightly softened, about 4–5 minutes.

2. Add the linguine to the skillet and toss. Drizzle remaining olive oil over the linguine while combining to coat evenly.

3. Add salt and pepper.

PER SERVING Calories: 537 | Fat: 22 g | Protein: 15 g | Sodium: 2,300 mg | Fiber: 12 g | Carbohydrates: 72 g | Sugar: 5 g

Veggie-Stuffed Shells

Brimming with vegetarian beauty, these morsels of goodness provide the amazing flavors of vegetables combined with the rich creaminess of cottage cheese and goat cheese.

INGREDIENTS | SERVES 4

1 tablespoon extra-virgin olive oil

1 yellow onion, chopped

1 cup red pepper, chopped

1 cup broccoli, chopped

1 cup zucchini, chopped

1 garlic clove, chopped

1 cup spinach, chopped

2 cups cottage cheese, or vegan cottage cheese

¼ cup ground flaxseed

8 ounces goat cheese, or vegan soft cheese, crumbled

1 teaspoon garlic powder

1 teaspoon all-natural sea salt

1 teaspoon cracked black pepper

12 cooked 100% whole-wheat pasta shells

There's Flaxseed in This?

When it comes to nutritious ingredients, some aren't always tempting to eat by the spoonful. Flaxseeds can be a difficult ingredient to just add to a recipe as a topping or a garnish. One of the best ways to sneak in some essential flaxseed nutrients in your favorite foods is to add ground flax to your favorite recipes in the cooking process. Acting as a thickening agent, and adding a slight nutty flavor, the quantity of flaxseed additions just need careful attention to ensure that recipes remain as tasty and textured as intended.

1. Preheat the oven to 350°F and prepare a 9" × 9" dish with olive oil spray.

2. In a skillet over medium heat, heat the olive oil and sauté the onion, red pepper, broccoli, zucchini, and chopped garlic until slightly softened but still crisp, about 6–8 minutes. Remove from heat and allow to cool for 5 minutes.

3. In a large bowl, mix together the sautéed vegetables, spinach, cottage cheese, ground flaxseed, and goat cheese until thoroughly combined. Add garlic powder, sea salt, and pepper.

4. Place the shells into the prepared dish, seam-side up, and stuff each shell full of the sautéed vegetable mixture.

5. Cover the dish, and bake for 30–35 minutes. Remove cover, and continue to bake for 10–15 minutes, or until shells are firm and stuffing is bubbly.

PER SERVING Calories: 517 | Fat: 26 g | Protein: 31 g | Sodium: 1,203 mg | Fiber: 10 g | Carbohydrates: 45 g | Sugar: 8 g

Light and Creamy Green Linguine

Spinach linguine gets topped with a delightful combination of light tofu brightened with the intense citrus flavor of lemon juice and the subtlety of vibrant spinach. Everything gets tossed together in a rich yogurt sauce that's deliciously clean and perfectly healthy!

INGREDIENTS | SERVES 2

1 package (14-ounce) extra-firm tofu

½ cup lemon juice

1 cup spinach

2 cups gluten-free spinach linguine, cooked and rinsed

1 cup nonfat Greek-style yogurt, or soy yogurt

1 teaspoon all-natural sea salt

1 teaspoon cracked black pepper

1 teaspoon garlic powder

1. In a large skillet, sauté the tofu in 2 tablespoons of the lemon juice until slightly golden and crispy.

2. Add the spinach to the skillet and toss until wilted, about 1 minute. Remove from heat.

3. Toss the pasta with the tofu and spinach, add the remaining lemon juice and the yogurt, and toss to combine thoroughly.

4. Season with the salt, pepper, and garlic powder.

PER SERVING Calories: 329 | Fat: 2.5 g | Protein: 15 g | Sodium: 1,342 mg | Fiber: 2 g | Carbohydrates: 52 g | Sugar: 9 g

Gluten-Free Pasta Varieties

Gluten-free pastas are now widely available. In a variety of types like shells, rotini, spaghetti, and linguine, and even flavored with spinach, tomato, garlic, or basil by adding those specific ingredients to the pasta in the manufacturing process, gluten-free pastas are simple to create and make for a perfect gluten-free substitution that doesn't change the rest of your favorite recipes. So, you can enjoy gluten-free pasta for whichever dish you choose any night of the week, simply and easily.

Simple Spaghetti with Sautéed Tofu and Onions

Simple may be in the title because this dish is quick and easy, but there's nothing simple about the taste!

INGREDIENTS | SERVES 2

1 Vidalia onion, sliced

3 tablespoons extra-virgin olive oil

1 (11-ounce) package extra-firm tofu

2 tablespoons balsamic vinegar

2 cups 100% whole-wheat spaghetti, cooked

1 teaspoon all-natural sea salt

1 teaspoon cracked black pepper

1 teaspoon garlic powder

1. In a large skillet over medium heat, sauté the onions in 2 tablespoons olive oil until slightly softened, about 4–6 minutes.

2. Add the tofu and balsamic vinegar to the skillet and sauté until tofu is browned and slightly crisp, about 6–8 minutes.

3. Add the spaghetti to the skillet and toss to combine, drizzling with the remaining olive oil until coated. Remove from heat, and season with the salt, pepper, and garlic powder.

PER SERVING Calories: 478 | Fat: 23 g | Protein: 16 g | Sodium: 1,178 mg | Fiber: 4 g | Carbohydrates: 48 g | Sugar: 3 g

Sweet and Savory Pepper Penne

Sautéed peppers and onions develop their natural sweetness, gain the intensity of sautéed garlic, then get tossed with tangy balsamic vinegar and penne for a pasta dish that packs a ton of flavor.

INGREDIENTS | SERVES 2

1 yellow onion, sliced

2 cloves garlic, minced

1 yellow pepper, sliced

1 red pepper, sliced

1 orange pepper, sliced

3 tablespoons extra-virgin olive oil

1 tablespoon balsamic vinegar

2 cups 100% whole-wheat penne, cooked

1 teaspoon all-natural sea salt

1 teaspoon cracked black pepper

1. In a large skillet over medium heat, sauté the onion, garlic, and peppers in 1 tablespoon of the oil until slightly softened but still crisp, about 4–6 minutes.

2. Add the balsamic vinegar to the skillet and toss to coat peppers and onions.

3. Add the penne to the skillet, drizzling remaining olive oil over penne and vegetables until evenly coated. Season with salt and pepper.

PER SERVING Calories: 468 | Fat: 22 g | Protein: 10 g | Sodium: 1,158 mg | Fiber: 6 g | Carbohydrates: 58 g | Sugar: 8.5 g

"Meat" Sauce Stuffed Shells

Traditional meat sauce is loaded with fat, calories, and . . . meat. This vegetarian spin on meat sauce makes for a hearty dish loaded with flavor and great nutrition.

INGREDIENTS | SERVES 2

1 cup yellow onion, minced

2 cups vegan "meat" crumbles

1 tablespoon extra-virgin olive oil

2 cups Tasty Tomato Sauce (see Chapter 5)

2 cups cottage cheese, or vegan cottage cheese

¼ cup ground flaxseed

1 teaspoon all-natural sea salt

1 teaspoon cracked black pepper

1 teaspoon garlic powder

6 100% whole-wheat shells, cooked

1. Preheat the oven to 350°F and prepare a 9" × 9" glass pan with olive oil spray.

2. In a large skillet over medium heat, sauté the yellow onion and meat crumbles in the tablespoon of oil until onions are soft and crumbles are crispy, about 5–7 minutes.

3. Add 1 cup tomato sauce to the skillet and combine well. Remove from heat, add the cottage cheese and flaxseed, and mix well. Add salt, pepper, and garlic powder.

4. Place the shells in the prepared glass dish seam-side up, and pack with the prepared mixture. Pour remaining cup of tomato sauce over top and bake uncovered for 30–35 minutes.

PER SERVING Calories: 562 | Fat: 24 g | Protein: 39 g | Sodium: 1,278 mg | Fiber: 10 g | Carbohydrates: 51 g | Sugar: 9 g

Wild Mushroom Risotto

Savor the flavors of mushrooms in this beautiful dish that's elegant enough for company and easy enough for weeknight wonders!

INGREDIENTS | SERVES 2

1 tablespoon extra-virgin olive oil

1 yellow onion, minced

2 tablespoons minced garlic

1⅓ cups long-grain brown rice, uncooked

3¾ cups water

6 cups baby portobello mushrooms, quartered

1 teaspoon all-natural sea salt

1 teaspoon cracked black pepper

2 teaspoons Italian seasoning

Risotto's Bad Rap

Many people don't make their own risotto because it's rumored to be so difficult: too wet, too dry, too sticky, or not sticky enough. But just stir constantly, use fresh ingredients, and watch closely for all the water to be absorbed, and you'll create a delicious risotto every time.

1. Drizzle the olive oil in a saucepan over medium heat, and sauté the minced onion and garlic until softened, about 5 minutes.

2. Add the uncooked rice to the saucepan and turn to coat in the oil, garlic, and onions. Stir over heat for 2 minutes.

3. Add the water, mushrooms, and seasonings to the saucepan, and stir to combine.

4. Bring to a boil, reduce heat to low, and simmer uncovered for 20 minutes, stirring frequently.

5. Risotto is done when the rice has absorbed all of the liquid and is sticky but cooked through.

PER SERVING Calories: 612 | Fat: 11 g | Protein: 16 g | Sodium: 1,225 mg | Fiber: 9 g | Carbohydrates: 115 g | Sugar: 9 g

CHAPTER 12

Splendid Sides

Tomato Garbanzos
204

Twice-Baked Potatoes
205

Sweet and Spicy
Brussels Sprouts
206

Garlicky Garbanzos and Spinach
207

Veggie-Stuffed Potatoes
208

Sautéed Spinach, Mushrooms,
and Potatoes
209

Acorn Squash Cups
210

Stuffed Mushrooms
211

Perfect Polenta
212

Spicy Broccolini
213

Roasted Red Potatoes
and Onions
213

Mediterranean Couscous
214

Broccoli-Cauliflower Bake
214

Zucchini Boats
215

Scalloped Potatoes with
Leeks and Olives
216

Garlic Mashed Potatoes
217

Not-Fried "Fried" Rice
218

Quinoa with Mixed Vegetables
219

Potato Fries
220

Scalloped Tomatoes with
Goat Cheese
221

Ultimate Spinach and
Mushroom Risotto
222

Tomato Garbanzos

Tempting tomato sauce–slathered garbanzos become splendid with spinach and garlic in this side dish that's tasty enough to be doubled for a main dish at any meal.

INGREDIENTS | SERVES 2

2 cups cooked garbanzo beans

2 cups Tasty Tomato Sauce (see Chapter 5)

1 cup baby spinach, chopped

1 teaspoon all-natural sea salt

1 teaspoon cracked black pepper

1 teaspoon garlic powder

Get Your Garbanzos Going!

When you're out of ideas for delicious side dishes, look no further than the delightful, creamy garbanzo bean. Whipped up in delicious flavors that can vary as widely as olive oil, with light citrus essences to thick and hearty tomato sauces, these protein-packed clean complex carbohydrate morsels of goodness pack a fabulous flavor that will fill you up without weighing you down.

1. In a large skillet over medium heat, combine the cooked garbanzo beans and Tasty Tomato Sauce. Sauté together until heated through, about 4–5 minutes.

2. Add chopped spinach and toss to combine, sautéing until spinach is wilted, about 2–3 minutes.

3. Remove from heat and add salt, pepper, and garlic powder.

PER SERVING Calories: 331 | Fat: 4.5 g | Protein: 18 g | Sodium: 1,234 mg | Fiber: 16 g | Carbohydrates: 58 g | Sugar: 10 g

Twice-Baked Potatoes

This clean variation on a classic favorite uses fresh vegetables and thick yogurt for a delightful filling in crispy skins that pack flavor and nutrition into every serving.

INGREDIENTS | SERVES 4

2 large Idaho potatoes

1 cup low-fat Greek-style yogurt, or soy yogurt

1 cup spinach, chopped

½ cup scallions, chopped

½ cup olives, chopped

1 teaspoon garlic powder

1 teaspoon all-natural sea salt

1 cup crumbled goat cheese, or vegan soft cheese

Rid Yourself of Restaurant Regret

When you find yourself in a restaurant rut that leads you down an unhealthy road, look to the cleaner homemade versions of restaurant foods to keep you happy at home. From potato skins to stuffed mushrooms and spinach and artichoke dip, all of your favorite restaurant foods can be cleaned up and created, guilt-free, right at home . . . without restaurant regret!

1. Preheat the oven to 400°F and bake potatoes unwrapped for 30–35 minutes, or until fork tender. Remove from heat and allow to cool for about 1 hour.

2. Halve potatoes and scoop out insides, leaving a thick enough skin intact to hold filling and remain sturdy, about ⅛". Place scooped potatoes in a mixing bowl, and return oven halves to preheated 400°F oven for about 10–15 minutes.

3. While potato skins are cooking, combine the scooped potatoes, yogurt, chopped spinach, scallions, olives, garlic powder, and sea salt.

4. Remove skins from oven, fill all 4 potato halves with equal amounts of the yogurt and potato mixture, and top with equal amounts of the crumbled goat cheese.

5. Return potatoes to oven and cook until cheese is melted and lightly golden.

PER SERVING Calories: 361 | Fat: 14 g | Protein: 18 g | Sodium: 992 mg | Fiber: 3.5 g | Carbohydrates: 40 g | Sugar: 6 g

Sweet and Spicy Brussels Sprouts

Brussels sprouts get a bad rap, but you'll be yearning for more when you whip up this batch of Brussels whirled in sweet and spicy flavors.

INGREDIENTS | SERVES 2

2 cups Brussels sprouts

¾ cup chopped shallots, about 2 large

1 yellow apple, peeled and minced

¼ cup water

2 teaspoons organic maple syrup

½ teaspoon red pepper flakes

1 teaspoon all-natural sea salt

1 teaspoon cracked black pepper

1. In a large skillet over medium heat, combine the Brussels sprouts, shallots, and apple with the ¼ cup of water. Drizzle the maple syrup over the skillet and sprinkle with the red pepper flakes. Steam and sauté together until onions and apples are soft and Brussels sprouts are fork tender, about 8–10 minutes.

2. Remove from heat and toss with sea salt and pepper.

PER SERVING Calories: 138 | Fat: 0.5 g | Protein: 4.5 g | Sodium: 1,198 mg | Fiber: 4.5 g | Carbohydrates: 32 g | Sugar: 14 g

Eat Outside the Box Once a Week

When was the last time you ate Brussels sprouts? How about lima beans? Tempeh? Pinto beans? Whatever ingredient it is that makes you glance at a recipe and flip right past it, try it this week! Think of all the foods you thought you hated as a kid but absolutely love as an adult. Think outside the box, then go there once a week . . . and think of how many delicious foods you can try over the next 52 weeks!

Garlicky Garbanzos and Spinach

Gorgeous garbanzo beans are brightened up with aromatic garlic and vibrant spinach in this delightful side dish that can accompany any vegetarian meal or act as an entrée all on its own.

INGREDIENTS | SERVES 2

1 tablespoon extra-virgin olive oil

2 garlic cloves, minced

2 cups cooked garbanzos

2 cups baby spinach leaves

8 ounces crumbled goat cheese, or vegan soft cheese

1 teaspoon garlic powder

1 teaspoon all-natural sea salt

1 teaspoon cracked black pepper

1. In a large skillet heat the olive oil and minced garlic over medium heat until garlic is golden and fragrant, about 1 minute. Add the garbanzo beans and spinach, and sauté until beans are heated through and spinach is wilted, about 2–3 minutes.

2. Add the goat cheese and toss until melted.

3. Remove from heat and add garlic powder, salt, and pepper.

PER SERVING Calories: 644 | Fat: 34 g | Protein: 36 g | Sodium: 1,520 mg | Fiber: 13 g | Carbohydrates: 49 g | Sugar: 9 g

Garbanzo Greatness . . . Squared!

You can double, trip, and even square the nutritional greatness of garbanzos by pairing them with foods that add even more quality nutrition. To the complex carbohydrates and proteins found in the dense, creamy chickpea, you can add even more complex carbs, fiber, essential vitamins and minerals—and even antioxidants—just by adding some more vibrant vegetables like spinach, tomatoes, broccoli, or a variety of other nutrient-dense foods.

Veggie-Stuffed Potatoes

Vibrant vegetables color these stuffed potatoes with delightful hues that make them a beautiful side dish that screams delicious nutrition.

INGREDIENTS | SERVES 4

2 large Idaho potatoes
1 tablespoon extra-virgin olive oil
½ cup chopped zucchini
½ cup mushrooms, sliced
½ cup chopped red onion
½ red pepper, chopped
1 teaspoon garlic powder
1 teaspoon all-natural sea salt
1 cup spinach, chopped
1 cup crumbled goat cheese, or vegan soft cheese

1. Preheat the oven to 400°F and bake potatoes unwrapped for 30–35 minutes, or until fork tender. Remove from heat and allow to cool for about 1 hour.

2. Halve potatoes and scoop out insides, leaving a thick enough skin intact to hold filling and remain sturdy, about ⅛". Return oven halves to the 400°F oven for about 10–15 minutes to bake until golden brown.

3. While potato skins are cooking, heat the tablespoon of olive oil in a large skillet over medium heat and sauté together the zucchini, mushrooms, onion, and red pepper until all are slightly softened, about 5–7 minutes. Season with garlic powder and sea salt, and add spinach. Sauté until spinach is wilted, about 1 minute, and remove from heat.

4. Remove skins from oven, fill all 4 potato halves with equal amounts of the vegetable mixture, and top with equal amounts of the crumbled goat cheese.

5. Return potatoes to oven and cook until cheese is melted and lightly golden.

PER SERVING Calories: 344 | Fat: 15 g | Protein: 15 g | Sodium: 813 mg | Fiber: 3 g | Carbohydrates: 37 g | Sugar: 3 g

Sautéed Spinach, Mushrooms, and Potatoes

A simple sauté of deep green spinach, woodsy mushrooms, and hearty potatoes delivers a whopping load of vitamins, minerals, and complex carbohydrates along with a depth of taste that makes it a perfect pairing to any dish.

INGREDIENTS | SERVES 4

5 red potatoes, cut into ¼" chunks

1 cup water

1 tablespoon minced garlic

1 cup sliced portobello mushrooms

3 cups whole baby spinach leaves

2 teaspoons garlic powder

1 teaspoon cracked black pepper

1 teaspoon all-natural sea salt

1. In a large skillet over medium to medium-high heat, combine the potatoes, water, and minced garlic and bring to a simmer for about 7–10 minutes or until potatoes are fork tender.

2. Move the potatoes from the skillet to a mixing bowl or large dish, and return skillet to heat with olive oil spray.

3. Add the mushrooms to the skillet and sauté until softened, about 3–5 minutes. Add the spinach leaves and fold until soft, about 2–3 minutes.

4. Combine the mushrooms and spinach with the potatoes, mix in seasonings, and blend well.

PER SERVING Calories: 203 | Fat: 0.5 g | Protein: 6 g | Sodium: 628 mg | Fiber: 7.5 g | Carbohydrates: 45.5 g | Sugar: 4 g

Acorn Squash Cups

This beautiful self-contained side of squash is the tastiest way to enjoy the wonderful winter variety. Sprinkled with cinnamon and sweetness, this makes the perfect sidekick to any savory main dish.

INGREDIENTS | SERVES 2

1 large acorn squash
1 tablespoon extra-virgin olive oil
1 tablespoon agave nectar
1 teaspoon cinnamon
1 teaspoon all-natural sea salt

1. Preheat the oven to 375°F. Cut the squash in half, and remove seeds and pulp.

2. Place the squash in a roasting pan with the hollowed insides facing up.

3. Coat the cut top edges and insides of the squash halves with the olive oil, drizzle the insides with the agave nectar, and sprinkle the cinnamon and salt on the top edges and insides of both.

4. Bake for 30–45 minutes, or until the insides of the squash are fork tender.

PER SERVING Calories: 180 | Fat: 7 g | Protein: 2 g | Sodium: 1,102 mg | Fiber: 4 g | Carbohydrates: 32 g | Sugar: 8 g

Stuffed Mushrooms

Beautiful button mushrooms get all jazzed up with crunchy zucchini and red pepper bits and creamy goat cheese on top. Tasty, tempting, and packed with natural ingredients, this guilt-free side dish pairs perfectly with any pasta entrée.

INGREDIENTS | SERVES 6

12 large white mushrooms

½ small zucchini

½ red pepper

1 teaspoon garlic powder

1 tablespoon water

¼ cup crumbled goat cheese, or vegan soft cheese

What Makes Goat Cheese Superior?

If you're wondering why goat cheese is "clean," while pasteurized, processed cheese isn't, it is because of the drastically different makeup of the cheeses. Cheese made from goats' milk is far superior to that of traditional dairy cheese made from cows' milk because there is no need to homogenize goats' milk. Goats' milk is naturally homogenized, while cows' milk must be homogenized in the manufacturing process. Without mechanical homogenization, valuable nutrition remains intact and the resulting product has shown to be far less allergenic and far less irritating to the human digestive system. In fact, even some lactose-intolerant people are able to consume it without problems.

1. Clean the mushrooms with a dry paper towel; remove and reserve stems.

2. Mince the zucchini, red pepper. Mince the mushroom stems separately.

3. Prepare a skillet with olive oil spray and place it over medium heat. Add the zucchini and red pepper. Sauté for about 2–3 minutes, and add mushroom stems and garlic powder and continue to sauté until all vegetables are tender, about 4–5 minutes. Add water to skillet, as needed, to prevent sticking and promote steaming.

4. Remove sautéed vegetables from heat and stuff mushroom caps full with the mixture.

5. Preheat oven to 375°F and use a small grate to place the mushrooms on in the oven.

6. Place the crumbled goat cheese in the tops, and bake for 20 minutes.

PER SERVING Calories: 56.5 | Fat: 3.5 g | Protein: 4 g | Sodium: 36 mg | Fiber: 1 g | Carbohydrates: 3 g | Sugar: 1.5 g

Perfect Polenta

When you're looking for the perfect side dish that adds color and flavor, but isn't too sweet, salty, or savory to overpower the main course, polenta is your clean answer.

INGREDIENTS | SERVES 12

8½ cups water

2 tablespoons extra-virgin olive oil

1 tablespoon all-natural sea salt

2 cups cornmeal

Polenta: The Perfect Answer to Snack and Mealtime Woes

Polenta is a low-fat, low-calorie dish that is delicious and versatile, but very few people enjoy it. When asked why they don't indulge in this tasty food that can be served in a million ways and at any meal-time, most people say they don't know how to make it. Yet it's absurdly easy to make! You can roll this delight into a log and freeze for easy cuttings of the perfect por-tions, or you can just store it in an airtight container in your refrigerator for simple sampling any time of day.

1. Bring the water and olive oil to a boil in a large pot over medium heat, and season with the sea salt. Pour the cornmeal into the pot, and whisk vigorously to prevent clumping.

2. The polenta will become thick. Keep stirring for 25–30 minutes, or until it becomes extremely thick.

3. Remove the polenta from the heat, and move to a cold, covered glass bowl.

4. Let stand for 10–15 minutes, covered, and serve, or wrap and refrigerate for later use.

PER SERVING Calories: 105 | Fat: 3 g | Protein: 2 g | Sodium: 596 mg | Fiber: 1 g | Carbohydrates: 18 g | Sugar: 0.5 g

Spicy Broccolini

This delicious dish of vibrant fiber-rich Broccolini, spiced up with robust red pepper flakes, makes for a simple side dish that tastes extraordinary in an unexpectedly spicy way.

INGREDIENTS | SERVES 2

1 tablespoon extra-virgin olive oil
1 tablespoon chopped garlic
1 pound Broccolini
1 teaspoon all-natural sea salt
1 teaspoon red pepper flakes

What Is Broccolini?

A part of the broccoli family (just a baby version of it), Broccolini is a delicious vegetable that many people eat raw. Find the gorgeous, long-stemmed variety in your grocer's fresh vegetable section and at many produce stands.

1. In a large skillet over medium heat, drizzle the tablespoon of olive oil and sauté the garlic for about 1 minute.

2. Add the Broccolini, sea salt, and red pepper flakes to the garlic and continue to sauté for 3–5 minutes.

3. Once the Broccolini is slightly softened but still crisp, remove from heat, plate, and serve.

PER SERVING Calories: 145 | Fat: 8 g | Protein: 7 g | Sodium: 1,254 mg | Fiber: 6 g | Carbohydrates: 17 g | Sugar: 4 g

Roasted Red Potatoes and Onions

Simple and fast, this recipe for roasted potatoes and onions only tastes like it took tons of time for intense prep and careful cooking.

INGREDIENTS | SERVES 4

8 red potatoes, cubed into 1" pieces
2 red onions, cut into 1" chunks
1 tablespoon extra-virgin olive oil
2 teaspoons garlic powder
1 teaspoon all-natural sea salt
1 teaspoon cracked black pepper
½ teaspoon turmeric

1. Preheat the oven to 400°F and spray a 9" × 13" baking dish with olive oil spray.

2. In a large resealable plastic bag, combine the potatoes and onions with the olive oil.

3. Sprinkle in the garlic powder, salt, pepper, and turmeric, and toss to coat.

4. Pour the potatoes and onion with the olive oil from the bag into the baking dish. Bake for 45 minutes or until potatoes are crispy on the outside and fork tender inside.

PER SERVING Calories: 353 | Fat: 4 g | Protein: 8 g | Sodium: 618.5 mg | Fiber: 11.5 g | Carbohydrates: 73.5 g | Sugar: 7 g

Mediterranean Couscous

The crunch of couscous and crisp vegetables and the creaminess of sharp goat cheese combine to take this dish to the next level.

INGREDIENTS | SERVES 4

¼ cup balsamic vinegar

1 cup roasted red pepper, chopped

1 cup steamed asparagus spears, chopped

1 cup black or green olives, chopped

3 cups couscous, cooked

1 cup crumbled goat cheese, or vegan soft cheese

1. In a large mixing bowl, combine the balsamic vinegar, chopped red pepper, asparagus, and olives, and toss to coat.

2. Add the couscous to the vegetables, and combine thoroughly until all couscous is coated with the balsamic vinegar.

3. Add the crumbled goat cheese and toss gently to distribute evenly throughout the couscous.

PER SERVING Calories: 408 | Fat: 19 g | Protein: 18 g | Sodium: 515 mg | Fiber: 9 g | Carbohydrates: 45 g | Sugar: 6 g

Broccoli-Cauliflower Bake

This delightful vegetable bake combines the delicious flavors and textures of broccoli and cauliflower with creamy goat cheese for a clean combination that pairs beautifully with any dish.

INGREDIENTS | SERVES 4

1 pound broccoli florets

1 pound cauliflower florets

2 tablespoons extra-virgin olive oil

1 cup crumbled goat cheese, or vegan soft cheese

1. Preheat the oven to 375°F and prepare a 9" × 13" casserole dish with olive oil spray.

2. In a large mixing bowl, combine the broccoli and cauliflower with the olive oil and goat cheese. Mix to coat.

3. Pour the mixture into the casserole dish, and bake for 30–45 minutes, or until the vegetables are tender and the cheese is melted.

PER SERVING Calories: 379 | Fat: 27.5 g | Protein: 22.5 g | Sodium: 264.5 mg | Fiber: 5 g | Carbohydrates: 14 g | Sugar: 5 g

Zucchini Boats

Just when you thought zucchini wasn't all that flavorful, along comes a side dish like this where zucchini takes center stage as the delicious main vegetable that packs quality nutrition into every vibrantly colored bite.

INGREDIENTS | SERVES 4

4 large zucchini
1 red pepper, minced
1 red onion, minced
1 cup mushrooms, minced
1 teaspoon garlic powder
1 teaspoon all-natural sea salt
1 teaspoon cracked black pepper
1 cup crumbled goat cheese, or vegan soft cheese

1. Preheat the oven to 400°F and prepare a small oven grate with olive oil spray.

2. Cut the zucchini in half lengthwise, and clean the seeds out of the center to make a large opening for the vegetables.

3. Prepare a large skillet with olive oil spray over medium heat.

4. Sauté the pepper, onion, and mushrooms with the garlic powder, salt, and pepper until vegetables are slightly softened.

5. Pack the sautéed vegetables into the centers of each zucchini, and top with the goat cheese.

6. Bake directly on the oven grate for 20 minutes, or until zucchini is tender and cheese is melted.

PER SERVING Calories: 311 | Fat: 21 g | Protein: 21 g | Sodium: 802 mg | Fiber: 3.5 g | Carbohydrates: 13 g | Sugar: 8 g

Scalloped Potatoes with Leeks and Olives

Traditional scalloped potatoes are loaded with heavy creams and sodium, making them anything but clean. This clean and delicious version utilizes the intense flavors of leeks and olives to max out the taste potential.

INGREDIENTS | SERVES 6

4 Idaho potatoes, sliced into ⅛" rounds

2 leeks, cut into ¼" pieces

1 cup sliced green olives

1 tablespoon extra-virgin olive oil

1 teaspoon garlic powder

1 teaspoon cracked black pepper

Satisfy Sodium Cravings with Savory Clean Components

Vegetables and spices that add a bite to meals can calm your cravings for salty foods. By getting creative with additions like olives, vinegars, and savory spices like cumin, cayenne, and many more can take a dish from mundane to daring, and satisfy that sodium need naturally and without the bloat.

1. Prepare a 9" × 13" baking dish with olive oil spray, and preheat the oven to 375°F.

2. In a large mixing bowl, combine the potato slices, leeks, and sliced olives with the olive oil, and pour into the baking dish.

3. Season with the garlic powder and pepper, and bake for 30–45 minutes.

PER SERVING Calories: 144 | Fat: 2.5 g | Protein: 3 g | Sodium: 210 mg | Fiber: 4 g | Carbohydrates: 28.5 g | Sugar: 3 g

Garlic Mashed Potatoes

Forget the fattening version of mashed potatoes and opt for this cleaned up potato plate instead. This recipe loads up on healthful ingredients to make for a great side that you can feel good about feeding to your family.

INGREDIENTS | SERVES 4

2 large Idaho potatoes, cut into ½" slices (leave skin on if you prefer)

2 tablespoons minced garlic

1 cup unsweetened almond milk

1 teaspoon all-natural sea salt

1 teaspoon cracked black pepper

Garlic Is Clean!

Traditional dishes that are normally prepared with butter, salt, and dangerous additives can, quickly and easily, be made healthier and more appealing by eliminating the poor ingredients and adding healthy ingredients that add tons of flavor naturally, instead . . . like garlic.

1. Place potatoes in a pot of water with the minced garlic.

2. Bring the potatoes to a boil over medium heat, and cook for 10–15 minutes, or until the potatoes are soft.

3. Remove the potatoes and garlic from the heat, drain, and pour into a large mixing bowl.

4. Add the almond milk gradually while mashing, and season with salt and pepper.

PER SERVING Calories: 101 | Fat: 0 g | Protein: 3 g | Sodium: 641 mg | Fiber: 2 g | Carbohydrates: 21 g | Sugar: 1 g

Not-Fried "Fried" Rice

Asian food just isn't the same if you don't have the traditional side of "fried" rice. But you can maintain your clean eating lifestyle and pack tons of flavor and tradition onto your plate with this "not fried" fried rice.

INGREDIENTS | SERVES 4

½ yellow onion, minced

2 eggs, beaten, or ½ cup vegan egg substitute

1 cup baby sweet peas

1 cup carrot, cut into matchsticks

2 cups cooked brown rice

1 tablespoon low-sodium soy sauce

Take-Out Takeover

Homemade "fried" rice is not only simple, but it's packed with natural vegetables and tons of flavor from each of the clean ingredients and spices. If you decide to get "real" fried rice from a restaurant, you can bet the rice is white and nutrition-depleted, the vegetables are anything but fresh, and the seasonings used most likely include large amounts of sodium and sugar.

1. Prepare a large skillet with olive oil spray over medium heat, and sauté the minced onion until slightly softened, for about 3–5 minutes.

2. Pour in the beaten eggs, and scramble until lightly fluffy, about 3–5 minutes. Break up the eggs into small pieces.

3. Add the peas and carrots and heat through, about 2 minutes, then remove skillet from heat.

4. Pour the rice in a large mixing bowl, and add the onions, eggs, carrots, and peas. Blend well.

5. Drizzle the soy sauce over the rice, and toss to coat completely.

PER SERVING Calories: 164 | Fat: 3.5 g | Protein: 6 g | Sodium: 280 mg | Fiber: 2.8 g | Carbohydrates: 27 g | Sugar: 2 g

Quinoa with Mixed Vegetables

Make quinoa that much tastier by adding fragrant flavors and vibrant vegetables to the mix! Packed with all-natural ingredients, this quinoa creation delivers taste, texture, and total nutrition.

INGREDIENTS | SERVES 2

1 cup dry organic quinoa

2 cups water

½ tablespoon garlic powder

½ tablespoon onion powder

½ red onion, chopped

1 cup broccoli florets

1 tablespoon extra-virgin olive oil

1 cup portobello mushrooms

1 teaspoon all-natural sea salt

1. Rinse the quinoa thoroughly and combine with the water in a medium saucepan over medium heat. Bring to a boil, reduce heat to low, add half of the garlic powder and half of the onion powder, and simmer for 15 minutes.

2. In a large sauté pan over medium heat, sauté the onion and broccoli in the olive oil for 7–10 minutes or until all are slightly softened.

3. Add the mushrooms and remaining half of the garlic and onion powders to the sauté pan and continue cooking until all vegetables are soft, about 5–7 minutes.

4. Remove the quinoa from the heat and transfer to a separate dish. Add the sautéed vegetables, and sprinkle with salt.

PER SERVING Calories: 408.5 | Fat: 12 g | Protein: 14.5 g | Sodium: 1,203 mg | Fiber: 8 g | Carbohydrates: 62 g | Sugar: 3 g

Potato Fries

Greasy fries get kicked to the curb when these clean, baked, better-for-you fries get served up next to your favorite sandwich fare.

INGREDIENTS | SERVES 4

6 Idaho potatoes, washed
1 tablespoon extra-virgin olive oil
1 teaspoon all-natural sea salt
1 teaspoon cracked black pepper
1 teaspoon paprika

1. Preheat the oven to 400°F and line a baking sheet with aluminum foil.

2. Cut the potatoes in half lengthwise, then in long strips about ¼"–½" in width.

3. In a large resealable plastic bag, toss the potatoes with the olive oil to coat.

4. In a small dish, combine the salt, pepper, and paprika.

5. Place the potato strips on the baking sheet and sprinkle with half of the seasonings. Bake for 15–20 minutes, or until crispy.

6. Turn the fries to bake the opposite sides, and sprinkle with remaining seasonings. Return to the oven and continue baking about 15 minutes, or until golden brown and crispy.

PER SERVING Calories: 285 | Fat: 4 g | Protein: 7 g | Sodium: 606 mg | Fiber: 4.5 g | Carbohydrates: 58.5 g | Sugar: 2 g

Scalloped Tomatoes with Goat Cheese

Bright red, juicy tomatoes get baked to gooey deliciousness and flavored to the extreme with basil, garlic, and goat cheese in this delicious side dish.

INGREDIENTS | SERVES 4

4 large tomatoes

¼ cup basil leaves, measured then chopped

1 tablespoon extra-virgin olive oil

1 cup crumbled goat cheese, or vegan soft cheese

1 teaspoon garlic powder

1 teaspoon all-natural sea salt

1 teaspoon cracked ground black pepper

1. Preheat the oven to 400°F, and prepare a 9" × 9" glass baking dish with olive oil spray.

2. Slice the tomatoes to ¼" thickness, and layer in the casserole dish.

3. Sprinkle the crumbled basil leaves over the tomatoes and drizzle with olive oil. Top the tomato and basil with the crumbled goat cheese, and season with the garlic powder, salt, and pepper.

4. Bake for 20 minutes, or until soft and slightly crisp.

PER SERVING Calories: 215 | Fat: 15 g | Protein: 12 g | Sodium: 801 mg | Fiber: 2.5 g | Carbohydrates: 8 g | Sugar: 5 g

Ultimate Spinach and Mushroom Risotto

Bright green spinach and beautiful baby portobellos add a visually appealing element to traditionally blank risotto for a side dish that tastes as great as it looks.

INGREDIENTS | SERVES 2

1 tablespoon extra-virgin olive oil

1 yellow onion, minced

2 tablespoons minced garlic

1⅓ cups long-grain brown rice, uncooked

3¾ cups water

6 cups baby portobello mushrooms, quartered

1 teaspoon all-natural sea salt

1 teaspoon cracked black pepper

2 teaspoons Italian seasoning

2 cups baby spinach, chopped

1. Drizzle the olive oil in a saucepan over medium heat, and sauté the minced onion and garlic until softened, about 5 minutes.

2. Add the uncooked rice to the saucepan and turn to coat in the oil, garlic, and onions. Stir over heat for 2 minutes.

3. Add the water, mushrooms, and seasonings to the saucepan, and stir to combine.

4. Bring to a boil, reduce heat to low, and simmer uncovered for 20 minutes, stirring frequently.

5. Risotto is done when the rice has absorbed all of the liquid and is sticky but cooked through. Fold in the chopped spinach, and stir over heat until the spinach is wilted and combined throughout, about 1–2 minutes.

PER SERVING Calories: 619 | Fat: 11.5 g | Protein: 17 g | Sodium: 1,235 mg | Fiber: 9.5 g | Carbohydrates: 116 g | Sugar: 9 g

CHAPTER 13

Delightful Desserts

Chia Pudding
224

Clean Chocolate Frosting
224

Chocolate Cake
225

Chocolate Chia Pudding
226

Blueberry Pie
226

Banana Pudding
227

Clean Vegan Pie Crust
228

Cherry Pie
229

Coconut Cream Pie
229

Maple Rice Pudding with Walnuts
230

Clean Carrot Cake
231

Clean Cranberry-Walnut Cookies
232

Carob-Walnut Cookies
232

Cocoa Café Brownies
234

Apple Crumble
235

Peach Tart
236

Tropical Paradise Pie
237

Bread Pudding with Maple-Cinnamon Walnuts
238

Bread Pudding with Fruits
239

Clean Whipped Cream
240

Chia Pudding

Omega-3-rich chia seeds get whipped up into a creamy pudding that has a delicious creamy texture similar to tapioca pudding. For a super-smooth consistency, try putting the concoction in the blender or food processor and emulsifying until no bits remain.

INGREDIENTS | SERVES 4

⅔ cup chia seeds
2 cups sweetened vanilla almond milk
½ teaspoon vanilla extract
3 teaspoons maple syrup

1. In a large glass bowl, combine the chia seeds, almond milk, and vanilla extract, and mix well.

2. Add maple syrup to taste, 1 teaspoon at a time.

3. Refrigerate 8 hours, or overnight, until set.

PER SERVING Calories: 151 | Fat: 10 g | Protein: 6 g | Sodium: 202 mg | Fiber: 7 g | Carbohydrates: 11 g | Sugar: 3 g

Clean Chocolate Frosting

To top the clean vegan chocolate cake, or to fill it up with even more clean chocolaty goodness, whip up this frosting for the perfect pairing that takes the chocolate cake experience to the next level.

INGREDIENTS | SERVES 8

1 cup carob chips
6 ounces silken tofu (½ package)
2 tablespoons coconut oil
¼ cup agave nectar
½ cup powdered carob (as needed)
½ cup almond milk

1. In a large glass mixing bowl, melt the carob chips in the microwave.

2. Using a mixer, beat together the melted carob chips with the tofu, coconut oil, and agave nectar until a smooth consistency is achieved.

3. As needed, add the additional powdered carob to thicken the frosting.

4. As needed, add the almond milk to thin the frosting.

PER SERVING Calories: 185 | Fat: 11 g | Protein: 3 g | Sodium: 13 mg | Fiber: 2 g | Carbohydrates: 27 g | Sugar: 16 g

Chocolate Cake

This vegan chocolate cake is so good, you'll wonder why everyone doesn't forego the eggs and bleached flour for smooth tofu and sweet agave.

INGREDIENTS | SERVES 8

1¼ cups whole-wheat pastry flour

2 teaspoons baking powder

2 teaspoons baking soda

1 teaspoon all-natural sea salt

1 cup carob chips, melted

1 (14-ounce) package silken tofu

1 cup powdered carob

1 cup agave nectar

1 tablespoon vanilla extract

Clean Chocolate Frosting (see recipe in this chapter)

1. Preheat the oven to 350°F and prepare two 8" round cake pans with olive oil spray and a light coating of the whole-wheat flour.

2. In a large mixing bowl, combine the flour, baking powder, baking soda, and salt. Mix well and set aside.

3. In the bowl of a stand mixer or large glass dish, combine the melted carob chips, silken tofu, powdered carob, agave nectar, and vanilla extract. Beat together until smooth and well combined.

4. Add the dry ingredients to the wet, 1 cup at a time, and incorporate well. Pour the cake batter evenly into the 2 cake pans and bake for 25 minutes, or until a butter knife inserted in the center comes out clean.

5. Allow to cool for 1 hour, remove from cake pans, and frost between layers and around the entire outside.

PER SERVING Calories: 260 | Fat: 1.5 g | Protein: 5 g | Sodium: 1 mg | Fiber: 5.5 g | Carbohydrates: 63 g | Sugar: 42 g

Chocolate Chia Pudding

You'd never even know that there's no dairy, no eggs, and no thickening agents added to this delicious pudding. The all-natural ingredients make this pudding the best you've ever had!

INGREDIENTS | SERVES 4

¾ cup chia seeds

2 cups sweetened almond milk

½ cup powdered carob

2 teaspoons vanilla extract

2 tablespoons agave nectar

1. In a large glass bowl, combine the chia seeds, almond milk, powdered carob, and vanilla. Pour the mixture into a blender or food processor container, and blend until the pudding is emulsified and thick, and no bits remain.

2. Add the agave nectar, a teaspoon at a time, while blending until desired sweetness is achieved.

3. Refrigerate 8 hours or overnight, until set.

PER SERVING Calories: 182 | Fat: 9 g | Protein: 9 g | Sodium: 43 mg | Fiber: 7 g | Carbohydrates: 18 g | Sugar: 9 g

Blueberry Pie

Overflowing with fresh blueberries that explode with vibrant taste and texture, this blueberry pie is one that makes clean eating a delicious delight!

INGREDIENTS | SERVES 8

3 dates, pitted

⅔ cup coconut milk

3 cups blueberries, washed

1 prepared Clean Vegan Pie Crust (see recipe in this chapter)

1. In a blender, combine the dates and coconut milk, and blend until emulsified and thickened.

2. In a small pot over medium heat, bring the coconut milk and date mixture to a boil. Reduce heat, add blueberries, and simmer for 5 minutes.

3. Remove the blueberries from the heat, and allow to cool for 5–10 minutes.

4. Pour the blueberries into the prepared pie shell, refrigerate, and allow to set for 3–5 hours, or overnight.

PER SERVING Calories: 159 | Fat: 9 g | Protein: 2 g | Sodium: 76 mg | Fiber: 2 g | Carbohydrates: 19.5 g | Sugar: 7.5 g

Banana Pudding

Sweet, creamy bananas pack this pudding dish with flavor and beauty.

INGREDIENTS | SERVES 4

⅔ cup chia seeds

3 cups sweetened vanilla almond milk

1 banana, peeled

½ teaspoon vanilla extract

1 teaspoon ground nutmeg

3 teaspoons maple syrup

1 banana, sliced for garnish

Go Bananas!

Adding texture, taste, and tons of nutrition to your favorite dessert recipes, bananas are a great ingredient to consider when cleaning up old favorites. Because of their naturally subtle taste, but unique flavor, bananas are a delightful addition to smooth out, add creaminess, or add a depth of flavor to sweet treats. With the added bonus of fiber, potassium, and B vitamins, bananas are a delicious and nutritious fruit that makes it okay to "go bananas"!

1. In a blender or food processor, combine the chia seeds, almond milk, 1 banana, vanilla extract, and the nutmeg, and blend or process until completely combined and smooth.

2. Add maple syrup to taste, 1 teaspoon at a time.

3. Refrigerate 8 hours, or overnight, until set.

4. Garnish with banana slices.

PER SERVING Calories: 229 | Fat: 13 g | Protein: 7 g | Sodium: 303 mg | Fiber: 9 g | Carbohydrates: 26 g | Sugar: 10 g

Clean Vegan Pie Crust

If you're going to make pies, store-bought pie crusts are a no-no! Simple and fast, this clean pie crust recipe takes the cake (or pie!) compared to any "who knows what it's made of" purchased variety.

INGREDIENTS | MAKES 1 PIE CRUST

1 cup hazelnuts
1 cup quick cooking oats
¼ cup Turbinado or Rapadura sugar
¼ cup rice flour
½ teaspoon fine all-natural sea salt
2 tablespoons coconut oil
¼ cup vanilla almond milk

Homemade No-Bake Pie Crust

When was the last time you enjoyed a pie crust that had no butter, sugar, or other unhealthy oils or ingredients? In addition to these not-so-clean ingredients, store-bought pie crusts can come loaded with chemicals, preservatives, and flavorings that you may not recognize, let alone be able to pronounce. Instead of the freezer aisle's pie crust, make a healthy homemade crust, quickly and easily, from all-natural ingredients.

1. Prepare a pie dish with olive oil spray.

2. In a food processor or coffee grinder, grind the hazelnuts and oats until fine.

3. In a mixing bowl, combine all dry ingredients and mix well.

4. Add the coconut oil and 2 tablespoons of the almond milk and blend until mixture becomes wet enough to hold together. If mixture is too dry, add remaining almond milk, 1 tablespoon at a time, until desired consistency is achieved.

5. Spoon the mixture into the pie pan, and press to ¼" thickness.

PER SERVING (⅛ CRUST) Calories: 204 | Fat: 13 g | Protein: 4 g | Sodium: 160 mg | Fiber: 2.5 g | Carbohydrates: 19 g | Sugar: 7 g

Cherry Pie

This amazing American classic gets even sweeter in this clean recipe that creates the flaky crust and unique taste of cherries we all know and love with all-natural ingredients.

INGREDIENTS | SERVES 8

3 dates, pitted
⅔ cup coconut milk
1 tablespoon Sucanat
3 cups cherries, pitted
1 prepared Clean Vegan Pie Crust (see recipe in this chapter)

1. In a blender, combine the dates and coconut milk, and blend until emulsified and thickened.

2. In a small pot over medium heat, bring the coconut milk and date mixture to a boil. Reduce heat, add the Sucanat and cherries, and simmer for 5 minutes.

3. Remove the cherries from the heat, and allow to cool for 5–10 minutes.

4. Pour the cherries into the prepared pie shell, refrigerate, and allow to set for 3–5 hours, or overnight.

PER SERVING Calories: 170 | Fat: 9 g | Protein: 2 g | Sodium: 75 mg | Fiber: 2 g | Carbohydrates: 21 g | Sugar: 11 g

Coconut Cream Pie

This pie's mile-high simple combination of clean ingredients creates a coconut cream confection that's easy to make and a delight to eat!

INGREDIENTS | SERVES 8

4 cups prepared Clean Whipped Cream (see recipe in this chapter)
½ cup Sucanat
2 cups plus 4 tablespoons unsweetened coconut flakes
1 prepared Clean Vegan Pie Crust (see recipe in this chapter)

1. In a large bowl, mix the Clean Whipped Cream and the Sucanat until well blended. Fold in 2 cups of the coconut flakes.

2. Sprinkle 2 tablespoons of the coconut flakes over the bottom of the prepared pie crust. Pour the coconut and whipped cream mixture into the pie shell, smooth the top, and sprinkle the remaining coconut flakes on top.

3. Refrigerate and chill for at least 2–4 hours, but best overnight.

PER SERVING Calories: 564 | Fat: 49.5 g | Protein: 4.5 g | Sodium: 118 mg | Fiber: 2.5 g | Carbohydrates: 16 g | Sugar: 15.5 g

Maple Rice Pudding with Walnuts

This recipe creates a rice pudding that hits the spot when your sweet tooth wants something scrumptious and your body wants something healthy. Easy and clean, this is the perfect pudding dish cold or hot.

INGREDIENTS | SERVES 12

3 cups uncooked brown rice
7 cups vanilla almond milk
¼ cup Sucanat
1 teaspoon vanilla extract
2 teaspoons cinnamon, divided
2 teaspoons nutmeg, divided
1 cup crushed walnuts
½ cup pure organic maple syrup

1. Preheat the oven to 325°F and prepare a 9" × 13" casserole dish with olive oil spray.

2. In a large mixing bowl, combine the rice, almond milk, Sucanat, vanilla, 1 teaspoon of the cinnamon, and 1 teaspoon of the nutmeg. Mix well to combine. Fold in the walnuts until evenly distributed throughout.

3. Pour the mixture into the prepared baking dish, drizzle with the maple syrup, and sprinkle the remaining cinnamon and nutmeg evenly over the top.

4. Bake for 2 hours, stirring occasionally.

PER SERVING Calories: 227 | Fat: 8 g | Protein: 3 g | Sodium: 83 mg | Fiber: 1 g | Carbohydrates: 32 g | Sugar: 21 g

Clean Carrot Cake

All clean eaters who love carrot cake can, now, indulge in their favorite confection guilt-free. With real carrots and natural ingredients, this is a carrot cake recipe that makes a good thing even better!

INGREDIENTS | SERVES 10

2 cups 100% whole-wheat flour

2 teaspoons baking soda

2 teaspoons baking powder

2 teaspoons cinnamon

¼ teaspoon nutmeg

1 teaspoon all-natural sea salt

2 cups grated carrots

½ cup carrot purée

1 cup vanilla almond milk

½ cup Sucanat

1½ cups unsweetened applesauce

2 teaspoons pure vanilla extract

½ cup agave nectar

½ cup crushed walnuts

Color Your Confections with Quality Nutrition

Knowing that fruits and vegetables are vibrant because of their high phytonutrients like beta-carotene, chlorophyll, immense vitamins and minerals, and powerful antioxidants, why wouldn't you use them in your favorite sweet treats, too? You can use them to create healthy desserts that you can actually feel good about eating.

1. Preheat the oven to 350°F. Spray a loaf pan with olive oil spray and cover with a thin coating of wheat flour.

2. In a large mixing bowl, combine flour, baking soda, baking powder, cinnamon, nutmeg, and salt. Mix well.

3. In a small bowl, combine the grated carrots, carrot purée, almond milk, Sucanat, applesauce, vanilla, and agave nectar. Mix well.

4. Add the carrot combination to the dry ingredients, and blend well. Add walnuts and mix in thoroughly.

5. Pour the batter into the bread pan. Bake for 30–45 minutes, or until a knife inserted in the center comes out clean. Feel free to top with the delicious Clean Whipped Cream (see recipe in this chapter)!

PER SERVING Calories: 207.5 | Fat: 4.5 g | Protein: 5 g | Sodium: 626.5 mg | Fiber: 5 g | Carbohydrates: 40 g | Sugar: 19 g

Clean Cranberry-Walnut Cookies

Cookie cravings can be calmed with the real thing when you have a delightful batch of these scrumptious cranberry- and walnut-packed cookies.

INGREDIENTS | MAKES 24 COOKIES

½ cup canola oil

½ cup Sucanat

1 teaspoon pure vanilla extract

1 egg, or ¼ cup vegan egg substitute

¼ cup water

1 cup old-fashioned oatmeal

⅔ cup 100% whole-wheat flour

1 cup unsweetened dried cranberries

1 cup crushed walnuts

½ teaspoon baking soda

½ teaspoon baking powder

Dash of all-natural sea salt

1. Preheat the oven to 350°F and prepare a baking sheet with aluminum foil and olive oil spray.

2. In a large mixing bowl, whisk together the canola oil, Sucanat, vanilla extract, egg or egg substitute, and water until thoroughly blended.

3. Add the oats, flour, dried cranberries, walnuts, baking soda, baking powder, and salt. Mix well.

4. Spoon the batter onto the prepared baking sheet by rounded spoonfuls, and bake for 10–15 minutes, or until golden brown.

PER SERVING Calories: 133 | Fat: 8.5 g | Protein: 2 g | Sodium: 46.5 mg | Fiber: 1.5 g | Carbohydrates: 10 g | Sugar: 8 g

The Hidden Sugars in Dried Fruits

When you have a craving for dried fruits, make sure you reach for the unsweetened variety. While just ⅓ cup of dried cranberries and other dried fruits constitutes an entire fruit serving, the amount of sugar in each serving can be surprising *and* overwhelming to your blood sugar and body's systems. Sweetening dried cranberries with additional sugars intensifies the sweetness, but adds unnecessary sugar and carbohydrates to an otherwise perfectly healthy food. So, look at the nutrition facts and ingredients on your next dried fruit's package to be sure you're getting all you want without all that you don't.

Carob-Walnut Cookies

Clean carob chips replace the not-so-natural store-bought chocolate chips to create a healthier version of America's favorite cookie. Adding walnuts for extra crunch, and a few omega-6s, this clean cookie is even tastier . . . and healthier, too.

INGREDIENTS | MAKES 24 COOKIES

1 cup 100% whole-wheat flour

1 cup oat flour

1 teaspoon baking soda

1 teaspoon baking powder

¾ cup unsweetened applesauce

½ cup Sucanat

¾ cup all-natural, organic honey

2 teaspoons pure vanilla extract

1 cup unsweetened carob chips

1 cup crushed natural walnuts

Carob Chips: A Great Alternative to Chocolate

Many recipes that contain chocolate chips have higher sugar and caffeine content than you'd want for your clean lifestyle; a simple swap for carob chips can make for a more nutritious, guilt-free, recipe alternative. Carob chips provide the same smooth texture with a hint of chocolaty goodness without all of the unnecessary processing, added sugars, and caffeine. Chocolate to carob: one great switch for healthy deliciousness!

1. Preheat the oven to 350°F and prepare a baking sheet with aluminum foil and olive oil spray.

2. In a large mixing bowl, combine the flours, baking soda, and baking powder, and blend well.

3. Add the applesauce, Sucanat, honey, and vanilla to the dry ingredients, and mix to combine.

4. Fold in the carob chips and walnuts.

5. Drop the cookie mix onto the baking sheet in rounded heaping teaspoons.

6. Bake for 10–15 minutes, or until golden brown.

PER SERVING Calories: 140.5 | Fat: 4 g | Protein: 3 g | Sodium: 76 mg | Fiber: 1.5 g | Carbohydrates: 20 g | Sugar: 14.5 g

Cocoa Café Brownies

These brownies deliver amazing taste and quality nutrition for a treat that only tastes naughty!

INGREDIENTS | SERVES 9

4 squares of unsweetened dark baking chocolate, about ¾ cup

½ cup strong black coffee

½ cup unsweetened applesauce

1 tablespoon agave nectar

½ cup Sucanat

3 eggs, or ¾ cup egg substitute

1 teaspoon vanilla extract

⅓ cup cocoa powder

½ cup 100% whole-wheat flour

1 teaspoon baking powder

1. Preheat the oven to 350°F and prepare a 9" × 9" baking pan with olive oil spray.

2. Melt the chocolate squares and set aside.

3. In a mixing bowl, combine the coffee, applesauce, agave nectar, Sucanat, eggs or egg substitute, and vanilla. Mix well. Add the melted chocolate to the wet ingredient mixture, and mix well to combine thoroughly.

4. In a separate mixing bowl, combine the cocoa powder, flour, and baking powder. Mix well, add to the wet ingredients, and combine thoroughly.

5. Pour the batter into the prepared baking dish and bake for 30 minutes, or until a fork inserted in the center comes out clean.

PER SERVING Calories: 121.5 | Fat: 8 g | Protein: 5 g | Sodium: 27 mg | Fiber: 4 g | Carbohydrates: 13.5 g | Sugar: 3.5 g

Apple Crumble

With a flaky crust, sweet softened apples, and a to-die-for crumble topping that tastes almost too good to be clean, this apple crumble has all of the goodness of classic apple pie.

INGREDIENTS | SERVES 2

4 cups Granny Smith apples, cored, peeled, and thinly sliced

¼ cup Sucanat

1 tablespoon cinnamon

½ cup crushed almonds

½ cup All-Natural Granola (see Chapter 5)

2 tablespoons coconut oil

Apples and Cinnamon for Appetite Suppressants

If you're in need of a sweet treat, but don't want to succumb to the temptation of an entire pie or cake, a delicious combination of apples and cinnamon may be the perfect solution. Because of the naturally occurring complex carbohydrates and fiber of apples, you achieve a feeling of fullness with much less than other foods. The cinnamon also adds a certain flavor that signals the brain and body to feel satiated. Apples and cinnamon may be the greatest combination ever to satisfy and sustain!

1. Prepare a 9" × 13" baking dish with olive oil spray, and preheat the oven to 375°F.

2. In a large mixing bowl, combine the apple slices, Sucanat, and cinnamon, and toss to coat. Pour the apples evenly into the prepared baking dish.

3. Combine the almonds, granola, and coconut oil together in a mixing bowl, and mix well. Crumble over top of the apples.

4. Bake for 35–45 minutes, or until topping is golden brown.

PER SERVING Calories: 723 | Fat: 34 g | Protein: 10.5 g | Sodium: 124 mg | Fiber: 11 g | Carbohydrates: 76 g | Sugar: 61.5 g

Peach Tart

Packed into a flaky clean crust, and topped with light and luscious whipped cream, this peach tart is, in a word, perfect.

INGREDIENTS | SERVES 8

4 cups peaches, peeled and sliced

¼ cup Sucanat

1 tablespoon freshly squeezed lemon juice

1 prepared Clean Vegan Pie Crust (see recipe in this chapter)

2 cups prepared Clean Whipped Cream (see recipe in this chapter)

Keep Your Favorite Fruits on Hand . . . in Your Freezer

If you're making a fruit recipe, you don't *always* have to wait until the fruit you crave is in season. Because manufacturers have perfected the art of flash-freezing fruits at their peak to preserve the nutrients and vitamins that we seek in the fresh versions, you can feel good about the ones you purchase frozen and store at home for quick use in any fruity cuisine you create.

1. In a mixing bowl, combine the peaches, Sucanat, and lemon juice, and toss to coat.

2. Pour the peaches into the prepared pie shell, refrigerate, and allow to set for about 3–5 hours, or overnight.

3. Before serving, top tart with Clean Whipped Cream.

PER SERVING Calories: 313 | Fat: 23 g | Protein: 3 g | Sodium: 93 mg | Fiber: 2 g | Carbohydrates: 18 g | Sugar: 13.5 g

Tropical Paradise Pie

The sensational tastes of tropical island flavors collide in this perfect pie for a flavor explosion.

INGREDIENTS | SERVES 8

3 dates, pitted

⅔ cup coconut milk

1 tablespoon Sucanat

4 cups fresh crushed pineapple

½ cup cherries, pitted

1 prepared Clean Vegan Pie Crust (see recipe in this chapter)

1. In a blender, combine the dates and coconut milk, and blend until emulsified and thickened.

2. In a small pot over medium heat, bring the coconut milk and date mixture to a boil. Reduce heat, add the Sucanat, pineapple, and cherries, and simmer for 5 minutes.

3. Remove the pineapple and cherries mixture from the heat, and allow to cool for 5–10 minutes.

4. Pour the pineapple and cherries mixture into the prepared pie shell. Refrigerate, and allow to set for about 3–5 hours, or overnight.

PER SERVING Calories: 180 | Fat: 9 g | Protein: 2 g | Sodium: 76 mg | Fiber: 2 g | Carbohydrates: 24 g | Sugar: 13 g

Bread Pudding with Maple-Cinnamon Walnuts

Simple bread pudding's gooey goodness gets sweetened, spiced, and nutty with the amazing addition of simple ingredients that maximize flavor and nutrition.

INGREDIENTS | SERVES 10

1 loaf stale whole-grain, 100% whole-wheat bread (torn into cubes)

1½ cups vanilla almond milk

1 tablespoon cinnamon

1 tablespoon pure vanilla extract

½ cup pure maple syrup

¼ cup unsweetened applesauce

4 eggs, or 1 cup vegan egg substitute

2 egg whites, or ½ cup vegan egg white substitute

1 cup crushed natural walnuts

1 teaspoon nutmeg

Pure Maple Syrup?

The traditional pancake syrup you grew up dousing your pancakes with probably was not natural maple syrup. When you need that specific taste for a recipe, sometimes you just have to use the real maple syrup that's now available in your local grocery store. Look for all-natural, organic maple syrup—it's the only product actually retrieved from maple trees and left unprocessed. The sugar content in this maple syrup is what's naturally occurring, rather than the chemically altered sugars in manufactured versions.

1. Prepare a 9" × 13" baking dish with olive oil spray.

2. Place the bread cubes in the prepared baking dish.

3. In a mixing bowl, combine the almond milk, cinnamon, vanilla, maple syrup, applesauce, eggs, and egg whites, and beat together to blend well.

4. Pour the liquid mixture over the bread cubes and sprinkle walnuts throughout; cover, refrigerate, and let the bread absorb the liquid overnight. Remove from the refrigerator 1 hour before baking.

5. Preheat the oven to 350°F, sprinkle the nutmeg over top, and bake for 35–45 minutes or until the pudding is firm and lightly browned.

PER SERVING Calories: 424.5 | Fat: 11.5 g | Protein: 16 g | Sodium: 650 mg | Fiber: 3.5 g | Carbohydrates: 65 g | Sugar: 13 g

Bread Pudding with Fruits

Vibrant fruits, citrus juice, creamy milk, and aromatic spices pack this bread pudding with so many naturally wonderful flavors that this clean recipe takeover of a traditionally heavy classic is surprisingly light and luscious.

INGREDIENTS | SERVES 10

1 loaf stale whole-grain, 100% whole-wheat bread (torn into cubes)

2 cups strawberries, tops removed and halved

2 cups blueberries, washed

2 cups mangoes, cubed

2 cups vanilla almond milk

4 tablespoons freshly squeezed orange juice

1 tablespoon pure vanilla extract

¼ cup unsweetened applesauce

4 eggs, or 1 cup vegan egg substitute

2 egg whites, or ½ cup vegan egg white substitute

1 teaspoon cinnamon

1 teaspoon nutmeg

1. Prepare a 9" × 13" baking dish with olive oil spray.

2. In a large mixing bowl, combine the bread and fruit, mix well, and place in the prepared baking dish.

3. In a mixing bowl, combine the almond milk, orange juice, vanilla, applesauce, eggs, and egg whites, and beat together to blend well.

4. Pour the liquid mixture over the bread and fruit and sprinkle with the cinnamon and nutmeg. Cover, refrigerate, and let the bread absorb the liquid overnight. Remove from the refrigerator 1 hour before baking.

5. Preheat the oven to 350°F, and bake for 35–45 minutes or until the pudding is firm and lightly browned.

PER SERVING Calories: 355 | Fat: 4 g | Protein: 14.5 g | Sodium: 660 mg | Fiber: 4.5 g | Carbohydrates: 65 g | Sugar: 13 g

Sugar, by Any Other Name, Is Still Sugar

High-fructose corn syrup, refined sugar, sugar substitute, and the list goes on and on, are all aliases for sugar, and they are all still sugar! Given scientific-sounding names or names that don't even relate to sugar or sweetness, sugar and sugar substitutes can be in almost anything you can purchase at a grocery store. Even products as simple as applesauce can be sugar traps, so it is of the utmost importance that you pay attention to the amount of sugar present, if any, in the clean products you buy. You can always sweeten your concoctions with honey, agave nectar, maple syrup, coconut sugar, and other natural sweeteners.

Clean Whipped Cream

Ditching the chemical-packed can and indulging in this healthy Clean Whipped Cream means you can have your dessert and actually eat it, too.

INGREDIENTS | MAKES 2 CUPS

2 (15-ounce) cans coconut milk

1½ tablespoons agave nectar

1½ tablespoons vanilla extract

Say "No!" to Deprivation

Clean eating is all about living healthier, not about deprivation. By using healthy, natural ingredients to create more nutritious versions of your favorite foods, you can indulge (in moderation) while still being health-focused. So, if you're faced with a craving that can't be calmed with fruit sweetness or vegetable crunch, shoot for the moon and try to clean up your favorite comfort food to have that same taste you love while being beneficial, too.

1. In a stainless steel mixing bowl, combine the coconut milk, agave nectar, and vanilla.

2. Using a high-speed handheld blender, whip the ingredients until thickened.

3. Refrigerate overnight.

PER SERVING (¼ CUP) Calories: 219 | Fat: 22.5 g | Protein: 2 g | Sodium: 14 mg | Fiber: 0.00 g | Carbohydrates: 6 g | Sugar: 3 g

CHAPTER 14

Radiant Raw Foods

Persimmon Pudding
242

Banana Strips
242

Peachy Parfait
243

Cinnamon Oatmeal
244

Clean Chia Porridge
245

Raw Granola Bars
246

Protein Squares
246

Seed and Grain Crackers
247

Apple-Flaxseed Loaf
247

Clean Curry Crackers
248

Raw Burritos
249

Raw Banana Bread
250

Pesto-Packed Kale Chips
251

Chunky Chocolate Chip Cookies
251

Pear Soup with Ginger and
Fennel
252

Simple Salsa
253

Tahini
253

Baba Gannouj
254

Mexican Pâté
255

Vanilla Almond Butter
255

Sprouted Burgers
256

Mint Chocolate Chip Ice Cream
256

Dairy-Free Almond Yogurt
257

Jicama Empanadas
258

Persimmon Pudding

Sweet, but rarely used, persimmons combine with delicious dates for a raw pudding that's fragrant and flavorful . . . with no need to dehydrate, sprout, or set.

INGREDIENTS | SERVES 2

2 fully ripe persimmons
¼ cup dates, pitted
½ cup sliced avocado
½ tablespoon raw carob powder
½ teaspoon mint extract, or 1 drop of peppermint essential oil

Persimmon Selection

Because persimmons have a chalky and bitter taste prior to becoming ripe, make sure you select ripe persimmons for your favorite persimmon presentations. You can ensure the fruit is ripe by testing for a soft outer shell and a jelly-like texture for the inner flesh.

1. Slice the persimmons in half and scoop out the soft fruit with a spoon.

2. Process all ingredients in a food processor with the S blade, or in a high-powered blender, until smooth. Serve immediately or refrigerate up to 3 days.

PER SERVING Calories: 126 | Fat: 3 g | Protein: 1 g | Sodium: 3 mg | Fiber: 3 g | Carbohydrates: 28 g | Sugar: 14 g

Banana Strips

The dehydrator makes this sweet treat a simple set-it-and-forget-it process that can be made in batches, stored for a week in plastic wrap, and be on hand for a variety of uses that all taste amazing!

INGREDIENTS | SERVES 6

4 cups sliced banana
1 tablespoon agave nectar
½ teaspoon vanilla extract

Fill 'er Up!

Banana strips make for great rollups that can taste sweet or savory, depending upon the ingredients you choose to fill them. Vibrant fruits and vegetables can be used to create simple, sweet, fruit-packed crepes or savory vegetable-stuffed soft tortilla rolls, and all can be made quickly and easily with strips that are made ahead of time and stored in tight plastic wrap for up to 7 days.

1. Place all the ingredients in a blender and purée until smooth.

2. Spread the mixture onto dehydrator trays with nonstick sheets. Dehydrate at 145°F for 2 hours. Turn down the temperature to 115°F and dehydrate for 8–12 hours.

3. Allow the leathers to cool, about 10–15 minutes. Peel them off the dehydrator tray, cut them into squares, and roll them tightly into a cylindrical shape. If you will be storing the leathers, wrap them tightly in plastic wrap.

PER SERVING Calories: 100 | Fat: 0 g | Protein: 1 g | Sodium: 1 mg | Fiber: 3 g | Carbohydrates: 25 g | Sugar: 15 g

Peachy Parfait

Delightful and light, this parfait uses vibrant fruits and homemade granola bars for an amazingly refreshing parfait that's packed with vitamins, minerals, and amazing antioxidants!

INGREDIENTS | SERVES 2

1 cup peaches, peeled and chopped

½ cup strawberries, sliced

2 tablespoons lemon juice

2 cups blueberries

1 cup young coconut meat

2 teaspoons cinnamon

1 teaspoon vanilla

1 cup Raw Granola Bars recipe (see recipe in this chapter), or small chunks of pecans or walnuts

¼ cup dried coconut flakes

Parfaits: The Perfect Canvas for Creativity

Your parfait can be made exactly how you want it, whenever you want it, simply by using your creativity. Jazz it up with fruits, nuts, grains, and seeds. Use a homemade yogurt as a base that can be infused with vanilla, almond, lemons, or a variety of other flavors. The fruits that color your parfaits can have as many possible combinations of color, flavor, and texture as your imagination can conceive. So morning, noon, or night, put your creativity to good use, and whip up an out-of-this-world parfait that's a stretch of *your* imagination!

1. Sprinkle the peach and strawberry slices with lemon juice and set aside.

2. Place 1½ cups blueberries and the coconut meat in a blender, and blend to create a cream. Add the cinnamon and vanilla. Blend until smooth.

3. In 2 tall, clear glasses, pour a thin layer of the blueberry cream. Top with a thin layer of granola.

4. Place a layer of peaches and strawberries onto the granola.

5. Pour a second layer of cream onto the fruit. Top with another layer of granola, a few more pieces of fruit, and then a thin drizzle of cream on the very top.

6. Garnish with remaining blueberries and coconut flakes.

PER SERVING Calories: 624 | Fat: 33 g | Protein: 11 g | Sodium: 12 mg | Fiber: 18 g | Carbohydrates: 72 g | Sugar: 34 g

Cinnamon Oatmeal

Raw oatmeal can be enjoyed without any need for heat! Soaking the oats and the berries allows the two main ingredients to develop amazing flavors and textures you're sure to enjoy any morning!

INGREDIENTS | SERVES 2

1½ cups dried oat groats, sprouted
¼ cup goji berries
2 cups Brazil nut milk
¼ cup fresh or dried blueberries
½ cup banana, sliced into rounds
1 tablespoon cinnamon
2 teaspoons maple syrup (optional)

Oat Groats for All

Packed with even more fiber and nutrition than traditional rolled oats, oat groats are a great complex carbohydrate to fill you up with heartiness and quality macro- and micronutrients any time of the day. Requiring a simple soak for raw vegetarians or traditional cooking methods for nonraw vegetarians, oat groats can be enjoyed in a variety of recipes with a variety of ingredients . . . with a small enough amount of gluten that those with gluten-intolerance and celiac disease have reported being able to eat them with no adverse reactions!

1. Soak the oat groats for 24 hours in a bowl of water. (Drain and rinse the oats after the first 12 hours and continue soaking another 12 hours in fresh water.)

2. Drain and rinse the oat groats again after soaking and allow them to dry in a colander for 30 minutes.

3. Soak the goji berries in water for 20 minutes.

4. Pour the oat groats into 2 cereal bowls. Add 1 cup Brazil nut milk to each bowl of oats. Garnish with the berries, bananas, cinnamon, and maple syrup (optional).

PER SERVING Calories: 806 | Fat: 30 g | Protein: 30 g | Sodium: 32 mg | Fiber: 17 g | Carbohydrates: 63 g | Sugar: 13 g

Clean Chia Porridge

Chia seeds' impressive versatility strikes again in this delightful recipe for porridge. With sprouted buckwheat and delicious fruits, this power-packed meal is a raw vegetarian's clean dream of porridge perfection.

INGREDIENTS | SERVES 2

½ cup buckwheat, sprouted

¼ cup chia seeds, soaked

2 cups sliced banana

¼ cup prunes, pitted

1 teaspoon cinnamon

1. Soak the buckwheat in water at room temperature for 6–8 hours. Soak the chia seeds in a separate bowl in ¾ cup water in the refrigerator for 6–8 hours. Stir the chia seeds a few times for the first 10 minutes.

2. Rinse and drain the buckwheat a few times, until the water is clear.

3. In a food processor or blender, blend the buckwheat until smooth. Add just enough water, a tablespoon at a time, to help it blend.

4. Add the banana, prunes, and cinnamon to the buckwheat and continue blending until smooth.

5. Stir in the chia seeds. Pour the porridge into serving bowls and serve.

PER SERVING Calories: 403 | Fat: 6 g | Protein: 10 g | Sodium: 10 mg | Fiber: 16 g | Carbohydrates: 52 g | Sugar: 26 g

Raw Granola Bars

Move over, store-bought granola bars! Even the raw varieties available for purchase can't come close to the taste, texture, or unique combination of delicious ingredients in these homemade bars!

INGREDIENTS | SERVES 8

1½ cups dry buckwheat (groats)

1 cup almonds, soaked (soaked for 24 hours is best)

½ cup dates or raisins, soaked for 1 hour

1 cup flaxseed, soaked (soaked for 12–24 hours is best)

½ cup young coconut meat

3 tablespoons raw honey or agave nectar

1 tablespoon pumpkin pie spice

2 teaspoons cinnamon

1. Soak the raw buckwheat groats in 4 cups water for 30 minutes. Drain, rinse, and sprout for 24 hours.

2. Using the S blade in a food processor, process all ingredients until well mixed. Do not over process—mixture should still be chunky.

3. Form mixture into rectangle bar shapes and place on dehydrator trays with nonstick sheets. Dehydrate at 145°F for 2–3 hours. Flip the bars over and continue dehydrating at 110°F for another 12 hours or until dry.

PER SERVING Calories: 367 | Fat: 19 g | Protein: 12 g | Sodium: 8 mg | Fiber: 12 g | Carbohydrates: 29 g | Sugar: 14 g

Protein Squares

Packed with clean protein, these nutrition-packed healthy homemade squares tote tasty ingredients that add delicious texture-varied elements to every bite. You can make these squares in bulk, wrap them in plastic wrap, and refrigerate to enjoy for weeks!

INGREDIENTS | SERVES 4

2 cups sprouted buckwheat

1 cup dried coconut

1 cup pistachios

¼ cup dates, pitted and chopped

2 tablespoons honey

1 tablespoon spirulina

1 tablespoon carob

1. Soak the raw buckwheat groats in 4 cups water for 30 minutes. Drain, rinse, and sprout for 24 hours.

2. Using the S blade in a food processor, process all ingredients until well mixed. Do not over process—mixture should still be chunky.

3. Form mixture into rectangle bar shapes and place on dehydrator trays with nonstick sheets. Dehydrate at 145°F for 2–3 hours. Flip the bars over and continue dehydrating at 110°F for another 12 hours or until dry.

PER SERVING Calories: 367 | Fat: 19 g | Protein: 12 g | Sodium: 8 mg | Fiber: 12 g | Carbohydrates: 45 g | Sugar: 20 g

Seed and Grain Crackers

*The dehydrator is put to great use in this delicious recipe for raw crackers.
Packed with heart-healthy grains and delicious seeds, these crackers have a slight
sweetness that makes the depth of each bite that much better!*

INGREDIENTS | SERVES 6

1 cup buckwheat groats
1 cup sunflower seeds
½ cup flaxseed
4 tablespoons agave nectar
1 teaspoon salt
2 tablespoons lemon juice
½ jalapeño pepper

1. Soak the buckwheat groats for 30 minutes. Rinse and drain. Soak the sunflower seeds for 1 hour. Rinse and drain. Soak the flaxseeds for 30 minutes in ½ cup water. Do not drain.

2. Place all ingredients in a food processor with an S blade and process until well mixed and chunky.

3. Spread the cracker batter on dehydrator trays with nonstick sheets and score into squares. Dehydrate at 145°F for 2 hours. Turn down heat to 110°F and dehydrate for 12 hours or until crunchy.

PER SERVING Calories: 330 | Fat: 19 g | Protein: 11 g | Sodium: 394 mg | Fiber: 9 g | Carbohydrates: 25 g | Sugar: 12 g

Apple-Flaxseed Loaf

*With natural ingredients that add tons of complementary flavors like sweet apples and sour lemon juice,
you're sure to enjoy every last bite of this bread that can be used with a nut spread or a sprout sandwich!*

INGREDIENTS | SERVES 6

4 cups flaxseed
1 cup sunflower seeds
2 cups apple, chunked
½ cup dates, pitted
4 tablespoons extra-virgin olive oil
3 tablespoons lemon juice
2 tablespoons agave nectar

1. Grind 2 cups flaxseed into a powder with a coffee grinder. Soak the remaining 2 cups flaxseed for 2 hours in water, and drain.

2. In a food processor, blend together the flaxseed (both ground and whole) and all the remaining ingredients until mixed but still chunky. Spread mixture about ¼" thick onto dehydrator trays with nonstick sheets. Score the batter into squares with a spatula.

3. Dehydrate at 145°F for 2 hours. Flip the bread over and continue dehydrating at 110°F for 8–12 hours.

PER SERVING Calories: 898 | Fat: 68 g | Protein: 26 g | Sodium: 37 mg | Fiber: 35 g | Carbohydrates: 51 g | Sugar: 19 g

Clean Curry Crackers

The warmth of curry spices swirl through every delightful bite of these perfect pumpkin-seed-packed crackers that tote delicious flavor with all of the quality nutrition you desire.

INGREDIENTS | SERVES 8

1 cup flaxseed
2 cups green pumpkin seeds
1 cup sunflower seeds
2 garlic cloves
1 tablespoon curry powder
¼ cup onion
¼ cup dates, pitted and chopped
1 teaspoon salt
1 cup orange juice

1. Grind the flaxseeds into a powder using a coffee grinder.

2. In a food processor with an S blade, process together all ingredients into a smooth batter.

3. Spread the batter ¼" thick onto dehydrator trays with nonstick sheets. Score the batter with a spatula into square or triangle shapes.

4. Start dehydrating at 145°F. After 2 hours, turn the dehydrator down to 110°F.

5. After 4 hours, remove the nonstick sheet and flip the crackers. Continue dehydrating for an additional 8–12 hours.

PER SERVING Calories: 436 | Fat: 34 g | Protein: 16 g | Sodium: 306 mg | Fiber: 9 g | Carbohydrates: 19 g | Sugar: 7 g

Raw Burritos

*Homemade tortillas with Mexican Pâté and Simple Salsa as main ingredients load up
on taste and texture with raw, wholesome goodness!*

INGREDIENTS | SERVES 4

2 cups young coconut meat

¼ cup red bell pepper, chopped

1 tablespoon beet juice

¼ teaspoon salt

½ cup Mexican Pâté (see recipe in this chapter)

1 cup Simple Salsa (see recipe in this chapter)

½ cup iceberg lettuce, shredded

Natural Colors

The dehydrated coconut meat mixture makes a soft and pliable tortilla wrap. You can add different colors of juice to change the colors of the wraps. Spinach juice will make green wraps, golden beet juice or turmeric will give them a golden color, and carrot juice will make them orange.

1. Prepare the burrito wraps the day before or the morning of, blending together the young coconut meat, red bell pepper, beet juice, and ¼ teaspoon salt.

2. Spread the burrito wrap mixture onto dehydrator trays with nonstick sheets. Dehydrate at 115°F for 4 hours.

3. Cut the burrito wraps into round tortilla shell shapes and lay flat on a dish.

4. Place 2–4 tablespoons of the Mexican Pâté onto each wrap. Place a heaping spoonful of salsa onto each wrap. Top with iceberg lettuce.

5. Lightly moisten one edge of the wrap and roll up the burrito.

PER SERVING Calories: 67 | Fat: 3 g | Protein: 2 g | Sodium: 460 mg | Fiber: 2 g | Carbohydrates: 15 g | Sugar: 5 g

Raw Banana Bread

Banana bread can be enjoyed by all with this scrumptious sweet raw recipe that packs in quality nutrition and tons of great taste.

INGREDIENTS | SERVES 6

2 cups ripe bananas

3 cups almond flour

¼ teaspoon salt

2 tablespoons liquid coconut oil

1 teaspoon vanilla extract

1 teaspoon cinnamon

1 cup flaxseed

Fresh Fruits in "Baked" Dishes

When your favorite fresh fruits start to take a turn in your fruit bowl, you can savor their flavors in raw "baked" goods by creating delicious breads. Apples, bananas, berries, and vegetables, too, can all be recycled into flavorful breads that maximize the flavorful fruits you love in breads. They can be frozen and enjoyed for far longer than the fresh fruit bowl.

1. In a food processor with an S blade, blend the bananas. Pour in the almond flour, salt, coconut oil, vanilla, and cinnamon, and continue processing until well mixed.

2. Grind the flaxseed into a coarse powder with a coffee grinder.

3. Pour the processed mixture into a large bowl and stir in the ground flaxseed.

4. Put half the batter back into the food processor and mix briefly. Then remove and repeat the process with the second half of the mixture.

5. Spread the batter about ¼" thick onto dehydrator trays with nonstick sheets. Use a spatula to score the batter into squares.

6. Dehydrate at 145°F. After 2–3 hours, flip the bread over. Turn heat down to 110°F and continue dehydrating for 8 hours.

PER SERVING Calories: 556 | Fat: 44 g | Protein: 18 g | Sodium: 126 mg | Fiber: 17 g | Carbohydrates: 29 g | Sugar: 8 g

Pesto-Packed Kale Chips

These crispy chips provide tons of natural nutrition like vitamins and essential minerals with the added benefit of being prepared in a raw process that retains it all!

INGREDIENTS | SERVES 4

6 cups kale
1 cup pine nuts
¼ cup nama shoyu
¼ cup lemon juice
¼ cup olive oil
1 tablespoon onion powder
1 clove garlic
½ teaspoon salt
¼ cup fresh chopped basil

1. Remove the stems from the kale and tear the leaves into big pieces. Place in a large bowl and set aside.

2. In a blender or food processor, blend all remaining ingredients, except the basil, until smooth. Add the basil last and briefly pulse until well mixed.

3. Mix the sauce with the kale. Use your hands to ensure the kale is well coated with the sauce.

4. Place the kale on dehydrator trays. Dehydrate at 115°F for 4 hours, until dry.

PER SERVING Calories: 417 | Fat: 37 g | Protein: 9 g | Sodium: 1,235 mg | Fiber: 4 g | Carbohydrates: 20 g | Sugar: 0 g

Chunky Chocolate Chip Cookies

You've got to enjoy the sweet side of life, and what better way than to whip up a batch of your favorite classic cookies. These top the charts in nutrition and taste, so dive in, guilt-free!

INGREDIENTS | SERVES 4

1 cup steel cut oats
¼ cup flaxseed
2 cups macadamia nuts
1 teaspoon vanilla extract
½ cup dried dates
½ cup liquid coconut oil
½ cup raw cacao nibs

1. Grind the oats and flaxseed into a powder using a coffee grinder.

2. Process the macadamia nuts in a food processor until they become a powder. Do not over process.

3. Mix in the oats, flaxseed, vanilla, dates, and liquid coconut oil and process until you achieve a creamy texture comparable to smooth peanut butter.

4. Stir in the cacao nibs by hand. Form into cookie shapes and dehydrate at 145°F for 2 hours.

PER SERVING Calories: 875 | Fat: 76 g | Protein: 11 g | Sodium: 23 mg | Fiber: 17 g | Carbohydrates: 60 g | Sugar: 32 g

Pear Soup with Ginger and Fennel

Sweet and spicy ginger and fennel add a depth of flavor to this no-need-to-heat bowl of natural pear goodness that will warm your heart and soul.

INGREDIENTS | SERVES 2

2 cups pear, cored and chopped

1 teaspoon ginger, juice or minced

1 cup fennel bulb, chopped

2 tablespoons lemon or lime juice

¼ teaspoon salt

1 clove garlic (optional)

1 teaspoon paprika

1 cup zucchini (optional garnish)

Fennel

Three parts of the fennel plant are used in gourmet cooking: the bulb, the leaves, and the seed. Fennel is a delicious vegetable that is often described as having a "licorice" taste. Rich in many phytonutrients, vitamins, and minerals including vitamin C, potassium, and folate, fennel is a beautiful, delicious, and nutritious addition to many delightful meals.

1. Place the pears into a blender or food processor and blend until smooth—the pear provides a liquid base for the soup. Add either 1 teaspoon minced ginger or ginger juice; blend until mixed.

2. Add all the remaining ingredients, except the paprika and zucchini, and blend until smooth. You may need to add a little water, one tablespoon at a time, to achieve a smooth texture.

3. If you'd like, you can garnish soup with cubes of chopped zucchini. Stir in the zucchini cubes and sprinkle the paprika on top.

PER SERVING Calories: 102 | Fat: 0 g | Protein: 1 g | Sodium: 315 mg | Fiber: 6 g | Carbohydrates: 28 g | Sugar: 15 g

Simple Salsa

With only four ingredients, this salsa couldn't get any simpler. Keeping the recipe's ingredients to a minimum means maxing out taste with powerful flavors from each unique one.

INGREDIENTS | SERVES 4

4 cups tomatoes, diced

½ cup white or red onion, diced

2 teaspoons salt

2 fresh jalapeño peppers, diced

Stir all the ingredients together in a bowl. Chill the salsa in the refrigerator for 1 hour to let the flavors marinate.

PER SERVING Calories: 43 | Fat: 0 g | Protein: 2 g | Sodium: 1,173 mg | Fiber: 3 g | Carbohydrates: 7 g | Sugar: 4 g

Tahini

The magical ingredient that most feel the need to find at a local grocery store can be made quickly and easily right at home with this vibrant raw recipe that takes the mystery out of the magic.

INGREDIENTS | SERVES 1

2 tablespoons sesame seeds

1 teaspoon sesame or olive oil

Pinch of salt (optional)

Pinch of cayenne, Italian seasoning, or raw chocolate (optional)

1. Grind the seeds to a powder in a coffee grinder or spice mill. Continue grinding until the seeds stick together and adhere to the walls of the grinder.

2. Remove from the grinder, add a small amount of oil (just enough to become smooth and creamy), stir with a fork, and add any desired seasoning.

PER SERVING Calories: 143 | Fat: 13 g | Protein: 3 g | Sodium: 2 mg | Fiber: 2 g | Carbohydrates: 4 g | Sugar: 0 g

Baba Gannouj

Fragrant, flavorful spices swirl through this delicious dish that takes eggplant to a new extreme! Bowls of beautiful baba gannouj goodness can be made quickly and easily, and enjoyed for days!

INGREDIENTS | SERVES 4

2 cups eggplant, sliced thinly

3 tablespoons lemon juice

2 tablespoons Tahini (see recipe in this chapter)

1 clove garlic, minced

1 teaspoon cumin

½ teaspoon black pepper

½ teaspoon salt

1 teaspoon paprika

1 teaspoon olive oil

2 tablespoons fresh chopped parsley

1. Place eggplant strips in a bowl or casserole dish and cover with 2 cups salt water. Add 1 teaspoon salt for every cup of water. Soften the eggplant by soaking it overnight in salt water, in the refrigerator, for 6–12 hours.

2. Drain the eggplant.

3. Place the eggplant, lemon juice, Tahini, garlic, cumin, black pepper, and salt in a food processor with an S blade, and process until smooth.

4. Pour mixture into serving bowls, sprinkle on paprika, and drizzle a little olive oil on top. Garnish with fresh parsley.

PER SERVING Calories: 59 | Fat: 4 g | Protein: 2 g | Sodium: 8 mg | Fiber: 2 g | Carbohydrates: 4 g | Sugar: 1 g

Mexican Pâté

With tacos or burritos, on crackers or kale chips, this pâté is a delicious side that packs a punch of interesting ingredients and knocks out nutrition deficiencies with protein, carbohydrates, vitamins, and minerals!

INGREDIENTS | SERVES 4

2 cups soaked sunflower seeds (12–24 hours is best)
1 cup corn, fresh cut off cob
¼ cup red or white onion, diced
2 tablespoons lime juice
½ teaspoon oregano
½ teaspoon cumin
½ teaspoon chili powder
¼ teaspoon salt
1 cup tomato, diced

1. Grind the sunflower seeds in a food processor until smooth. Add the remaining ingredients, except the tomatoes, and process until chunky.

2. Add the tomatoes and pulse briefly.

PER SERVING Calories: 320 | Fat: 25 g | Protein: 12 g | Sodium: 159 mg | Fiber: 6 g | Carbohydrates: 27 g | Sugar: 5 g

Vanilla Almond Butter

Store-bought almond butter can have questionable ingredients, but you can use this recipe to create luscious nut butters flavored with fragrant vanilla right in your home . . . with no questions about the purity or processing.

INGREDIENTS | SERVES 6

2 cups almonds, soaked
2 tablespoons olive, sesame, or flax oil
½ teaspoon salt
1 teaspoon vanilla extract

1. Homogenize the almonds in a masticating juicer. Alternatively, process the almonds in a food processor with an S blade until the almonds stick to the walls.

2. Gradually add in the oil, salt, and vanilla until creamy.

PER SERVING Calories: 296 | Fat: 26 g | Protein: 10 g | Sodium: 194 mg | Fiber: 6 g | Carbohydrates: 6 g | Sugar: 1 g

Almond Butter

It is difficult to create the same smooth consistency and texture of the almond butter sold in stores. The companies that make almond butter use heavy-duty machines to homogenize the nuts. However, a food processor or masticating juicer will create a creamy nut butter that comes close to the texture of the store-bought variety.

Sprouted Burgers

Beef burgers, turkey burgers, and veggie burgers can't compare to the raw goodness of these sprouted burgers that load up with all-natural ingredients for an impressive blast of taste and nutrients.

INGREDIENTS | SERVES 4–6

2 cups sunflower seeds, soaked (12–24 hours is best)

2 tablespoons flaxseed, ground

½ cup mixed sprouts (alfalfa, fenugreek, mung, lentil, green pea)

¼ cup chopped celery

¼ cup chopped red or white onion

4 tablespoons agave nectar

1 clove garlic, minced

1 tablespoon nama shoyu

1 tablespoon Italian seasoning

1. Using a food processor with an S blade, mix all ingredients together. Leave some texture and chunks in the mixture.

2. Form the mixture into 4–6 burger patties and dehydrate at 110°F for 4 hours. Flip burgers over and continue to dehydrate for 2–4 more hours.

PER SERVING Calories: 323 | Fat: 26 g | Protein: 11 g | Sodium: 160 mg | Fiber: 5 g | Carbohydrates: 34 g | Sugar: 19 g

Mint Chocolate Chip Ice Cream

Ice cream from the store can be packed with a surprising amount of preservatives and unnatural ingredients. Avoid all of the unknown by blessing your body with homemade ice cream goodness you can actually feel good about!

INGREDIENTS | SERVES 2

2 tablespoons liquid coconut oil

1 cup cashews

⅓ cup dates

1 tablespoon cacao nibs

2 tablespoons fresh chopped mint

1. Warm the coconut oil to a liquid by placing the container in a bowl of warm water for a few minutes.

2. Place all the ingredients in a blender and blend until smooth.

3. Pour mixture into ice cream trays or molds. Freeze for 3 hours or until mixture becomes solid.

PER SERVING Calories: 585 | Fat: 44 g | Protein: 13 g | Sodium: 14 mg | Fiber: 6 g | Carbohydrates: 35 g | Sugar: 21 g

Dairy-Free Almond Yogurt

No need to search store shelves for vegan or raw varieties of yogurt when you've got a delightful batch of this beautiful dairy-free yogurt at home!

INGREDIENTS | SERVES 2

2 cups raw almonds
2 cups water or young coconut water
½ teaspoon salt
1 tablespoon miso or 1 teaspoon probiotic powder

Skip Store-Bought Yogurts

When trying to adhere to a vegan or raw food diet, it can be challenging to find basic foods you love that don't include certain ingredients or involve certain processing. By creating delicious basics like milks, yogurts, and butters at home, you can save time, save money, and know that your ingredients and procedures follow the guidelines you put in place.

1. Soak the almonds in water for 12–24 hours. Drain the water and replace with fresh water after 6 hours.

2. Drain and rinse the almonds. Blend them with water or young coconut water, salt, and miso or the probiotic powder until creamy.

3. Place mixture into a yogurt maker, or use a glass jar and cover the opening with a cheesecloth. Fasten cheesecloth to the jar with a rubber band or string.

4. Let the mixture sit at room temperature for 6–8 hours, then serve.

PER SERVING Calories: 393 | Fat: 72 g | Protein: 33 g | Sodium: 1,152 mg | Fiber: 21 g | Carbohydrates: 20 g | Sugar: 3 g

Jicama Empanadas

Who'd have thought you could savor the flavors of amazing empanadas any time you'd like . . . and benefit from all of the nutrients that remain intact because they're natural and prepared raw!

INGREDIENTS | SERVES 2

½ jicama
4 tablespoons lime juice
4 tablespoons olive oil
1 teaspoon cumin
½ teaspoon salt
1 cup walnuts
2 tablespoons green pumpkin seeds
1 tablespoon onion powder
½ clove garlic, minced
½ teaspoon cinnamon
½ tablespoon jalapeño pepper, diced
1 tablespoon fresh minced oregano or
1 teaspoon dried

1. Prepare the empanada shell by slicing the jicama with a mandoline slicer or cheese grater. Cut the jicama into long, thin slices.

2. Prepare a dressing by stirring together the lime juice, olive oil, ½ teaspoon cumin, and salt. Brush each jicama slice to lightly coat them with the dressing.

3. Prepare the filling by blending together the walnuts, pumpkin seeds, onion powder, garlic, remaining ½ teaspoon cumin, cinnamon, jalapeño, and oregano.

4. Lay the jicama slices flat. Place a small scoop of the filling onto one half of each jicama slice. Fold over the jicama to create a pocket. Serve immediately, or dehydrate for 2 hours at 145°F and serve warm.

PER SERVING Calories: 541 | Fat: 51 g | Protein: 11 g | Sodium: 590 mg | Fiber: 8 g | Carbohydrates: 23 g | Sugar: 4 g

CHAPTER 15

Healthy Holidays

Hearty Mushroom and
Herb Stuffing
260

"Sausage" Soufflé
261

Sweet Potato Casserole with
Sweet Walnut Topping
262

Chunky Cranberry-Walnut
Stuffing
263

Mashed Potatoes and
Cauliflower
264

Mashed Sweet Potato Perfection
265

Creamy, Dreamy Asparagus
Casserole
266

Clean Green Bean Casserole
267

Pecan-Packed Pie
268

Protein-Packed Pumpkin Pie
269

Clean Green Beans Almondine
270

Sweet and Savory Corn Pudding
271

Clean Corn Bread
272

Merry Mushroom Gravy
273

Cleaned Up Cranberry Sauce
274

Scalloped Potatoes
275

Creamy Potato Hash with
"Sausage," Sage, and
Mushrooms
276

Hearty Mushroom and Herb Stuffing

Vibrant vegetables and tons of mouth-watering mushrooms pack this stuffing with savory flavors that make ordinary stuffing extraordinary stuffing!

INGREDIENTS | SERVES 8

2 tablespoons extra-virgin olive oil

1 (16-ounce) package sliced button mushrooms

1 cup chopped celery

1 cup chopped yellow or white onions

1 cup Simple Stock (see Chapter 7)

1 (16-ounce) package whole button mushrooms

2 teaspoons ground sage

2 teaspoons dried rosemary

2 teaspoons dried basil

2 teaspoons all-natural sea salt

2 teaspoons cracked black pepper

8 slices stale 100% whole-wheat bread, torn

Keep It Light to Keep It Clean

A tip to keep your at-home meals flowing: When you find yourself planning a meal, make sure you keep the meal preparation fun, stress-free, and creative. If you plan ahead, and plan smart, you can create delicious homemade fixings to go on your everyday dinner table (or even your family's holiday dinner table!) that are healthy, clean, and creative. Always remember, make whatever you can ahead of time to free up valuable time on the holiday itself.

1. In a large skillet over medium heat, combine ½ tablespoon of the olive oil with the sliced mushrooms and chopped celery and onions. Sauté for about 3–5 minutes, or until slightly softened.

2. Add ½ cup of the Simple Stock and simmer uncovered, reduce, and sauté until completely absorbed, about 5 minutes.

3. Add the whole mushrooms to the skillet, and season with 1 teaspoon each of the sage, rosemary, basil, sea salt, and pepper. Add ¼ cup stock and sauté until vegetables and herbs are cooked through, about 5–7 minutes.

4. In a large serving dish, toss the vegetable sauté (and all of the juices that remain) with the torn bread pieces.

5. Add the remaining stock, olive oil (if needed), and spices to the stuffing, and toss.

6. Serve hot.

PER SERVING Calories: 134 | Fat: 4.5 g | Protein: 6 g | Sodium: 718 mg | Fiber: 2.5 g | Carbohydrates: 19 g | Sugar: 4.5 g

"Sausage" Soufflé

The intense flavors of coriander and garlic pair up with vibrant vegetables and vegan sausage crumbles to create a light and fluffy egg-stravagant eating experience!

INGREDIENTS | SERVES 16

1 pound (4 cups) vegan sausage substitute, crumbled

2 tablespoons coriander seeds

2 teaspoons garlic powder

2 teaspoons onion powder

2 teaspoons all-natural sea salt

2 teaspoons cracked black pepper

1 tablespoon extra-virgin olive oil

1 cup onions, diced

1 cup mushrooms, diced

1 cup green pepper, diced

1 cup red pepper, diced

12 eggs, or 3 cups vegan egg substitute

2 cups unsweetened almond milk

1 cup crumbled goat cheese, or vegan soft cheese

Try the Potato-Packed Version for More Complex Carbohydrates!

If you're looking for a meal that provides tons of nutrition and healthy helpings of complex carbohydrates, recipes that can substitute potatoes or other combinations of hearty vegetables make for the perfect "option recipes" that give you the choice in the nutritional composition of the meal. It's simple to turn this soufflé into a vegetarian dish. Just replace the "sausage" and coriander with 4 cups of hash brown potatoes! Add them when you beat together the eggs (or egg substitute), milk, and goat cheese, and voilà!

1. Preheat the oven to 375°F and prepare a baking dish with olive oil spray.

2. In a large mixing bowl, combine the "sausage" crumbles, coriander seeds, and 1 teaspoon each of the garlic and onion powders, salt, and pepper. Combine well.

3. In a large skillet over medium heat, warm the olive oil and sauté the onions, mushrooms, and peppers until slightly softened, about 5–7 minutes Add the "sausage" mixture to the pan, and sauté until cooked through, about 5–7 minutes. Remove from heat, and allow to cool for 15 minutes.

4. In the large mixing bowl, beat together the eggs, almond milk, goat cheese, and remaining spices until well combined. Add the sautéed "sausage" and vegetables to the beaten eggs, and combine well.

5. Pour the mixture into the prepared baking dish and bake for 1 hour, or until golden brown and cooked through.

PER SERVING Calories: 248 | Fat: 16 g | Protein: 17 g | Sodium: 468 mg | Fiber: 2 g | Carbohydrates: 7.5 g | Sugar: 2.5 g

Sweet Potato Casserole with Sweet Walnut Topping

That's right, carrot cake isn't the only way to serve vegetables for dessert!
Topped with omega-rich walnuts and swirled with antioxidant-packed cinnamon,
this dish is one you can feel great about serving to your family.

INGREDIENTS | SERVES 10

3 large sweet potatoes, peeled and cubed

1½ cups vanilla almond milk

2 eggs, or ½ cup vegan egg substitute

1 teaspoon pure vanilla extract

1 teaspoon cinnamon

1 teaspoon ground cloves

½ cup Sucanat, divided

1 teaspoon ginger

2 cups crushed walnuts

½ cup coconut oil

1. In a large pot over medium heat, boil sweet potato cubes until soft.

2. Prepare a 9" × 13" baking dish with olive oil spray, and preheat the oven to 400°F.

3. Drain the sweet potatoes, and mash completely. Add the almond milk, eggs, vanilla, cinnamon, cloves, ¼ cup of the Sucanat, and ginger, and blend well.

4. Pour the sweet potato mixture into the prepared baking dish.

5. In a small bowl, combine the walnuts, remaining ¼ cup of Sucanat, and coconut oil, and blend well. Sprinkle the walnut mixture over the sweet potatoes, and bake for 35–45 minutes, or until the top is golden brown.

PER SERVING Calories: 348.5 | Fat: 27 g | Protein: 6 g | Sodium: 64.5 mg | Fiber: 3 g | Carbohydrates: 11.5 g | Sugar: 13.5 g

Chunky Cranberry-Walnut Stuffing

Chunks of fresh cranberries and crunchy walnuts combine in this spiced up savory stuffing that has just the right amount of sweetness for an unexpected extraordinary taste sensation.

INGREDIENTS | SERVES 4

8 slices of stale 100% whole-wheat bread, torn

2 tablespoons extra-virgin olive oil

2 teaspoons ground sage

2 teaspoons dried rosemary

2 teaspoons dried basil

2 teaspoons all-natural sea salt

2 teaspoons cracked black pepper

2 cups unsweetened dried cranberries

2 cups crushed natural walnuts

Getting Creative with Fresh Ingredients

Some people tend to stick to the traditional holiday staples when preparing a holiday feast, but there's no harm in thinking outside the box . . . literally! Adding fresh ingredients like cranberries and walnuts to your homemade stuffing can add a surprisingly pleasant and unexpected twist. With nontraditional seasonings—and taste and texture combinations you wouldn't normally use—you can end up with a delicious side that may become a requested staple for future occasions.

1. Preheat the oven to 400°F and line a baking sheet with olive oil spray.

2. In a large mixing bowl, combine the torn bread pieces with 1 tablespoon of olive oil, and 1 teaspoon each of the sage, rosemary, basil, sea salt, and pepper. Toss the bread to coat evenly.

3. Layer the bread pieces evenly on the prepared baking dish, and toast (tossing frequently) in the oven until slightly crunchy. Remove from heat, and pour into a large serving dish.

4. Add the remaining olive oil and spices to the stuffing, and toss to coat.

5. Fold in the dried cranberries and walnuts until well combined.

6. Serve warm.

PER SERVING Calories: 767 | Fat: 47.5 g | Protein: 13 g | Sodium: 1,523 mg | Fiber: 9 g | Carbohydrates: 84 g | Sugar: 43 g

Mashed Potatoes and Cauliflower

This recipe combines potatoes and cauliflower for the same great flavor and texture as traditional mashed potatoes, but with a wider variety of vitamins and nutrients from two vegetables instead of just one!

INGREDIENTS | SERVES 6

1 pound Idaho potatoes, peeled, washed, and cubed

1 pound cauliflower florets

2 teaspoons garlic powder

1 teaspoon onion powder

1 teaspoon all-natural sea salt

1 teaspoon cracked black pepper

2 cups unsweetened almond milk

1 tablespoon chopped scallions

Sneak In the Nutrition

While potatoes have loads of nutrition and tons of health benefits, there are healthy alternatives that offer different nutritional value. Adding cauliflower to your pot of boiling potatoes will result in a creamy bowl of mashed delight that's not far off from the original. The added bonus to the lower calorie load of the dish is a better variety of nutrients that come from combining a starchy root vegetable with a cruciferous, fiber-rich one.

1. In a large pot over medium heat, bring the potato cubes to a boil, reduce heat to low, and simmer for 10 minutes.

2. Add the cauliflower to the pot and simmer for an additional 10 minutes, or until the cauliflower is fork tender.

3. Remove the pot from the heat, drain, and move the potatoes and cauliflower to a large serving bowl. Season with the garlic powder, onion powder, salt, and pepper.

4. Mash or beat the potatoes and cauliflower, adding the almond milk, ¼ cup at a time, until desired texture is achieved.

5. Sprinkle the scallions over top, and serve hot.

PER SERVING Calories: 89 | Fat: 0.5 g | Protein: 3 g | Sodium: 481 mg | Fiber: 4 g | Carbohydrates: 17 g | Sugar: 2.5 g

Mashed Sweet Potato Perfection

Vibrant orange, sweet, and creamy, sweet potatoes need only TLC to taste amazing, but adding a couple all-natural, sweet-treat ingredients to heighten the sweet potato experience makes a holiday that much more memorable.

INGREDIENTS | SERVES 8

3 large sweet potatoes, peeled and cubed

2 tablespoons agave nectar

1 teaspoon cinnamon

1 teaspoon nutmeg

1 cup vanilla almond milk

Hooray for Leftovers!

After every holiday meal, it seems like there's more food in the fridge than there was on the table. Because most people love all of the holiday fixins—but don't want to have it for breakfast, lunch, and dinner the entire week following your favorite family gathering—sometimes you have to get creative with how to reuse food. Sandwiches, wraps, soups, and salads are all different ways to create healthy meals and snacks with the leftovers in your fridge.

1. In a large pot over medium heat, bring the sweet potatoes to a boil.

2. Reduce heat to low, and simmer until fork tender, about 30 minutes.

3. Remove the potatoes from the heat, drain, and return to the pot.

4. Add the agave nectar, cinnamon, and nutmeg to the sweet potatoes. Mash or beat until smooth, adding the almond milk, ¼ cup at a time, until desired consistency is reached.

5. Pour the sweet potatoes into a serving dish, and sprinkle lightly with cinnamon just in the center of the top.

6. Serve hot.

PER SERVING Calories: 71 | Fat: 0.5 g | Protein: 1 g | Sodium: 44.5 mg | Fiber: 2 g | Carbohydrates: 16.5 g | Sugar: 8 g

Creamy, Dreamy Asparagus Casserole

Bunches of beautiful asparagus spears get combined with sautéed onions,
creamy yogurt and almond milk, and delightfully subtle but tasty spices that all come together
to create a bright green dish of tasty nutrition fit for any holiday feast.

INGREDIENTS | SERVES 8

1 cup yellow onion, diced

1 tablespoon extra-virgin olive oil

1 cup unsweetened almond milk

1 cup plain nonfat Greek-style yogurt, or vegan yogurt

6 cups asparagus spears, cleaned

2 teaspoons all-natural sea salt

2 teaspoons white pepper

1 teaspoon garlic powder

1. In a skillet over medium heat, sauté the onions in the olive oil until soft and cooked through, about 5–7 minutes. Remove from heat and place in a mixing bowl.

2. Add the almond milk and yogurt to the onions, and stir to combine.

3. Add the asparagus, salt, pepper, and garlic powder to the cream, and combine well.

4. Preheat the oven to 400°F and prepare a 9" × 13" baking dish with olive oil spray.

5. Pour the asparagus mixture into the prepared casserole dish, and bake for 25–35 minutes, or until bubbly.

6. Remove the dish from the oven, and allow the casserole to cool for about 15 minutes before eating.

PER SERVING Calories: 69 | Fat: 2 g | Protein: 6 g | Sodium: 630 mg | Fiber: 3 g | Carbohydrates: 8 g | Sugar: 4 g

Clean Green Bean Casserole

While the traditional green bean casserole recipes use ingredients that add tons of unwanted sodium, fat, calories, and preservatives, this clean recipe maximizes the tastes and textures of all-natural ingredients by using complementary spices and varying the cooking processes for more depth and less fluff.

INGREDIENTS | SERVES 8

1 cup white mushrooms, minced

1 tablespoon extra-virgin olive oil

1 cup almond milk

1 cup nonfat plain Greek-style yogurt, or vegan yogurt

6 cups cooked green beans, cleaned and halved

2 teaspoons all-natural sea salt

2 teaspoons white pepper

1 teaspoon garlic powder

1 teaspoon onion powder

Feel Good about *Your* Food

In some holiday recipes, heavy cream, condensed milk, and whole milk are the main creaming ingredients, but you can keep your favorite recipes delicious and still clean them up with healthier substitutions. You have to keep in mind that providing your body and those of the ones you love with great-tasting food that actually promotes health and well-being is the goal, not creating great-tasting food that handicaps health. By replacing the fattening ingredients with fresh, more nutritious ones, you can achieve the same great taste and texture . . . and add healthful helpings of nutrients to your favorite foods.

1. In a skillet over medium heat, sauté the mushrooms in the olive oil until soft and cooked through, about 4–6 minutes. Remove from heat, place in a mixing bowl, and allow to cool for 10 minutes.

2. Add the almond milk and yogurt to the mushrooms, and stir to combine.

3. Add the green beans, salt, pepper, garlic powder, and onion powder to the cream, and combine well.

4. Preheat the oven to 400°F and prepare a baking dish with olive oil spray.

5. Pour the green bean mixture into the prepared casserole dish, and bake for 25–35 minutes, or until bubbly.

6. Remove the dish from the oven, and allow the casserole to cool for about 15 minutes before eating.

PER SERVING Calories: 82 | Fat: 2 g | Protein: 5.5 g | Sodium: 623.5 mg | Fiber: 3 g | Carbohydrates: 12 g | Sugar: 4.5 g

Pecan-Packed Pie

Pecan pie can be a tasty, but unhealthy, holiday tradition. Clean it up by eliminating the fat- and sugar-laden ingredients with healthier alternatives that maintain that same great taste and crunch.

INGREDIENTS | SERVES 8

4 cups natural pecans, divided

¾ cup coconut oil

1 cup honey or agave nectar

1½ cups dates, pitted

1 teaspoon ground nutmeg

1 teaspoon cinnamon

1 teaspoon ground cloves

1 prepared Clean Vegan Pie Crust (see Chapter 13)

Pecan Pie Gets a Clean Makeover

Pecan pie is a holiday dream that's a dieter's nightmare, right? Wrong! Pecans are an amazing source of protein and healthy fats and, when combined with fresh natural ingredients, can deliver the same great taste as the traditional but not-anywhere-near-as-healthy versions of pecan pie. Clean, packed with benefits for the body and the brain, and amazingly delicious, this is a pecan pie that's delicious and nutritious from the crust to the filling to the topping!

1. In a food processor, process 3 cups of the pecans, coconut oil, honey or agave nectar, and dates until thickened. Move to a mixing bowl, and add the nutmeg, cinnamon, and cloves to the pecan mix, and blend well.

2. Set out the prepared pie shell.

3. Pour the pecan mix into the pie shell, and top with the remaining pecans. Press them lightly into the pie, and allow the pie to set for 3–4 hours.

PER SERVING Calories: 864.5 | Fat: 64.5 g | Protein: 7 g | Sodium: 75.5 mg | Fiber: 9 g | Carbohydrates: 77 g | Sugar: 58 g

Protein-Packed Pumpkin Pie

Pumpkin may be a vibrant complex carbohydrate, but adding protein-rich ingredients like almond milk and yogurt brings this pie to an extraordinary protein-providing level like never before!

INGREDIENTS | SERVES 8

1 prepared Clean Vegan Pie Crust (see Chapter 13)

1 (15-ounce) can pure puréed pumpkin

1 cup vanilla almond milk

2 tablespoons plain nonfat Greek-style yogurt, or vegan yogurt

2 eggs, or ½ cup vegan egg substitute

½ cup honey, or agave

2 tablespoons Sucanat

2 teaspoons cinnamon

½ teaspoon pumpkin pie spice

½ teaspoon ground cloves

Canned *Can* Be Okay

With canned pumpkin purée readily available at most grocery stores, it would be a little nonsensical to steam, mash, or purée your own at triple the cost and triple the time. Make sure that your canned pumpkin is pure pumpkin with no added ingredients; the ingredient list should contain one thing and one thing only: pumpkin.

1. Preheat the oven to 375°F and set out the prepared pie crust.

2. In a mixing bowl, combine the pumpkin purée, almond milk, yogurt, eggs or egg substitute, and honey or agave nectar, and mix well.

3. Add the Sucanat, cinnamon, pumpkin pie spice, and cloves, and mix thoroughly.

4. Pour the pie mixture into the prepared pie crust, and bake 45–60 minutes, or until center is set and a knife inserted in the center comes out clean.

PER SERVING Calories: 205 | Fat: 6 g | Protein: 4 g | Sodium: 111 mg | Fiber: 1 g | Carbohydrates: 32 g | Sugar: 24 g

Clean Green Beans Almondine

Most people douse their green beans in butter and layer on the salt, but clean recipes like this one make the most of green beans' natural flavor by adding ingredients that brighten their flavor and slivered almonds to accentuate their natural crunch.

INGREDIENTS | SERVES 6

1 pound green beans, cleaned and trimmed

2 tablespoons extra-virgin olive oil

½ cup slivered almonds

1 teaspoon freshly squeezed lemon juice

1 teaspoon all-natural sea salt

Holiday Appetizers: Clean and Delicious!

Creating healthy holiday appetizers can get a little tricky if you're trying to adhere to a clean lifestyle. Creating natural "shells" for "fillings," both out of vibrant vegetables and fruits like bell peppers, squash, onions, artichokes, oranges, mushrooms, etc., that can support fillings or fill up supporters is easy, healthy, *and* smart. Avoiding cheeses, high-fat creams, and unnecessary white flour and sugar, you can still create a wide variety of delicious appetizers that will please *and* promote health. Homemade chips and dips, salsas, salads, and even meatless entrées can be whipped up in a flash and plated to serve many.

1. In a medium saucepan of water, bring the green beans to a boil, reduce heat, and simmer until tender but still crisp, about 6–8 minutes.

2. Remove the green beans from the heat, and drain.

3. Place the green beans in a large serving dish, and toss with the olive oil, almonds, lemon juice, and sea salt until well combined.

PER SERVING Calories: 109 | Fat: 8.5 g | Protein: 3 g | Sodium: 5 mg | Fiber: 3 g | Carbohydrates: 7 g | Sugar: 3 g

Sweet and Savory Corn Pudding

Corn pudding has taken a delightful turn for the savory side in this dish that is beautiful, delicious, and actually nutritious, too!

INGREDIENTS | SERVES 6

2 cups sweet corn kernels, fresh or thawed

1 cup unsweetened almond milk

¼ cup plain nonfat Greek-style yogurt, or vegan yogurt

2 eggs, or ½ cup vegan egg substitute

2 teaspoons all-natural sea salt

2 teaspoons cracked black pepper

2 teaspoons garlic powder

1 cup scallions, chopped

1 cup chopped red bell peppers

¼ cup cornmeal

1 cup Garlic and Herb Tortilla Chips (see Chapter 5), processed to chunky crumbs

1. Preheat the oven to 350°F and prepare a 9" × 13" casserole dish with olive oil spray.

2. In a blender or food processor, combine half of the corn kernels, half of the almond milk, and the yogurt, and blend together until smooth.

3. In a large mixing bowl, combine the remaining almond milk, eggs, and seasonings, and whisk to combine thoroughly.

4. Add to the mixing bowl the processed purée, remaining corn, scallions, red pepper, cornmeal, and ½ cup of the tortilla chip crumbs, and mix well.

5. Pour the mixture into the casserole dish, top with remaining tortilla crumbs, and bake for 30 minutes, or until the pudding has thickened and the top is golden brown.

PER SERVING Calories: 308 | Fat: 12 g | Protein: 9 g | Sodium: 1,255 mg | Fiber: 4 g | Carbohydrates: 41.5 g | Sugar: 5 g

Clean Corn Bread

Corn bread has received a bad reputation, but in clean varieties like this one, nutritious ingredients add flavor and quality nutrients in every luscious bite.

INGREDIENTS | SERVES 6

2 tablespoons 100% whole-wheat flour (for coating of pan)

1 cup plain nonfat yogurt, or soy yogurt

2 tablespoons plain low-fat Greek-style yogurt, or vegan yogurt

2 eggs, or ½ cup vegan egg substitute

2 tablespoons applesauce

1 tablespoon Sucanat

2 cups kernel corn, fresh or frozen

1 cup self-rising cornmeal

1. Preheat the oven to 375°F and coat a loaf pan with olive oil spray and whole-wheat flour.

2. In a large mixing bowl, combine the yogurts, eggs or egg substitute, applesauce, Sucanat, and corn, and mix well.

3. Add the cornmeal gradually, and combine thoroughly.

4. Pour the mix into the prepared bread pan, and bake for 20–30 minutes, or until golden brown and a knife inserted in the center comes out clean.

PER SERVING Calories: 201 | Fat: 4 g | Protein: 7.5 g | Sodium: 49 mg | Fiber: 2.5 g | Carbohydrates: 34 g | Sugar: 7.5 g

Merry Mushroom Gravy

Gravy can be thick and delicious without being fattening and filled with undesirable ingredients. At your next holiday get-together, whip up this mushroom-packed masterpiece that gives gravy a clean spin.

INGREDIENTS | MAKES 4 CUPS

1 tablespoon extra-virgin olive oil

5 cups sliced portobello mushrooms

1 teaspoon garlic powder

1 teaspoon cracked black pepper

2 teaspoons all-natural sea salt

4 tablespoons oat flour

4 cups unsweetened almond milk

1. In a saucepan over medium heat, combine the olive oil, mushrooms, garlic powder, pepper, and 1 teaspoon of the sea salt. Sauté the mushrooms until they are soft and tender, about 6–8 minutes.

2. Whisk the flour and remaining teaspoon of salt into the almond milk until well blended.

3. Add the almond milk to the mushrooms gradually, ¼ cup at a time, stirring constantly. Reduce heat to low.

4. Once the sauce begins to thicken, continue to simmer for 1–2 minutes, then remove from heat. Allow to set about 5 minutes, and serve.

PER SERVING (¼ CUP) Calories: 38.5 | Fat: 1.5 g | Protein: 1.5 g | Sodium: 343 mg | Fiber: 1 g | Carbohydrates: 3.5 g | Sugar: 1 g

Cleaned Up Cranberry Sauce

Canned varieties of cranberry sauce can be riddled with excess . . . everything. Slim down the ingredient list to simple, all-natural ingredients, and your taste buds and your body will be happy and healthier.

INGREDIENTS | SERVES 6

1 cup freshly squeezed orange juice

¼ cup agave nectar

1 tablespoon orange zest

1 pound cranberries, washed

The Magic Ingredient That Complements Everything

If you're wondering what to have for dinner on a random evening, don't forget about cranberry sauce recipes like this one! Topping salads, rice, vegetables, and pastas, this cranberry sauce makes for a great sweet addition that perfectly complements a slightly salty entrée.

1. In a large pot over medium heat, bring the orange juice, agave nectar, and orange zest to a boil. Reduce the heat to low, and simmer.

2. Add the washed cranberries to the pot, and simmer for about 10–15 minutes, or until the cranberries begin to burst.

3. Remove from heat, stir, and allow the sauce to thicken.

4. Serve warm or cold.

PER SERVING Calories: 98.5 | Fat: 0.5 g | Protein: 1 g | Sodium: 3 mg | Fiber: 3.5 g | Carbohydrates: 26 g | Sugar: 18 g

Scalloped Potatoes

Ditch the blatantly unhealthy scalloped potatoes that load up on cheese, cream, and salt, and whip up a batch of these thinly sliced, perfectly seasoned potatoes that will calm those cravings and kill the guilt.

INGREDIENTS | SERVES 6

6 large Idaho potatoes

2 cups unsweetened almond milk

2 cups crumbled goat cheese, or vegan soft cheese

1 cup scallions, chopped

2 teaspoons garlic powder

2 teaspoons onion powder

1 teaspoon cracked black pepper

1. With a mandoline, slice the potatoes thinly.

2. In a large mixing bowl, combine the potatoes, almond milk, goat cheese, scallions, garlic powder, onion powder, and pepper.

3. Preheat the oven to 400°F and prepare a 9" × 13" casserole dish with olive oil spray.

4. Pour the potato mixture into the casserole dish, and bake for 45–60 minutes, or until bubbly and golden brown.

5. Remove from heat, and allow to set and thicken for about 10–15 minutes before serving.

PER SERVING Calories: 509 | Fat: 27 g | Protein: 27 g | Sodium: 335 mg | Fiber: 6 g | Carbohydrates: 37.5 g | Sugar: 5 g

Creamy Potato Hash with "Sausage," Sage, and Mushrooms

*Vegan sausage substitute can add hearty depth to an entrée, and
be a valuable addition for taste and texture purposes.*

INGREDIENTS | SERVES 4

4 small red potatoes, cut into ¼" pieces

1 tablespoon minced garlic

1¼ cup water

1 pound vegan sausage substitute, crumbled

1 teaspoon coriander

1 teaspoon dried sage

1 cup sliced baby portobello mushrooms

2 cups nonfat Greek-style yogurt, or vegan yogurt

1 teaspoon garlic powder

1 teaspoon all-natural sea salt

1 teaspoon cracked black pepper

1. In a large skillet over medium heat, combine the potatoes, minced garlic, and 1 cup water, and simmer for 7–10 minutes or until potatoes are fork tender but still firm. Transfer the potatoes to a bowl, and return skillet to heat.

2. Add the sausage substitute, coriander, and sage to the skillet, and sauté until browned, about 6–8 minutes.

3. Add the mushrooms and ¼ cup water, and sauté until all water is evaporated and mushrooms are reduced. Remove skillet from heat and transfer vegetables and sausage to a mixing bowl, allowing to cool for about 5 minutes.

4. Fold yogurt into vegetables, coating all evenly.

5. Season with garlic powder, salt, and pepper.

PER SERVING Calories: 248 | Fat: 3.5 g | Protein: 18 g | Sodium: 500 mg | Fiber: 3.5 g | Carbohydrates: 40 g | Sugar: 12 g

CHAPTER 16

Kid-Friendly Fun

Creamy Tofu and Veggie Pasta
278

Black Bean and Corn Quesadilla
279

Raspberry Sorbet
279

Pineapple-Banana Freeze
280

Perfectly Sweet Oatmeal
280

All-Natural Fruit Bake
281

Blueberry Cobbler with
Almond Crumble
282

Almond Butter Cookies
283

Creamy Corn Pudding
284

Almond Butter, Flax, and
Jelly Rollups
285

Sweet Potato Fries
286

Protein-Packed Lettuce Wraps
287

Almond Butter Granola Balls
288

Peanut Butter and Jelly Bars
289

Fruit Kebabs
290

Almond Butter Banana Pitas
290

Fun Fruit Pops
291

Cinnamon Tortilla Chips
291

Banana Sorbet
292

Decorative Pineapple with
Fruit Skewer Fun
292

Citrus Tofu Kebabs
293

Creamy Tofu and Veggie Pasta

Picky eaters love this simple pasta tossed with sweet peas, corn, and carrots, with the light addition of sautéed tofu. While none of the ingredients are strong or overpowering, each provides an abundant amount of vitamins, minerals, and nutrients that promote quality system functioning growing bodies need.

INGREDIENTS | SERVES 2

1 cup gluten-free spiral pasta
½ cup matchstick carrots
1 (14-ounce) package extra-firm tofu
½ cup kernel corn, fresh or thawed
½ cup sweet peas
½ cup low-fat Greek-style yogurt, or vegan yogurt
1 teaspoon all-natural sea salt

1. In a large pot of boiling water, cook the pasta and matchstick carrots until the pasta is soft and cooked through and the carrots are soft and tender.

2. Drain the pasta and carrots, rinse, and transfer to a glass bowl.

3. Prepare a medium skillet with olive oil spray and place it over medium heat. Sauté the tofu until lightly golden and slightly crunchy, about 7–9 minutes.

4. Add the corn and peas, and sauté until cooked through, about 2–4 minutes. Remove skillet from heat and transfer tofu and vegetables to the pasta bowl.

5. Fold the yogurt into the pasta until all ingredients are equally smothered, and season with salt.

PER SERVING Calories: 344 | Fat: 7 g | Protein: 23 g | Sodium: 1,200 mg | Fiber: 5 g | Carbohydrates: 47 g | Sugar: 12 g

Black Bean and Corn Quesadilla

Because black beans have a creamy texture and corn lends a sweet flavor, many kids enjoy the combination of the two and will happily devour these crispy quesadillas.

INGREDIENTS | SERVES 2

2 100% whole-wheat tortillas
1 cup black beans, mashed
1 cup kernel corn, cooked
1 teaspoon all-natural sea salt

1. Preheat a broiler or toaster oven to 400°F.

2. Lay the tortillas flat and cover the entire surface of each with ½ cup of the mashed black beans.

3. Scatter the corn kernels evenly throughout the tortillas on ½ only, and sprinkle sea salt over top. Fold the tortilla over to enclose, and press down lightly to secure.

4. Broil or toast for 5 minutes on each side, or until golden brown.

PER SERVING Calories: 244 | Fat: 2 g | Protein: 10 g | Sodium: 1,300 mg | Fiber: 10 g | Carbohydrates: 49 g | Sugar: 5 g

Raspberry Sorbet

This chilling fresh fruit treat is the perfect healthy snack to satisfy a sweet tooth and daily recommended essential fruit servings all at the same time.

INGREDIENTS | SERVES 6

4 cups frozen raspberries
2 teaspoons agave nectar
2 teaspoons vanilla
1 teaspoon mint leaves, chopped

1. In a high-speed blender, combine the raspberries, agave nectar, vanilla, and mint, and purée.

2. Once fully puréed, pour the raspberry mixture into 6 cups, and freeze for 10 minutes.

3. Serve with a spoon.

PER SERVING Calories: 80 | Fat: 0.5 g | Protein: 1 g | Sodium: 1 mg | Fiber: 2 g | Carbohydrates: 19 g | Sugar: 11 g

Pineapple-Banana Freeze

Sweet and slightly tart, this splendid blend of bananas and pineapple creates a delicious and nutritious treat that will cool off any hot summer day.

INGREDIENTS | SERVES 6

2 bananas

2 cups pineapple

2 teaspoons vanilla

1 cup ice

1. In a high-speed blender, combine the bananas, pineapple, and vanilla, and purée. Add ice and blend until smooth.

2. Once smooth, pour the mixture into 6 cups, and freeze for 10 minutes.

3. Serve with a spoon.

PER SERVING Calories: 66 | Fat: 0 g | Protein: 1 g | Sodium: 1 mg | Fiber: 2 g | Carbohydrates: 16 g | Sugar: 10 g

Perfectly Sweet Oatmeal

Oatmeal doesn't have to be littered with unhealthy ingredients to taste great. By using protein-packed almond milk and a hint of sweetness from mineral-rich maple syrup, you can whip up healthy oatmeal that provides essential nutrition without unhealthy additives.

INGREDIENTS | SERVES 2

2 cups rolled oats

2 cups vanilla almond milk

1 tablespoon maple syrup

1. Pour 1 cup of the rolled oats into each of 2 bowls.

2. Mix in 1 cup of almond milk and ½ tablespoon of maple syrup in each bowl.

3. Microwave on high for 2–3 minutes, or until the oats have completely absorbed all of the almond milk.

4. Stir to combine, allow to cool, and serve.

PER SERVING Calories: 417 | Fat: 7 g | Protein: 11.5 g | Sodium: 146 mg | Fiber: 8 g | Carbohydrates: 76.5 g | Sugar: 21 g

All-Natural Fruit Bake

Kids love this sweet treat because they can help make it! Washing the fruit, preparing the fruit, tossing, pouring, and presenting can all be clever ways to show your kids the fun of creating healthy foods.

INGREDIENTS | SERVES 8

2 cups blueberries, washed

2 cups strawberries, quartered

2 cups sliced peaches

2 cups sliced pears

1 tablespoon freshly squeezed lemon juice

2 tablespoons agave nectar

1 teaspoon freshly grated lemon zest

How to Grate Citrus

To grate citrus, first scrub the skin vigorously to remove dirt, germs and allergens, and harmful chemicals or pesticides. Once the fruit's skin is clean, use a fine grater or Microplane to scrape the outer peel over a bowl. Continuously circling the fruit as you grate is the most effective method, and can prevent overgrating into the bitter white part of the flesh.

1. Preheat the oven to 350°F and prepare a 9" × 13" baking dish with olive oil spray.

2. In a mixing bowl, toss all of the fruit together with the lemon juice, agave nectar, and lemon zest.

3. Pour the fruit into the baking dish, and bake at 350°F for 25–35 minutes, or until all fruit is tender.

PER SERVING Calories: 84.5 | Fat: 0.5 g | Protein: 1 g | Sodium: 2 mg | Fiber: 3 g | Carbohydrates: 22 g | Sugar: 16.5 g

Blueberry Cobbler with Almond Crumble

Light and irresistible, this sweet and crunchy treat is a great improvement upon traditional recipes that include excessive amounts of butter, refined flour and sugar, and few natural ingredients.

INGREDIENTS | SERVES 2

4 tablespoons water
2 tablespoons agave nectar
2 pints blueberries, washed
2 tablespoons coconut oil
1 cup crushed almonds
½ cup All-Natural Granola (see Chapter 5)

Combining Antioxidants and Healthy Fats for Optimum Health

Phytonutrients and polyphenols like *anthocyanins* (strong plant chemicals that create the deep colors of healthy fruit) are warriors that work wonders for providing a youthful, healthy existence. Healthy fats like rich omegas help the body to digest and absorb fibrous fruits and vegetables that contain these important nutrients. By combining omega-rich foods like nuts, fish, and oils with antioxidant-rich foods, you end up getting more out of every bite of the delicious and nutritious morsels you already enjoy.

1. In a small pot, combine the water and agave nectar over medium heat, stir, and bring to a boil.

2. Reduce heat to low, add blueberries to the pot, and simmer for about 2–4 minutes (stirring constantly).

3. Pour the blueberries evenly into 2 medium soufflé cups, and allow to thicken.

4. Return the same pot to medium heat and melt the coconut oil.

5. Add the almonds and granola to the coconut oil, and mix well.

6. Top the blueberries with the almonds and granola, and chill.

PER SERVING Calories: 776 | Fat: 45 g | Protein: 17 g | Sodium: 13 mg | Fiber: 16 g | Carbohydrates: 87 g | Sugar: 55 g

Almond Butter Cookies

These sweet cookies make for a delicious and nutritious alternative to the traditional peanut butter cookies. Just like peanut butter cookies, they're protein-packed and a favorite with kids!

INGREDIENTS | MAKES 24 COOKIES

2 cups rice flour

1 teaspoon baking powder

1 cup natural almond butter

¼ cup unsweetened applesauce

½ cup agave nectar

1 egg, or ¼ cup vegan egg substitute

Nut Butter Buyers Beware!

When purchasing a nut butter, pay close attention to its ingredients and nutrition facts. While the label may say "organic," "natural," or use other buzzwords to capture your attention, you shouldn't skip over the nutrition facts and buy the product on good faith. Look for a quality amount (approximately 10 g) of protein per serving with low sodium (less than 60 mg) and low sugar (less than 10 g) counts. You should not find "partially hydrogenated oils," which are also known as trans fats, in the ingredient list. Be an informed consumer!

1. Preheat the oven to 350°F and prepare a baking sheet with aluminum foil and olive oil spray.

2. In a large mixing bowl, combine the flour and baking powder, and blend well.

3. Add the almond butter, applesauce, agave nectar, and egg (or egg substitute) to the dry ingredients, and mix to combine.

4. Drop the cookie mix onto the baking sheet in rounded heaping teaspoons.

5. Bake for 10–15 minutes, or until golden brown.

PER SERVING Calories: 117 | Fat: 3 g | Protein: 2 g | Sodium: 24 mg | Fiber: 1 mg | Carbohydrates: 21 g | Sugar: 9 g

Creamy Corn Pudding

This is a sweet version of the amazingly thick and yummy traditional corn pudding. Using almond milk and Greek-style yogurt makes this dish protein-packed, and the fresh corn makes for a healthful helping of a sweet fresh vegetable packed with complex carbohydrates.

INGREDIENTS | SERVES 6

3 cups sweet corn kernels, fresh or thawed

1 cup vanilla almond milk

¼ cup plain low-fat Greek-style yogurt, or vegan yogurt

2 eggs, or ½ cup vegan egg substitute

1 tablespoon organic maple syrup

¼ cup cornmeal

1 cup Cinnamon Tortilla Chips (see recipe in this chapter), processed to chunky crumbs

Benefits of Natural Corn

While it is true that corn has been taken from the fields, chemically or genetically altered, and manufactured into hundreds of thousands of different products ranging from candy bars to corn chips, the natural corn kernel itself (fresh or flash-frozen) is a healthy provider of valuable nutrition. Packed with vitamins and minerals that have been shown to prevent illness and promote lung function, and complex carbohydrates that contribute to the body's essential energy stores, corn is a healthy vegetable option . . . in its natural form.

1. Preheat the oven to 350°F and prepare a casserole dish with olive oil spray.

2. In a blender or food processor, combine half of the corn kernels, half of the almond milk, and the yogurt, and blend together until smooth.

3. In a large mixing bowl, combine the remaining almond milk, eggs, and maple syrup, and whisk to combine thoroughly.

4. Add to the mixing bowl the processed purée, remaining corn, cornmeal, and ½ cup of the processed tortilla chip crumbs, and mix well.

5. Pour the mixture into the casserole dish, top with remaining tortilla chip crumbs, and bake for 30 minutes, or until the pudding has thickened and the top is golden brown.

PER SERVING Calories: 324 | Fat: 13 g | Protein: 9 g | Sodium: 546.5 mg | Fiber: 3.5 g | Carbohydrates: 46 g | Sugar: 6 g

Almond Butter, Flax, and Jelly Rollups

If plain peanut butter and jelly sandwiches don't feel healthy enough to give for a snack, try these wraps that provide essential omega-3s, protein, and antioxidants in every sweet, creamy, crunchy bite.

INGREDIENTS | SERVES 2

2 100% whole-wheat tortillas

4 tablespoons almond butter

4 tablespoons mashed strawberries

2 tablespoons ground flaxseed

Start Small

Almost every child has a special treat that they would eat all day, every day if they could. If you want to make that treat a little healthier, try one substitute at a time. Start sprinkling a teaspoon of ground flaxseed on peanut butter sandwiches, peanut butter–covered brown rice cakes, or muffins and gradually increase the amount; your little buddy will barely notice the new addition, will eventually be accustomed to the taste and texture, and will be open to healthy foods like flax in the long run. Plus, the added flax will help you pump up your child's omega-3 intake.

1. Lay tortillas on a flat surface.

2. Spread 2 tablespoons of the almond butter on each tortilla and cover with 2 tablespoons of the mashed strawberries.

3. Sprinkle a tablespoon of the ground flaxseeds over the jelly evenly on each tortilla and roll tightly.

PER SERVING Calories: 264 | Fat: 13 g | Protein: 7 g | Sodium: 193.5 mg | Fiber: 5 g | Carbohydrates: 33 g | Sugar: 12 g

Sweet Potato Fries

Fries don't have to be a no-no anymore. Vibrant vitamin A–packed sweet potatoes provide essential vitamins and minerals with a sweet, creamy taste that gets crispy and even more delicious when prepared for fries.

INGREDIENTS | SERVES 4

2 sweet potatoes (peeled or with skin intact)

1 tablespoon olive oil

1 teaspoon all-natural sea salt

Your Favorite of Your Child's Favorite Vegetables

Rich in vitamins and minerals like vitamin A, vitamin C, and lutein that remedy vitamin D deficiencies, promote healthy eyesight, and prevent illnesses like asthma by strengthening the lungs, sweet potatoes may be one of your favorite vegetables to prepare for your little one. Luckily for everyone involved, because of their sweetness and versatility, there's sure to be at least one way to cook a sweet potato that will appeal to your child.

1. Preheat the oven to 400°F and line a baking sheet with aluminum foil and olive oil spray.

2. Cut the sweet potatoes into 2"–3" long strips about ¼" in width.

3. Pour the sweet potatoes and olive oil into a large resealable plastic bag, and toss to coat.

4. Line the sweet potatoes on the baking sheet, sprinkle with half of the salt, and bake for 15–20 minutes, or until slightly crisp.

5. Flip the fries, sprinkle the remaining salt, and continue baking for 15–20 minutes, or until crispy and fork tender.

PER SERVING Calories: 86 | Fat: 3.5 g | Protein: 1 g | Sodium: 626 mg | Fiber: 2 g | Carbohydrates: 13 g | Sugar: 3 g

Protein-Packed Lettuce Wraps

Kids like anything that looks cool and can be wrapped up . . . especially if they can do it on their own. Delicious, crispy, crunchy, and packed with nutritious deliciousness, these lettuce wraps are a great sandwich alternative anytime.

INGREDIENTS | SERVES 4

1 cup plain nonfat yogurt, or vegan yogurt

1 cup cooked ground extra-firm tofu, crumbled

1 cup finely chopped walnuts

1 cup green seedless grapes, quartered

½ tablespoon organic honey or agave nectar

1 tablespoon ground flaxseed

4 crisp butter lettuce leaves

1. In a large mixing bowl, combine the yogurt, tofu crumbles, walnuts, grapes, honey or agave nectar, and flaxseed. Combine thoroughly.

2. Lay the lettuce leaves flat, and spoon ¼ of the mixture into the center of each leaf.

3. Wrap tightly, and serve.

PER SERVING Calories: 285 | Fat: 22 g | Protein: 9 g | Sodium: 37 mg | Fiber: 3 g | Carbohydrates: 17 g | Sugar: 11 g

Make Alterations to Fit Your Child's Tastes

Don't be afraid to remove, add, or change items in recipes so they're more likely to appeal to your child's tastes. If you know your child will like most of the ingredients in a recipe, but a single element would make the meal a disaster, go ahead and replace that single disliked ingredient. *You know your child's likes and dislikes, so use that knowledge to your advantage* and do what you can to have the most nutritious foods be the ones consumed most often. Plus, if it's important enough, you can always wait a few months and try that disliked ingredient again.

Almond Butter Granola Balls

Homemade granola, almond butter, maple syrup, and ground flaxseed combine in these yummy bite-sized balls that are packed with clean carbohydrates, protein, antioxidants, and minerals that make anytime a great time for snack time.

INGREDIENTS | SERVES 5

1 cup all-natural almond butter

2 tablespoons organic maple syrup

2 cups All-Natural Granola (see Chapter 5)

2 tablespoons ground flaxseed

Almond Butter and Granola for Greatness

What could be better than a clean combination of carbohydrates and protein that fuel and repair your child's body before, during, and after healthy activity? Almond Butter Granola Balls contain protein, carbohydrates, and clean healthy fats, all rolled up, literally, into great balls of goodness that help fuel and repair your child's body no matter what activity is going on.

1. In a large mixing bowl, combine the almond butter and maple syrup, and mix until fully combined and smooth.

2. Add the granola and ground flaxseed, and stir to combine thoroughly.

3. Form the mixture into ¾"–1" balls and line up in a storage container.

4. Refrigerate for 1 hour, and serve.

PER SERVING Calories: 381 | Fat: 20 g | Protein: 12 g | Sodium: 17 mg | Fiber: 7.5 g | Carbohydrates: 50 g | Sugar: 25 g

Peanut Butter and Jelly Bars

Peanut butter and jelly sandwiches become a handy "on-the-go" treat of simplicity and balanced nutrition with these easy to create, clean, and scrumptious bars that any kid would love!

INGREDIENTS | MAKES 16 BARS

3 cups all-natural peanut butter

¼ cup coconut oil

½ cup agave nectar

4 cups rolled oats

2 cups mashed strawberries

Ditch the Store-Bought Jelly

Although many jellies and jams claim to be healthy, sugar-free, and whatever else may appeal to consumers, there is no comparison between the nutrition in store-bought jellies and those made at home with natural ingredients. By creating jelly from scratch using fresh berries or other fruits you can handpick with the kiddies at local farms—mashed or puréed, sweetened with natural sweeteners or absolutely nothing at all—homemade jelly has no empty ingredients to speak of and can be enjoyed in a wide variety of ways in, on, or with a million different dishes. Inexpensive, easy, and delicious, your own jelly will be the best you've ever had . . . and the most fun your kids will ever have making their own!

1. Prepare a medium saucepan with olive oil spray over medium heat, and combine the peanut butter, the coconut oil, and the agave nectar. Stirring constantly, mix until well blended and melted, about 5–8 minutes.

2. Add the oats to the mixture, and stir to combine. Once well blended, remove from the heat.

3. Prepare a 9" × 9" baking dish with olive oil spray. Pour half of the peanut butter–oatmeal mixture into the dish and press firmly to mold the mix as an even layer on the bottom of the pan.

4. Pour the mashed fruit over the bottom layer and spread evenly.

5. Allow the fruit layer to set for about 5 minutes, and then layer the remaining peanut butter–oatmeal mixture evenly over the top.

6. Refrigerate for 1 hour, or overnight for best results. Cut into 16 rectangles.

PER SERVING Calories: 429 | Fat: 29 g | Protein: 15 g | Sodium: 224 mg | Fiber: 5 g | Carbohydrates: 33 g | Sugar: 14 g

Fruit Kebabs

After being told for years, "Put down that sharp stick!," your little one will love to spend the time skewering the vibrant fresh fruit of his or her choice to create an edible masterpiece all his or her own.

INGREDIENTS | SERVES 4

1 cup green seedless grapes
1 cup pineapple chunks
1 cup halved strawberries
1 cup red seedless grapes
1 cup blueberries

1. Prepare a platter with all of the fruit, and start skewers with a green grape, a pineapple chunk, a strawberry half, a red grape, and a blueberry or two.

2. Continue skewering fruit and condense firmly.

3. Serve skewers.

4. For children under seven, remove fruit from skewers, and serve as a fruit salad instead.

PER SERVING Calories: 105 | Fat: 0.5 g | Protein: 1 g | Sodium: 2.5 mg | Fiber: 3 g | Carbohydrates: 27 g | Sugar: 21 g

Almond Butter Banana Pitas

Slathered with delicious almond butter and packed to the brim with sweet, creamy bananas, these simple pitas pack clean protein and tons of taste in a handheld snack your kids are sure to love!

INGREDIENTS | SERVES 2

1 stone-ground 100% whole-wheat pita
4 tablespoons almond butter
1 tablespoon agave nectar
1 banana, peeled and sliced

1. Cut the pita in half and open the pockets.

2. Slather the inside of each pita with the almond butter and drizzle with ½ tablespoon of agave nectar in each.

3. Evenly layer the banana slices on one side of each pita half. Tightly close and serve.

PER SERVING Calories: 261.5 | Fat: 9 g | Protein: 4.5 g | Sodium: 99 mg | Fiber: 3.5 g | Carbohydrates: 43.5 g | Sugar: 26.5 g

Fun Fruit Pops

No need to add anything for sweetness in this delicious snack that's whipped up quickly, frozen, and on hand for an all-natural fruit packed treat healthy enough for breakfast, snacks, or dessert.

INGREDIENTS | SERVES 6

1 banana
1 cup strawberries, tops removed
1½ cups freshly squeezed orange juice

Homemade Ice Pops = Fruit, Fun, and . . . a Stick!

There's just something whimsical about food on a stick. Even adults are drawn to foods that, for some reason, become more appealing once put on a stick. Taking into consideration that kids love sweetness, sticks, and frozen treats, frozen fruit pops have it all wrapped up in a single delicious serving!

1. In a high-speed blender, combine the banana, strawberries, and orange juice.

2. Pour the smoothie mixture into 6 individual pop makers.

3. Freeze overnight, and remove by running the pop makers under warm water until the pops release.

PER SERVING Calories: 55.5 | Fat: 0.5 g | Protein: 1 g | Sodium: 1 mg | Fiber: 1 g | Carbohydrates: 13.5 g | Sugar: 9 g

Cinnamon Tortilla Chips

Store-bought cinnamon chips are made using questionable ingredients and, sometimes, even more questionable methods. Skip the mystery bags of sugar-laden chips and opt for these homemade all-natural cinnamon-y tortilla crisps instead.

INGREDIENTS | MAKES 40 CHIPS

4 100% whole-wheat tortillas
2 teaspoons cinnamon
½ teaspoon salt

Make Snacking Healthy and Delicious

If you have a hankering for some chips and dip, but want to refrain from the salty, store-bought variety of both, you can combine these clean chips with Fruit Salsa (see Chapter 5), low-fat yogurt, or agave-sweetened Greek-style yogurt to make a great guiltless snack for adults and kids alike!

1. Tear each tortilla into 10–12 pieces.

2. Preheat the oven to 350°F. Line a baking sheet with aluminum foil and spray with olive oil spray.

3. Layer the tortilla pieces evenly on the baking sheet, spray with olive oil, and sprinkle with the cinnamon and salt.

4. Bake for 10–15 minutes, or until crispy.

PER SERVING (4 CHIPS) Calories: 38.5 | Fat: 1 g | Protein: 1 g | Sodium: 195 mg | Fiber: 0.5 g | Carbohydrates: 6.5 g | Sugar: 0.5 g

Banana Sorbet

Simple and quick, this banana sorbet is not only natural, sweet, and delicious, it's homemade so you can control the quality and amounts of each ingredient to fit your specific tastes and needs.

INGREDIENTS | SERVES 6

4 frozen whole bananas (peeled and bagged prior to freezing)
2 teaspoons vanilla
1 teaspoon nutmeg
1 teaspoon agave nectar

Simplicity Can Be Key

When creating delicious and nutritious meals that appeal to kids, keep it simple. They may be hesitant to eat a dish that combines too many flavors—even if it's just one flavor they dislike among many they love. Keep it to a handful of ingredients, and add more, little by little, as they grow up.

1. In a high-speed blender, combine the bananas and vanilla, and purée.

2. While blending, add the nutmeg and agave nectar.

3. Once fully puréed, pour the banana mixture into 6 cups, and freeze for 10 minutes.

4. Serve with a spoon.

PER SERVING Calories: 80 | Fat: 0.5 g | Protein: 1 g | Sodium: 1 mg | Fiber: 2 g | Carbohydrates: 19.5 g | Sugar: 11 g

Decorative Pineapple with Fruit Skewer Fun

Party snacks don't have to be creamy and heavy to look and taste great! If you're looking to add fruit to a party's platter, try skewering fruit and poking it in a pineapple for a beautiful centerpiece that packs fresh fruit fun on every individual skewer.

INGREDIENTS | SERVES 20

1 large pineapple
4 cups pineapple, in cubes
4 cups strawberries
1 pound green seedless grapes
1 pound red seedless grapes
4 cups clementine segments
4 cups blueberries
20–30 skewers, 10–12"

1. Place the pineapple in the center of a serving tray.

2. Skewer the fruit in the following order: pineapple, strawberries, grapes, clementines, and blueberries until all skewers are completed.

3. Stab the skewers into the pineapple with the largest fruit flush against the pineapple.

4. Rotate the pineapple, and continue adding the skewers evenly throughout the pineapple's surface until all are completely set.

PER SERVING Calories: 77 | Fat: 0.5 g | Protein: 1 g | Sodium: 2 mg | Fiber: 2.5 g | Carbohydrates: 20 g | Sugar: 15 g

Citrus Tofu Kebabs

*Because kids aren't ingrained with the "pass the salt" habit yet, these kebabs
are perfect just as they are. Sweet citrus fruits flavor tofu on a handy kebab that's easy to eat.
Just remember that kids shouldn't be left unattended with sharp skewers.*

INGREDIENTS | SERVES 4

1 pound extra-firm tofu, cubed
1 grapefruit, inside sections removed
½ pineapple, cut into 1" cubes

Tofu: The Blank Canvas Kids Love

Packed with protein, tofu is a great high-protein food your kids can enjoy in a number of ways. Whether they prefer to have it plain, with dip, or topped with every extra dash of spice and topping, tofu is a versatile and easy to prepare food for children. Tofu can take on the flavors of anything you combine with it, which makes it a wonderful companion for delicious fresh fruit, vibrant vegetables, or carbohydrate-rich pasta or rice. Sweet and tangy flavors from your child's favorite fruits make each bite of tempting tofu delicious and nutritious.

1. Prepare a grill with olive oil spray and set to medium heat.

2. Skewer the tofu, grapefruit, and pineapple in the same rotation throughout.

3. Lay the skewers on the grill grate and grill for 5–7 minutes. Turn the skewers and continue grilling for 7 minutes, or until the tofu is completely cooked through and golden brown.

4. Remove the skewers from the grill and serve.

5. For children under seven, remove the tofu, grapefruit, and pineapple from the skewers onto a plate and serve.

PER SERVING Calories: 138 | Fat: 2 g | Protein: 9 g | Sodium: 71 mg | Fiber: 2.5 | Carbohydrates: 22 g | Sugar: 16 g

Eating Clean Meal Plan

	BREAKFAST	SNACK	LUNCH	SNACK	DINNER
Day 1	Clean Huevos Rancheros (2)	Ginger-Citrus-Apple Salad	Tomato, Basil, and Mozzarella Wrap	Simple Strawberry-Banana Smoothie	Clean Cashew Stir-Fry with Not-Fried "Fried" Rice
Day 2	Apple-Cinnamon Pancakes (2)	Clean Green Go-Getter Smoothie	Black Bean-Garbanzo Burger	Colorful Vegetable-Pasta Salad	Italian Tofu Bake
Day 3	Spinach, Red Onion, and Mushroom Frittata	Strawberry-Walnut-Flaxseed Salad	Spicy Cinnamon-Almond Smoothie	Black Bean and Yellow Rice Wrap	Thai Vegetable Curry
Day 4	Fruity French Toast Sandwiches	Cucumber-Tabbouleh Salad	Marvelous Mediterranean Wrap	Dreamy Melon Cream Smoothie	Pesto-Painted Tofu Sauté
Day 5	Best-Ever Breakfast Bars (2)	Baked Apples and Pears with Leafy Greens	Perfect Pineapple-Banana Blend	Grilled Veggie Wrap-Up	Vegetarian Meat Loaf with Perfect Polenta
Day 6	Baked Fruit with Cinnamon and Spice	Tropical Island Salad	Asian-Infused Tofu Burger	Mango Medley Smoothie	Good-For-You Gumbo
Day 7	Banana Bread with Walnuts and Flaxseed (1 slice)	Lighter Waldorf Salad	Pear Paradise Smoothie	Perfect Portobello Burger	Creamy Curry Tempeh with Vegetables
Day 8	Sunshine Corn Muffins (2)	Clean "Chocolate"–Almond Butter Smoothie	Chick Patty	Tex-Mex Salad	Creamy Tomato-Basil Soup with Acorn Squash Cups
Day 9	Toasted Almond Butter Banana Sandwiches	Blueberry Cobbler Smoothie	Spicy Zucchini Stacker	Creamy Onion-Fennel Soup	Sweet Tofu with Summer Squash
Day 10	Poached Eggs with Spicy Chive Cream	Cucumber-Melon Salad	Savory Spinach, Tomato, and Garlic Smoothie	Spicy Sweet Potato Soup	Vegan Chili
Day 11	Over-the-Top Cinnamon Walnut Oatmeal	Roasted Fennel, Tomato, and Chickpea Toss	Peachy Protein Smoothie	Sweet Carrot, Cabbage, and Cucumber Wrap with Hummus	Five-Alarm Enchilada (1) with Spicy Broccolini
Day 12	Veggie and Egg White Omelet	Lemon-Scented Rice with Fruit Salsa Salad	Roasted Red Pepper and Onion Wrap with Spicy Chickpea Sauce	Sweet Citrus Smoothie	Lemon-Basil Tofu with Stuffed Baked Onions
Day 13	Protein-Packed Parfaits	Tomato, Mozzarella, and Spinach Salad	Crunchy Chai Confection Smoothie	Quick Quinoa and Black Bean Burger	Tofu Piccata with Veggie-Stuffed Potatoes
Day 14	Fruity Egg White Frittata	Bean and Couscous Salad	Artichoke-Mozzarella Wrap	Spiced Apple Surprise Smoothie	Sautéed Tofu with Balsamic Onions and Mushrooms with Potato Fries

Standard U.S./Metric Measurement Conversions

VOLUME CONVERSIONS

U.S. Volume Measure	Metric Equivalent
⅛ teaspoon	0.5 milliliters
¼ teaspoon	1 milliliters
½ teaspoon	2 milliliters
1 teaspoon	5 milliliters
½ tablespoon	7 milliliters
1 tablespoon (3 teaspoons)	15 milliliters
2 tablespoons (1 fluid ounce)	30 milliliters
¼ cup (4 tablespoons)	60 milliliters
⅓ cup	90 milliliters
½ cup (4 fluid ounces)	125 milliliters
⅔ cup	160 milliliters
¾ cup (6 fluid ounces)	180 milliliters
1 cup (16 tablespoons)	250 milliliters
1 pint (2 cups)	500 milliliters
1 quart (4 cups)	1 liter (about)

WEIGHT CONVERSIONS

U.S. Weight Measure	Metric Equivalent
½ ounce	15 grams
1 ounce	30 grams
2 ounces	60 grams
3 ounces	85 grams
¼ pound (4 ounces)	115 grams
½ pound (8 ounces)	225 grams
¾ pound (12 ounces)	340 grams
1 pound (16 ounces)	454 grams

OVEN TEMPERATURE CONVERSIONS

Degrees Fahrenheit	Degrees Celsius
200 degrees F	95 degrees C
250 degrees F	120 degrees C
275 degrees F	135 degrees C
300 degrees F	150 degrees C
325 degrees F	160 degrees C
350 degrees F	180 degrees C
375 degrees F	190 degrees C
400 degrees F	205 degrees C
425 degrees F	220 degrees C
450 degrees F	230 degrees C

BAKING PAN SIZES

American	Metric
8 x 1½ inch round baking pan	20 x 4 cm cake tin
9 x 1½ inch round baking pan	23 x 3.5 cm cake tin
11 x 7 x 1½ inch baking pan	28 x 18 x 4 cm baking tin
13 x 9 x 2 inch baking pan	30 x 20 x 5 cm baking tin
2 quart rectangular baking dish	30 x 20 x 3 cm baking tin
15 x 10 x 2 inch baking pan	30 x 25 x 2 cm baking tin (Swiss roll tin)
9 inch pie plate	22 x 4 or 23 x 4 cm pie plate
7 or 8 inch springform pan	18 or 20 cm springform or loose bottom cake tin
9 x 5 x 3 inch loaf pan	23 x 13 x 7 cm or 2 lb narrow loaf or pate tin
1½ quart casserole	1.5 liter casserole
2 quart casserole	2 liter casserole

Index

Note: Page numbers in **bold** indicate category recipe lists.

Appetizers, **141**–58
about: dip versatility, 154
Balsamic Mushroom Skewers, 150
Coconut Crusted Tofu Strips, 152
Cool and Crunchy Spinach and Artichoke
Dip, 144
Delicious Deviled Eggs, 157
Fantastic Falafel, 147
Ginger-Vegetable Spring Rolls, 148
Great Guacamole, 143
Herbed Potato Patties, 149
Layered Bean Dip, 156
Perfect Pinto Bean Pesto, 158
Roasted Red Pepper and Artichoke Dip,
155
Roasted Veggie Dip with a Kick, 146
Spicy Clean Refried Beans, 144
Spicy Jalapeño Poppers, 153
Spicy Spinach and Artichoke Dip, 143
Stuffed Baked Onions, 151
Stuffed Pepper Poppers, 142
Tomato-Basil Hummus, 158
Veggie Dip Stuffed Tomatoes, 155
Veggie-Packed Potato Skins, 145
Yogurt-Veggie Dip, 154
Apples
about: suppressing appetite, 235
Apple-Cinnamon Pancakes, 46
Apple Crumble, 235
Apple-Flaxseed Loaf, 247
Baked Apples and Pears with Leafy Greens,
133
Baked Fruit with Cinnamon and Spice, 55
Ginger-Citrus-Apple Salad, 129
Lighter Waldorf Salad, 139
Spiced Apple Surprise smoothie, 68
Waldorf Wrap, 92
Apricot, Cranberry, Almond Bars, 89
Artichokes
Antipasto Salad, 129
Artichoke-Mozzarella Wraps, 100
Baked Veggie Pasta, 190
Cool and Crunchy Spinach and Artichoke
Dip, 144

Linguine with Leeks, Artichokes, and Garlic,
197
Roasted Red Pepper and Artichoke Dip, 155
Spicy Spinach and Artichoke Dip, 143
Asparagus
Creamy, Dreamy Asparagus Casserole, 266
Creamy Asparagus Soup, 124
Mushroom and Asparagus Bake, 166
Avocados
Avocados and Greens, 132
Great Guacamole, 143
Lime-Avocado Dipping Sauce, 87
Sweet and Spicy Avocado Burger, 106
Terrific Tortillas, 163

Baba Gannouj, 254
Bananas
about, 227
Almond Butter Banana Pitas, 290
Banana Bread with Walnuts and Flaxseed,
57
Banana Pudding, 227
Banana Sorbet, 292
Banana Strips, 242
Fun Fruit Pops, 291
Pineapple-Banana Freeze, 280
Raw Banana Bread, 250
smoothies with. *See* Smoothies
Toasted Almond Butter Banana Sandwiches,
55
Barley, in Best-Ever Vegetable-Barley Soup,
114
Bars and balls
Almond Butter Granola Balls, 288
Apricot, Cranberry, Almond Bars, 89
Best-Ever Breakfast Bars, 48
Clean Protein Power Bars, 49
Peanut Butter and Jelly Bars, 289
Perfect Pumpkin Pie Snack Bars, 88
Protein Squares, 246
Raw Granola Bars, 246
Basil
Creamy Tomato-Basil Soup, 121
Lemon-Basil Tofu, 172

Linguine with Fire-Roasted Tomatoes,
Basil, and Mozzarella, 193
Peppy Pesto, 90
Perfect Pinto Bean Pesto, 158
Pesto and Pine Nut Penne, 190
Pesto-Painted Tofu Sauté, 172
Roasted Red Pepper Pesto, 75
Tomato, Basil, and Mozzarella Wraps, 99
Tomato-Basil Hummus, 158
Tomato-Basil Rigatoni, 197
Beans and legumes. *See also* Green beans;
Peas
about: black beans, 45; garbanzos, 204,
207; lentils, 113
Bean and Couscous Salad, 140
Black Bean and Corn Quesadilla, 279
Black Bean and Yellow Rice Wraps, 92
Black Bean-Garbanzo Burgers, 97
Chick Patties, 108
Clean Black Bean Huevos Rancheros, 45
Fantastic Falafel, 147
Garlicky Garbanzos and Spinach, 207
Layered Bean Dip, 156
Lentil-Vegetable Soup, 112
Over-Stuffed Bean Burritos, 162
Perfect Pinto Bean Pesto, 158
Protein-Packed Breakfast Burritos, 43
Quick Quinoa and Black Bean Burger, 103
Refreshing Red Lentil Soup, 113
Roasted Fennel, Tomato, and Chickpea
Toss, 138
Saucy Southwestern Soup, 116
Slow Cooker Red Beans and Rice, 188
Spicy Chickpea Sauce, 105
Spicy Clean Refried Beans, 144
Sweet Green Chickpea Soup, 119
Tangy Three-Bean Salad, 139
Terrific Tortillas, 163
Tex-Mex Quesadillas, 80
Tex-Mex Salad, 137
Tomato-Basil Hummus, 158
Tomato Garbanzos, 204
Vegan Chili, 169
Veggie Burgers, 102

Benefits, of clean vegetarian diet, 18–21, 26–27
Berries
about: cranberries, 134
All-Natural Fruit Bake, 281
Apricot, Cranberry, Almond Bars, 89
Blueberry Cobbler with Almond Crumble, 282
Blueberry Pie, 226
Bread Pudding with Fruits, 239
Chunky Cranberry-Walnut Stuffing, 263
Clean Cranberry-Walnut Cookies, 232
Cleaned Up Cranberry Sauce, 274
Decorative Pineapple with Fruit Skewer Fun, 292
Fast Fruit-Oatmeal Bowls, 52
Fruit Kebabs, 290
Fruit Salsa, 76
Fruity Egg White Frittata, 53
Fun Fruit Pops, 291
Peachy Parfait, 243
Raspberry Sorbet, 279
smoothies with. See Smoothies
Strawberry-Walnut-Flaxseed Salad, 135
Sweet and Spicy Cabbage with Cranberries and Walnuts, 134
Blenders, 30–31
Bloat, beating, 166
Blueberries. See Berries
Brain functioning, 19–20
Bread puddings, 238–39
Breads. See also Sandwiches and wraps
about: sprouted grain, 50; whole-wheat, 100
Banana Bread with Walnuts and Flaxseed, 57
Clean Corn Bread, 272
Raw Banana Bread, 250
Sunshine Corn Muffins, 59
Zucchini Bread, 83
Breakfasts, 41–60
Apple-Cinnamon Pancakes, 46
Baked Fruit with Cinnamon and Spice, 55
Banana Bread with Walnuts and Flaxseed, 57
Best-Ever Breakfast Bars, 48
Cinnamon Oatmeal, 244
Clean Black Bean Huevos Rancheros, 45
Clean Chia Porridge, 245
Clean Huevos Rancheros, 44

Clean Protein Power Bars, 49
Fast Fruit-Oatmeal Bowls, 52
Fruity Egg White Frittata, 53
Fruity French Toast Sandwiches, 50
Homemade Scallion Hash Brown Cakes, 54
Over-the-Top Cinnamon Walnut Oatmeal, 56
Perfectly Sweet Oatmeal, 280
Poached Eggs with Spicy Chive Cream, 60
Protein-Packed Breakfast Burritos, 43
Protein-Packed Parfaits, 51
Simple Sweet Potato Pancakes, 47
Spinach, Red Onion, and Mushroom Frittata, 42
Sunshine Corn Muffins, 59
Toasted Almond Butter Banana Sandwiches, 55
Veggie and Egg White Omelets, 58
Broccoli
Broccoli-Cauliflower Bake, 214
Clean Cashew Stir-Fry, 171
Clean Green Go-Getter smoothie, 71
Cream of Broccoli Soup, 115
Great Greens Pasta Pot, 195
Quinoa with Mixed Vegetables, 219
Sweet and Spicy Veggie Stir-Fry, 179
Sweet Green Chickpea Soup, 119
Veggie and Egg White Omelets, 58
Broccolini
Potato-Broccolini Soup, 123
Spicy Broccolini, 213
Brussels sprouts, sweet and spicy, 206
Bulgur, in Cucumber-Tabbouleh Salad, 128
Burgers. See Sandwiches and wraps
Burritos, 43, 162, 249

Cabbage
about: nutrition benefits, 74
Colorful Cabbage Rolls, 74
Ginger-Vegetable Spring Rolls, 148
Sweet and Spicy Cabbage with Cranberries and Walnuts, 134
Sweet Carrot, Cabbage, and Cucumber Wraps, 97
Calories, daily, 17
Carbohydrates, complex, 32–34, 261
Carob
about: as chocolate alternative, 233
Carob-Walnut Cookies, 233
Chocolate Cake, 225

Chocolate Chia Pudding, 226
Clean Chocolate Frosting, 224
Carrots
Clean Carrot Cake, 231
Clean Cashew Stir-Fry, 171
Gardener's Pie, 160
Not-Fried "Fried" Rice, 218
Simple Sweet and Spicy Carrot Soup, 114
Sweet Carrot, Cabbage, and Cucumber Wraps, 97
Cauliflower
about: nutrition benefits, 171; sneaking into dishes, 264
Broccoli-Cauliflower Bake, 214
Clean Cashew Stir-Fry, 171
Clean Green Go-Getter smoothie, 71
Gardener's Pie, 160
Mashed Potatoes and Cauliflower, 264
Cheese
about: fresh vs. processed, 189; goat, 211
pasta with. See Pasta
Scalloped Tomatoes with Goat Cheese, 221
Stuffed Mushrooms, 211
Tomato, Mozzarella, and Spinach Salad, 136
wraps with. See Sandwiches and wraps
Cherries
Cherry Pie, 229
Cherry-Pineapple Pucker, 63
Chickpeas. See Beans and legumes
Chili, vegan, 169
Chips, 80, 84, 86, 251, 291
Chocolate
about: carob as alternative to, 233. See also Carob
Chunky Chocolate Chip Cookies, 251
Clean "Chocolate"–Almond Butter Smoothie, 71
Cocoa Café Brownies, 234
Mint Chocolate Chip Ice Cream, 256
Choline, 35
Cilantro, in Spicy Cilantro-Tomato Salad, 132
Citrus
about: grating, 281; lemon benefits, 90
Asian Almond-Mandarin Salad, 136
Citrus, Fennel, and Spinach Salad, 128
Citrus Tofu Kebabs, 293
Ginger-Citrus-Apple Salad, 129
Lemon, Leek, and Fennel Soup, 119
Lemon-Basil Tofu, 172

Lemon-Scented Rice with Fruit Salsa Salad, 140
Lime-Avocado Dipping Sauce, 87
smoothies with. *See* Smoothies
Clean vegetarian diet. *See* Vegetarian diet, clean
Coconut
    Clean Whipped Cream, 240
    Coconut Cream Pie, 229
    Coconut Crusted Tofu Strips, 152
    Raw Burritos, 249
    smoothies with milk of. *See* Smoothies
    Tropical Island Salad, 131
Containers, glass, 30
Cooking methods, 108
Coolers, insulated, 31
Corn
    about: cornmeal, 59; nutrition benefits, 284
    Black Bean and Corn Quesadilla, 279
    Clean Corn Bread, 272
    Clean Creamy Corn Chowder, 115
    Creamy Corn Pudding, 284
    Creamy Veggie Casserole, 165
    Gardener's Pie, 160
    Mexican Pâté, 255
    Perfect Polenta, 212
    Sunshine Corn Muffins, 59
    Sweet and Savory Corn Pudding, 271
    Tex-Mex Salad, 137
Couscous
    Bean and Couscous Salad, 140
    Mediterranean Couscous–Stuffed Tomato Poppers, 78
    Mediterranean Couscous, 214
Crackers. *See* Raw foods
Cranberries. *See* Berries
Cream, alternative, 184
Cream, whipped, 240
Cucumbers
    about: nutrition benefits, 128
    Cucumber-Melon Salad, 131
    Cucumber-Tabbouleh Salad, 128
    Sweet Carrot, Cabbage, and Cucumber Wraps, 97
Cutting boards, 30

Desserts, **223**–40. *See also* Raw foods
    about: no-bake pie crust, 228; refined sugars and, 16; vegetables in, 231
    All-Natural Fruit Bake, 281

Almond Butter Cookies, 283
Apple Crumble, 235
Banana Pudding, 227
Banana Sorbet, 292
Blueberry Pie, 226
Bread Pudding with Fruits, 239
Bread Pudding with Maple-Cinnamon Walnuts, 238
Carob-Walnut Cookies, 233
Cherry Pie, 229
Chia Pudding, 224
Chocolate Cake, 225
Chocolate Chia Pudding, 226
Clean Carrot Cake, 231
Clean Chocolate Frosting, 224
Clean Cranberry-Walnut Cookies, 232
Clean Vegan Pie Crust, 228
Clean Whipped Cream, 240
Cocoa Café Brownies, 234
Coconut Cream Pie, 229
Creamy Corn Pudding, 284
Maple Rice Pudding with Walnuts, 230
Peach Tart, 236
Pecan-Packed Pie, 268
Pineapple-Banana Freeze, 280
Protein-Packed Pumpkin Pie, 269
Raspberry Sorbet, 279
Tropical Paradise Pie, 237
Drinking clean, 15. *See also* Water and hydration

Eggplant
    about: nutrition benefits, 84, 101
    Baba Gannouj, 254
    Crunchy Garlic Eggplant Chips, 84
    Eggplant, Portobello, Spinach, and Mozzarella Stacks, 101
    Italian Eggplant Sandwiches, 107
    Ratatouille, 180
    Roasted Eggplant Dip, 85
    Roasted Veggie Dip with a Kick, 146
    Thai Vegetable Curry, 163
Eggs
    Clean Black Bean Huevos Rancheros, 45
    Clean Huevos Rancheros, 44
    Delicious Deviled Eggs, 157
    Fruity Egg White Frittata, 53
    Fruity French Toast Sandwiches, 50
    Poached Eggs with Spicy Chive Cream, 60
    Protein-Packed Breakfast Burritos, 43

"Sausage" Soufflé, 261
Spicy Spanish Egg Quesadilla, 81
Spinach, Red Onion, and Mushroom Frittata, 42
Veggie and Egg White Omelets, 58
Enchiladas, 173–76
Energy, increasing, 19, 26–27
Entrées, **159**–82
    about: combining vegetables, 180; salads as meals, 137
    Best-Ever Tofu Enchiladas, 173
    Clean Cashew Stir-Fry, 171
    Creamy Curry Tempeh with Vegetables, 178
    Creamy Veggie Casserole, 165
    Five-Alarm Enchiladas, 174
    Gardener's Pie, 160
    Garlic Tofu Stir-Fry, 168
    Ginger-Lime Tofu, 182
    Good-For-You Gumbo, 177
    Italian Tofu Bake, 167
    Lemon-Basil Tofu, 172
    Mushroom and Asparagus Bake, 166
    Over-Stuffed Bean Burritos, 162
    Pesto-Painted Tofu Sauté, 172
    Ratatouille, 180
    Rustic Roasted Root Vegetables, 161
    Sautéed Tofu with Balsamic Onions and Mushrooms, 181
    Spinach Enchiladas, 175
    Sweet and Spicy Veggie Stir-Fry, 179
    Sweet Tofu with Summer Squash, 170
    Tasty Tomatillo Enchiladas, 176
    Terrific Tortillas, 163
    Thai Vegetable Curry, 163
    Tofu Piccata, 179
    Vegan Chili, 169
    Vegetarian Meat Loaf, 164
Equipment, 29–31

Falafel, 147
Fats, clean, 34, 147, 282
Fennel
    about, 252
    Citrus, Fennel, and Spinach Salad, 128
    Creamy Onion-Fennel Soup, 117
    Lemon, Leek, and Fennel Soup, 119
    Pear Soup with Ginger and Fennel, 252
    Roasted Fennel, Tomato, and Chickpea Toss, 138

Filé powder, 177
Food processors, 31
Fruits. *See also specific fruits*
    about: in "baked" dishes, 250; as complex carbohydrate source, 33; dried, hidden sugars in, 232; freezing, 236; making jellies, 289; SOD production, 133; stocking pantry, 33–34
    Baked Fruit with Cinnamon and Spice, 55
    Best-Ever Breakfast Bars, 48
    Bread Pudding with Fruits, 239
    Decorative Pineapple with Fruit Skewer Fun, 292
    Fruit Kebabs, 290
    Fruity French Toast Sandwiches, 50
    Fun Fruit Pops, 291

Garbanzos. *See* Beans and legumes
Gardener's Pie, 160
Garlic
    about: healthy flavor of, 217
    Garlic Tofu Stir-Fry, 168
    Linguine with Leeks, Artichokes, and Garlic, 197
    Savory Spinach, Tomato, and Garlic Smoothie, 67
Gazpacho, 120
Ginger, 95
    Ginger-Citrus-Apple Salad, 129
    Ginger-Lime Tofu, 182
    Ginger-Vegetable Spring Rolls, 148
Glass containers, 30
Goals, defining, 26–27
Grains, **183**. *See also* Couscous; Oats; Pasta; Rice
    about: as complex carbohydrate source, 32; stocking pantry, 32
    Almond Butter Granola Balls, 288
    Best-Ever Vegetable-Barley Soup, 114
    Clean Chia Porridge, 245
    Cucumber-Tabbouleh Salad, 128
    Protein Squares, 246
    Raw Granola Bars, 246
    Seed and Grain Crackers, 247
Granola, 79. *See also* Bars and balls
Grapes
    Decorative Pineapple with Fruit Skewer Fun, 292
    Fruit Kebabs, 290
    Lighter Waldorf Salad, 139

Protein-Packed Lettuce Wraps, 287
    Waldorf Wrap, 92
Green beans
    Balsamic Green Beans with Quinoa, 185
    Best-Ever Vegetable-Barley Soup, 114
    Clean Green Bean Casserole, 267
    Clean Green Beans Almondine, 270
    Gardener's Pie, 160
    Great Greens Pasta Pot, 195
Gumbo, 177

Health benefits, of clean vegetarian diet, 18–21, 26
Holiday recipes, **259**–76
    Chunky Cranberry-Walnut Stuffing, 263
    Clean Corn Bread, 272
    Cleaned Up Cranberry Sauce, 274
    Clean Green Bean Casserole, 267
    Clean Green Beans Almondine, 270
    Creamy, Dreamy Asparagus Casserole, 266
    Creamy Potato Hash with "Sausage," Sage, and Mushrooms, 276
    Hearty Mushroom and Herb Stuffing, 260
    Mashed Potatoes and Cauliflower, 264
    Mashed Sweet Potato Perfection, 265
    Merry Mushroom Gravy, 273
    Pecan-Packed Pie, 268
    Protein-Packed Pumpkin Pie, 269
    "Sausage" Soufflé, 261
    Scalloped Potatoes, 275
    Sweet and Savory Corn Pudding, 271
    Sweet Potato Casserole with Sweet Walnut Topping, 262
Hummus, 75, 158
Hydration. *See* Water and hydration

Immersion blenders, 30
Immunity, stronger, 20
Ingredients
    avoiding specific ones, 37
    complex carbohydrates (clean), 32–34
    experimenting with new, 36
    fats (clean), 34, 147, 282
    fresh, 169
    proteins (clean), 32
    stocking pantry, 32–35
    sweeteners (clean and nonclean), 34–35

Jellies, making, 289
Jicama Empanadas, 258

Kale chips, 251
Kid-friendly recipes, **277**–93
    about: altering to fit child's tastes, 287
    All-Natural Fruit Bake, 281
    Almond Butter, Flax, and Jelly Rollups, 285
    Almond Butter Banana Pitas, 290
    Almond Butter Cookies, 283
    Almond Butter Granola Balls, 288
    Banana Sorbet, 292
    Black Bean and Corn Quesadilla, 279
    Blueberry Cobbler with Almond Crumble, 282
    Cinnamon Tortilla Chips, 291
    Citrus Tofu Kebabs, 293
    Creamy Corn Pudding, 284
    Creamy Tofu and Veggie Pasta, 278
    Decorative Pineapple with Fruit Skewer Fun, 292
    Fruit Kebabs, 290
    Fun Fruit Pops, 291
    Peanut Butter and Jelly Bars, 289
    Perfectly Sweet Oatmeal, 280
    Pineapple-Banana Freeze, 280
    Protein-Packed Lettuce Wraps, 287
    Raspberry Sorbet, 279
    Sweet Potato Fries, 286
Kitchen equipment, 29–31
Kiwis, in Fruit Salsa, 76
Knives, 29

Lacto-ovo vegetarians, 13
Lacto-vegetarians, 13
Leeks
    Lemon, Leek, and Fennel Soup, 119
    Linguine with Leeks, Artichokes, and Garlic, 197
    Scalloped Potatoes with Leeks and Olives, 216
    Sweet Green Chickpea Soup, 119
Leftovers, 162, 265
Lemon. *See* Citrus
Lentils. *See* Beans and legumes

Mangoes
    Bread Pudding with Fruits, 239
    Fruit Salsa, 76
    Mango Medley smoothie, 66
Maple Rice Pudding with Walnuts, 230
Maple syrup, 170, 238
Meal plans, 27–28, 294

Measurement conversion chart, 295
Measuring equipment, 31
Meatless products. *See also* Soy; Tofu
    about: protein intake and, 21–22
    Creamy Curry Tempeh with Vegetables,
        178
    Creamy Potato Hash with "Sausage," Sage,
        and Mushrooms, 276
    "Meat" Sauce Stuffed Shells, 201
    Paella, 187
    "Sausage" Soufflé, 261
    Vegetarian Meat Loaf, 164
Melons
    Cucumber-Melon Salad, 131
    Dreamy Melon Cream Smoothie, 68
Metabolism, improved, 19, 60
Mint Chocolate Chip Ice Cream, 256
Motivation, maintaining, 35–37
Mushrooms
    about: nutrition benefits, 96, 150;
        Portobellos, 96
    Baked Veggie Pasta, 190
    Balsamic Mushroom Skewers, 150
    Cheesy Mushroom and Sweet Pea Pasta,
        196
    Creamy Veggie Casserole, 165
    Eggplant, Portobello, Spinach, and
        Mozzarella Stacks, 101
    Hearty Mushroom and Herb Stuffing, 260
    Merry Mushroom Gravy, 273
    Mushroom and Asparagus Bake, 166
    Pasta Primavera, 191
    Perfect Portobello Burgers, 96
    Quinoa with Mixed Vegetables, 219
    Red Pepper Rice with Mushrooms and
        Sweet Peas, 185
    Sautéed Spinach, Mushrooms, and
        Potatoes, 209
    Sautéed Tofu with Balsamic Onions and
        Mushrooms, 181
    Spinach, Red Onion, and Mushroom
        Frittata, 42
    Stuffed Baked Onions, 151
    Stuffed Mushrooms, 211
    Ultimate Spinach and Mushroom Risotto,
        222
    Vegan Stroganoff, 184
    Vegetarian Lasagna, 189
    Vegetarian Meat Loaf, 164
    Wild Mushroom Risotto, 202

Notebook, 31
Nutrition, maximizing, 17–18, 94
Nuts and seeds
    about: almond butter, 255, 288; flaxseed
        benefits, 49, 198; making almond milk,
        70; nut butter precautions, 283; sesame
        seed benefits, 77; walnut benefits, 56, 57
    All-Natural Granola, 79
    Almond Butter, Flax, and Jelly Rollups, 285
    Almond Butter Banana Pitas, 290
    Almond Butter Cookies, 283
    Almond Butter Granola Balls, 288
    Apple-Flaxseed Loaf, 247
    Apricot, Cranberry, Almond Bars, 89
    Asian Almond-Mandarin Salad, 136
    Banana Bread with Walnuts and Flaxseed,
        57
    Banana-Nut Smoothie, 70
    Bread Pudding with Maple-Cinnamon
        Walnuts, 238
    Carob-Walnut Cookies, 233
    Chia Pudding, 224
    Chocolate Chia Pudding, 226
    Chunky Cranberry-Walnut Stuffing, 263
    Clean Cashew Stir-Fry, 171
    Clean Chia Porridge, 245
    Clean "Chocolate"–Almond Butter
        Smoothie, 71
    Clean Cranberry-Walnut Cookies, 232
    Clean Curry Crackers, 248
    Clean Protein Power Bars, 49
    Clean Vegan Pie Crust, 228
    Creamy Cashew Dipping Sauce, 82
    Dairy-Free Almond Yogurt, 257
    Jicama Empanadas, 258
    Lighter Waldorf Salad, 139
    Maple Rice Pudding with Walnuts, 230
    Mexican Pâté, 255
    Over-the-Top Cinnamon Walnut Oatmeal, 56
    Peanut Butter and Jelly Bars, 289
    Pecan-Packed Pie, 268
    Pesto and Pine Nut Penne, 190
    Protein-Packed Lettuce Wraps, 287
    Roasted Red Pepper and Pine Nut
        Hummus, 75
    Seed and Grain Crackers, 247
    Spicy Cinnamon-Almond Smoothie, 66
    Sprouted Burgers, 256
    Strawberry-Walnut-Flaxseed Salad, 135
    Sweet and Spicy Cabbage with Cranberries
        and Walnuts, 134

    Sweet and Spicy Sesame Tofu Strips, 77
    Sweet Potato Casserole with Sweet Walnut
        Topping, 262
    Tahini, 253
    Toasted Almond Butter Banana
        Sandwiches, 55
    Tropical Island Salad, 131
    Vanilla Almond Butter, 255
    Waldorf Wrap, 92

Oats
    about: groats, 244; nutrition benefits, 52;
        soaking, 244
    All-Natural Granola, 79
    Best-Ever Breakfast Bars, 48
    Cinnamon Oatmeal, 244
    Clean Protein Power Bars, 49
    Fast Fruit-Oatmeal Bowls, 52
    Over-the-Top Cinnamon Walnut Oatmeal,
        56
    Perfectly Sweet Oatmeal, 280
Okra, in Good-For-You Gumbo, 177
Olives
    Antipasto Salad, 129
    Scalloped Potatoes with Leeks and Olives,
        216
Onions
    about: shallots, 175
    Clean Cashew Stir-Fry, 171
    Clean French Onion Soup, 118
    Creamy Onion-Fennel Soup, 117
    Homemade Scallion Hash Brown Cakes, 54
    Roasted Red Pepper and Onion Wrap with
        Spicy Chickpea Sauce, 105
    Roasted Red Potatoes and Onions, 213
    Roasted Veggie Dip with a Kick, 146
    Sautéed Tofu with Balsamic Onions and
        Mushrooms, 181
    Simple Spaghetti with Sautéed Tofu and
        Onions, 200
    Spinach, Red Onion, and Mushroom
        Frittata, 42
    Stuffed Baked Onions, 151
    Sweet and Spicy Veggie Stir-Fry, 179
    Veggie and Egg White Omelets, 58
Ovo-vegetarians, 13

Pancakes, 46, 47
Pantry, stocking, 32–35
Parfaits, 243
Pasta, **183**

about: choosing type, 196; gluten-free, 199
Asian Tofu Sauté with Rice Noodles, 186
Baked Veggie Pasta, 190
Cheesy Mushroom and Sweet Pea Pasta, 196
Cheesy Spinach Shells, 194
Colorful Vegetable-Pasta Salad, 130
Creamy Tofu and Veggie Pasta, 278
Creamy Veggie Casserole, 165
Great Greens Pasta Pot, 195
Light and Creamy Green Linguine, 199
Linguine with Fire-Roasted Tomatoes, Basil, and Mozzarella, 193
Linguine with Leeks, Artichokes, and Garlic, 197
"Meat" Sauce Stuffed Shells, 201
Pasta Primavera, 191
Pesto and Pine Nut Penne, 190
Simple Spaghetti with Sautéed Tofu and Onions, 200
Sweet and Savory Pepper Penne, 200
Tofu Spaghetti, 193
Tomato-Basil Rigatoni, 197
Vegan Stroganoff, 184
Vegetarian Lasagna, 189
Veggie-Stuffed Shells, 198
Peaches
All-Natural Fruit Bake, 281
Baked Fruit with Cinnamon and Spice, 55
Fast Fruit-Oatmeal Bowls, 52
Peach Tart, 236
Peachy Parfait, 243
Peachy Protein Smoothie, 65
Pears
about: SOD production, 133
All-Natural Fruit Bake, 281
Baked Apples and Pears with Leafy Greens, 133
Baked Fruit with Cinnamon and Spice, 55
Pear Paradise smoothie, 64
Pear Soup with Ginger and Fennel, 252
Peas
Cheesy Mushroom and Sweet Pea Pasta, 196
Clean Cashew Stir-Fry, 171
Creamy Veggie Casserole, 165
Gardener's Pie, 160
Great Greens Pasta Pot, 195
Not-Fried "Fried" Rice, 218
Paella, 187

Red Pepper Rice with Mushrooms and Sweet Peas, 185
Sweet and Spicy Veggie Stir-Fry, 179
Sweet Green Chickpea Soup, 119
Peppers
Baked Veggie Pasta, 190
Colorful Vegetable-Pasta Salad, 130
Grilled Veggie Wrap-Up, 94
Ratatouille, 180
Roasted Red Pepper and Artichoke Dip, 155
Roasted Red Pepper and Onion Wrap with Spicy Chickpea Sauce, 105
Roasted Red Pepper and Pine Nut Hummus, 75
Roasted Red Pepper Pesto, 75
Spicy Jalapeño Poppers, 153
Stuffed Pepper Poppers, 142
Sweet and Savory Pepper Penne, 200
Sweet Pepper Sandwich Stacker, 93
Sweet Rice and Sweeter Peppers, 186
Performance, improved, 19
Persimmon Pudding, 242
Personalizing plan, 27–29
Pineapples
Cherry-Pineapple Pucker, 63
Clean Piña Colada, 72
Decorative Pineapple with Fruit Skewer Fun, 292
Fruit Kebabs, 290
Fruit Salsa, 76
Perfect Pineapple-Banana Blend, 65
Pineapple-Banana Freeze, 280
Sweet Citrus Smoothie, 63
Tropical Island Salad, 131
Tropical Paradise Pie, 237
Polenta, 212
Portion sizes, 21
Potatoes. See also Sweet potatoes
about: nutrition benefits, 54
Baked Potato Chips, 86
Creamy Potato Hash with "Sausage," Sage, and Mushrooms, 276
Gardener's Pie, 160
Garlic Mashed Potatoes, 217
Herbed Potato Patties, 149
Homemade Scallion Hash Brown Cakes, 54
Mashed Potatoes and Cauliflower, 264
Potato Fries, 220
Roasted Red Potatoes and Onions, 213

Rustic Roasted Root Vegetables, 161
Sautéed Spinach, Mushrooms, and Potatoes, 209
Scalloped Potatoes, 275
Scalloped Potatoes with Leeks and Olives, 216
Twice-Baked Potatoes, 205
Veggie-Packed Potato Skins, 145
Veggie-Stuffed Potatoes, 208
Processed foods, 15–16
Proteins. See also specific protein sources
about: clean, sources/ingredients, 32; intake, vegetarian diet and, 21–22; quinoa and, 103
Clean Protein Power Bars, 49
Peachy Protein Smoothie, 65
Protein-Packed Breakfast Burritos, 43
Protein-Packed Lettuce Wraps, 287
Protein-Packed Parfaits, 51
Protein-Packed Pumpkin Pie, 269
Protein Squares, 246
Pumpkin
about: canned, 269; nutrition benefits, 122
Curried Pumpkin Bisque, 122
Perfect Pumpkin Pie Snack Bars, 88
Protein-Packed Pumpkin Pie, 269

Quesadillas, 80, 81
Quinoa
about: protein from, 103
Balsamic Green Beans with Quinoa, 185
Quick Quinoa and Black Bean Burger, 103
Quinoa with Mixed Vegetables, 219

Raspberries. See Berries
Ratatouille, 180
Raw foods, **241**–58
about: parfaits, 243
Apple-Flaxseed Loaf, 247
Baba Gannouj, 254
Banana Strips, 242
Chunky Chocolate Chip Cookies, 251
Cinnamon Oatmeal, 244
Clean Chia Porridge, 245
Clean Curry Crackers, 248
Dairy-Free Almond Yogurt, 257
Jicama Empanadas, 258
Mexican Pâté, 255
Mint Chocolate Chip Ice Cream, 256
Peachy Parfait, 243

Pear Soup with Ginger and Fennel, 252
Persimmon Pudding, 242
Pesto-Packed Kale Chips, 251
Protein Squares, 246
Raw Banana Bread, 250
Raw Burritos, 249
Raw Granola Bars, 246
Seed and Grain Crackers, 247
Simple Salsa, 253
Sprouted Burgers, 256
Tahini, 253
Vanilla Almond Butter, 255
Raw vegans, 14
Rice
    about: risotto, 202
    Black Bean and Yellow Rice Wraps, 92
    Good-For-You Gumbo, 177
    Lemon-Scented Rice with Fruit Salsa
        Salad, 140
    Maple Rice Pudding with Walnuts, 230
    Not-Fried "Fried" Rice, 218
    Paella, 187
    Red Pepper Rice with Mushrooms and
        Sweet Peas, 185
    Slow Cooker Red Beans and Rice, 188
    Stuffed Pepper Poppers, 142
    Summer Squash Casserole, 192
    Sweet Rice and Sweeter Peppers, 186
    Ultimate Spinach and Mushroom Risotto,
        222
    Vegetarian Meat Loaf, 164
    Wild Mushroom Risotto, 202
Roasting, 105

Salads, **127**–40
    about: dip versatility, 154; for meals, 137;
        sneaking nutrition into, 135
    Antipasto Salad, 129
    Asian Almond-Mandarin Salad, 136
    Avocados and Greens, 132
    Baked Apples and Pears with Leafy Greens,
        133
    Bean and Couscous Salad, 140
    Citrus, Fennel, and Spinach Salad, 128
    Colorful Vegetable-Pasta Salad, 130
    Crisp Romaine Salad with Balsamic
        Tomatoes, 129
    Cucumber-Melon Salad, 131
    Cucumber-Tabbouleh Salad, 128
    Ginger-Citrus-Apple Salad, 129

Lemon-Scented Rice with Fruit Salsa
    Salad, 140
Lighter Waldorf Salad, 139
Roasted Fennel, Tomato, and Chickpea
    Toss, 138
Spicy Cilantro-Tomato Salad, 132
Strawberry-Walnut-Flaxseed Salad, 135
Sweet and Spicy Cabbage with Cranberries
    and Walnuts, 134
Tangy Three-Bean Salad, 139
Tex-Mex Salad, 137
Tomato, Mozzarella, and Spinach Salad,
    136
Tropical Island Salad, 131
Sandwiches and wraps, **91**–108
    about: cooking methods, 108; sprouted
        grain bread, 50; whole-wheat, 100
    Almond Butter, Flax, and Jelly Rollups, 285
    Almond Butter Banana Pitas, 290
    Artichoke-Mozzarella Wraps, 100
    Asian-Infused Tofu Burgers, 95
    Black Bean and Yellow Rice Wraps, 92
    Black Bean-Garbanzo Burgers, 97
    Chick Patties, 108
    Eggplant, Portobello, Spinach, and
        Mozzarella Stacks, 101
    Fruity French Toast Sandwiches, 50
    Grilled Veggie Wrap-Up, 94
    Italian Eggplant Sandwiches, 107
    Lean, Mean Sloppy Joes, 104
    Marvelous Mediterranean Wraps, 99
    Over-Stuffed Bean Burritos, 162
    Perfect Portobello Burgers, 96
    Protein-Packed Breakfast Burritos, 43
    Protein-Packed Lettuce Wraps, 287
    Quick Quinoa and Black Bean Burger, 103
    Raw Burritos, 249
    Roasted Red Pepper and Onion Wrap with
        Spicy Chickpea Sauce, 105
    Spicy Zucchini Stacker, 98
    Sprouted Burgers, 256
    Sweet and Spicy Avocado Burger, 106
    Sweet Carrot, Cabbage, and Cucumber
        Wraps, 97
    Sweet Pepper Sandwich Stacker, 93
    Toasted Almond Butter Banana
        Sandwiches, 55
    Tomato, Basil, and Mozzarella Wraps, 99
    Veggie Burgers, 102
    Waldorf Wrap, 92

Sauces and dips
    Cool and Crunchy Spinach and Artichoke
        Dip, 144
    Creamy Cashew Dipping Sauce, 82
    Fresh Salsa, 76
    Fruit Salsa, 76
    Great Guacamole, 143
    Layered Bean Dip, 156
    Lime-Avocado Dipping Sauce, 87
    Merry Mushroom Gravy, 273
    Peppy Pesto, 90
    Perfect Pinto Bean Pesto, 158
    Roasted Eggplant Dip, 85
    Roasted Red Pepper and Artichoke Dip,
        155
    Roasted Red Pepper and Pine Nut
        Hummus, 75
    Roasted Red Pepper Pesto, 75
    Roasted Veggie Dip with a Kick, 146
    Simple Salsa, 253
    Spicy Chickpea Sauce, 105
    Spicy Chive Cream, 60
    Spicy Spinach and Artichoke Dip, 143
    Tangy Tomatillo Salsa Verde, 79
    Tasty Tomato Sauce, 82
    Tomato-Basil Hummus, 158
    Yogurt-Veggie Dip, 154
"Sausage". *See* Meatless products
Seeds. *See* Nuts and seeds
Serving sizes, 21
Side dishes, **203**–22
    Acorn Squash Cups, 210
    Broccoli-Cauliflower Bake, 214
    Garlicky Garbanzos and Spinach, 207
    Garlic Mashed Potatoes, 217
    Mediterranean Couscous, 214
    Not-Fried "Fried" Rice, 218
    Perfect Polenta, 212
    Potato Fries, 220
    Quinoa with Mixed Vegetables, 219
    Roasted Red Potatoes and Onions, 213
    Sautéed Spinach, Mushrooms, and
        Potatoes, 209
    Scalloped Potatoes with Leeks and Olives,
        216
    Scalloped Tomatoes with Goat Cheese, 221
    Spicy Broccolini, 213
    Stuffed Mushrooms, 211
    Sweet and Spicy Brussels Sprouts, 206
    Tomato Garbanzos, 204

Twice-Baked Potatoes, 205
Ultimate Spinach and Mushroom Risotto, 222
Veggie-Stuffed Potatoes, 208
Zucchini Boats, 215
Sloppy Joes, 104
Slow cooker, cracks in, 182
Smoothies, **61**–72
about: making almond milk for, 70
Banana-Nut Smoothie, 70
Blueberry Cobbler Smoothie, 62
Cherry-Pineapple Pucker, 63
Clean "Chocolate"–Almond Butter Smoothie, 71
Clean Green Go-Getter, 71
Clean Piña Colada, 72
Crazy for Cranberry-Orange, 69
Crunchy Chai Confection, 64
Dreamy Melon Cream Smoothie, 68
Mango Medley, 66
Peachy Protein Smoothie, 65
Pear Paradise, 64
Perfect Pineapple-Banana Blend, 65
Savory Spinach, Tomato, and Garlic Smoothie, 67
Simple Strawberry-Banana Smoothie, 67
Spiced Apple Surprise, 68
Spicy Cinnamon-Almond Smoothie, 66
Sweet Citrus Smoothie, 63
Sweet Potato Pie Smoothie, 69
Tofu Berry Smoothie, 62
Snacks, **73**–90. *See also* Kid-friendly recipes
about: making healthy, 291
All-Natural Granola, 79
Apricot, Cranberry, Almond Bars, 89
Baked Potato Chips, 86
Colorful Cabbage Rolls, 74
Mediterranean Couscous–Stuffed Tomato Poppers, 78
Creamy Cashew Dipping Sauce, 82
Crunchy Garlic Eggplant Chips, 84
Fresh Salsa, 76
Fruit Salsa, 76
Garlic and Herb Tortilla Chips, 80
Lime-Avocado Dipping Sauce, 87
Peppy Pesto, 90
Perfect Pumpkin Pie Snack Bars, 88
Roasted Eggplant Dip, 85
Roasted Red Pepper and Pine Nut Hummus, 75

Roasted Red Pepper Pesto, 75
Spicy Spanish Egg Quesadilla, 81
Sweet and Spicy Sesame Tofu Strips, 77
Tangy Tomatillo Salsa Verde, 79
Tasty Tomato Sauce, 82
Tasty Tostadas, 87
Tex-Mex Quesadillas, 80
Zucchini Bread, 83
Sodium cravings, 216
SOD production, 133
Soups, **109**–26
about: batch size, 110; "hearty", 123
Best-Ever Vegetable-Barley Soup, 114
Clean Creamy Corn Chowder, 115
Clean Creamy Zucchini Soup, 125
Clean French Onion Soup, 118
Cream of Broccoli Soup, 115
Creamy Asparagus Soup, 124
Creamy Onion-Fennel Soup, 117
Creamy Tomato-Basil Soup, 121
Curried Pumpkin Bisque, 122
Gazpacho, 120
Lemon, Leek, and Fennel Soup, 119
Lentil-Vegetable Soup, 112
Miso Soup, 126
Pear Soup with Ginger and Fennel, 252
Potato-Broccolini Soup, 123
Refreshing Red Lentil Soup, 113
Saucy Southwestern Soup, 116
Simple Stock, 110
Simple Sweet and Spicy Carrot Soup, 114
Spicy Sweet Potato Soup, 111
Squash and Sage Soup, 121
Sweet Green Chickpea Soup, 119
Soy. *See also* Tofu
about: alternatives to, 24; benefits, 23–24; history of, 22–23; production of, 23; questionable consequences of, 24
Miso Soup, 126
Spicy foods, 60, 174
Spinach
about: nutrition benefits, 42; sneaking into dishes, 194
Avocados and Greens, 132
Baked Veggie Pasta, 190
Cheesy Spinach Shells, 194
Citrus, Fennel, and Spinach Salad, 128
Clean Green Go-Getter smoothie, 71
Cool and Crunchy Spinach and Artichoke Dip, 144

Eggplant, Portobello, Spinach, and Mozzarella Stacks, 101
Garlicky Garbanzos and Spinach, 207
Sautéed Spinach, Mushrooms, and Potatoes, 209
Savory Spinach, Tomato, and Garlic Smoothie, 67
Spicy Spinach and Artichoke Dip, 143
Spinach, Red Onion, and Mushroom Frittata, 42
Spinach Enchiladas, 175
Tomato, Mozzarella, and Spinach Salad, 136
Ultimate Spinach and Mushroom Risotto, 222
Spring rolls, 148
Squash. *See also* Zucchini
Acorn Squash Cups, 210
Grilled Veggie Wrap-Up, 94
Ratatouille, 180
Roasted Veggie Dip with a Kick, 146
Squash and Sage Soup, 121
Summer Squash Casserole, 192
Sweet Tofu with Summer Squash, 170
Stock, simple, 110
Strawberries. *See* Berries
Stuffing, 260, 263
Sugars, in dried fruits, 232
Sugars, refined, 16, 239
Sweeteners, 16, 34–35, 48, 170, 238, 239
Sweet potatoes
about: nutrition benefits, 111, 286
Mashed Sweet Potato Perfection, 265
Simple Sweet Potato Pancakes, 47
Spicy Sweet Potato Soup, 111
Sweet Potato Casserole with Sweet Walnut Topping, 262
Sweet Potato Fries, 286
Sweet Potato Pie Smoothie, 69

Tahini, 253
Tempeh, creamy curry with vegetables, 178
Textures, 160
Thai Vegetable Curry, 163
Thickeners, 164
Tofu
about: deviled egg alternative, 157; for kids, 293; as meat substitute, 167
Asian-Infused Tofu Burgers, 95
Asian Tofu Sauté with Rice Noodles, 186

Best-Ever Tofu Enchiladas, 173
Chocolate Cake, 225
Citrus Tofu Kebabs, 293
Clean Chocolate Frosting, 224
Coconut Crusted Tofu Strips, 152
Creamy Tofu and Veggie Pasta, 278
Five-Alarm Enchiladas, 174
Garlic Tofu Stir-Fry, 168
Ginger-Lime Tofu, 182
Italian Tofu Bake, 167
Lean, Mean Sloppy Joes, 104
Lemon-Basil Tofu, 172
Light and Creamy Green Linguine, 199
Marvelous Mediterranean Wraps, 99
Pesto-Painted Tofu Sauté, 172
Protein-Packed Lettuce Wraps, 287
Sautéed Tofu with Balsamic Onions and
    Mushrooms, 181
Simple Spaghetti with Sautéed Tofu and
    Onions, 200
Spinach Enchiladas, 175
Sweet and Spicy Sesame Tofu Strips, 77
Sweet Tofu with Summer Squash, 170
Tasty Tomatillo Enchiladas, 176
Tofu Berry Smoothie, 62
Tofu Piccata, 179
Tofu Spaghetti, 193
Vegan Stroganoff, 184
Tomatillos
    Tangy Tomatillo Salsa Verde, 79
    Tasty Tomatillo Enchiladas, 176
Tomatoes
    Mediterranean Couscous–Stuffed Tomato
        Poppers, 78
    Creamy Tomato-Basil Soup, 121
    Crisp Romaine Salad with Balsamic
        Tomatoes, 129
    Gazpacho, 120
    Linguine with Fire-Roasted Tomatoes,
        Basil, and Mozzarella, 193
    Roasted Fennel, Tomato, and Chickpea
        Toss, 138
    sauces with. See Sauces and dips
    Savory Spinach, Tomato, and Garlic
        Smoothie, 67
    Scalloped Tomatoes with Goat Cheese, 221
    Simple Salsa, 253
    Spicy Cilantro-Tomato Salad, 132
    Tex-Mex Salad, 137
    Tomato, Basil, and Mozzarella Wraps, 99

Tomato-Basil Hummus, 158
Tomato-Basil Rigatoni, 197
Tomato Garbanzos, 204
Veggie Dip Stuffed Tomatoes, 155
Tortillas. See also Sandwiches and wraps
    Best-Ever Tofu Enchiladas, 173
    Black Bean and Corn Quesadilla, 279
    Cinnamon Tortilla Chips, 291
    Clean Black Bean Huevos Rancheros, 45
    Clean Huevos Rancheros, 44
    Five-Alarm Enchiladas, 174
    Garlic and Herb Tortilla Chips, 80
    Spicy Spanish Egg Quesadilla, 81
    Spinach Enchiladas, 175
    Tasty Tomatillo Enchiladas, 176
    Tasty Tostadas, 87
    Terrific Tortillas, 163
    Tex-Mex Quesadillas, 80
Tostadas, 87
Travel, eating clean and, 37–39

Vanilla Almond Butter, 255
Vanilla extract, 53
Vegan options/substitutions, 39–40, 148
Vegans, 14
Vegetables. See also Salads
    about: combining for flavor and nutrition,
        180; as complex carbohydrate source,
        33; in desserts, 231; eating rainbow of,
        94; at every meal, 165; roasting, 105;
        stocking pantry, 33
    Grilled Veggie Wrap-Up, 94
    main dishes. See Entrées
    pasta with. See Pasta
    Quinoa with Mixed Vegetables, 219
    soups with. See Soups
    Veggie-Stuffed Potatoes, 208
    Yogurt-Veggie Dip, 154
Vegetarian diet
    about: overview of, 11
    classes of vegetarians, 12–14
    lacto-ovo vegetarians, 13
    lacto-vegetarians, 13
    ovo-vegetarians, 13
    protein intake, 21–22
    raw vegans, 14
    vegans, 14
Vegetarian diet, clean
    about: getting started, 25; overview of,
        14–15

avoiding processed foods, 15–16
avoiding specific ingredients, 27
away from home, 37–39
benefits, 18–21, 26–27
daily calories, 17
drinking clean, 15
eating every three to four hours, 16–17,
    20–21
eating rainbow daily, 94
eliminating refined sugars, 16
explained, 14–18
goals for, 26–27
kitchen equipment, 29–31
maximizing nutrition, 17–18
meal plans, 27–28, 294
personalizing plan, 27–29
reasons for, 12
staying motivated, 35–37
stocking pantry, 32–35
variety and vibrancy, 18
vegan options/substitutions, 39–40
water and hydration, 15, 20, 28–29, 37, 39

Water and hydration, 15, 20, 28–29, 37, 39
Weight loss, 26

Yogurt
    about, 51; heavy cream alternative, 184;
        making, 257
    creamy soups with. See Soups
    Dairy-Free Almond Yogurt, 257
    Protein-Packed Parfaits, 51
    Spicy Chive Cream, 60
    Yogurt-Veggie Dip, 154

Zucchini
    about: nutrition benefits, 83, 125
    Clean Creamy Zucchini Soup, 125
    Colorful Vegetable-Pasta Salad, 130
    Grilled Veggie Wrap-Up, 94
    Roasted Veggie Dip with a Kick, 146
    Spicy Zucchini Stacker, 98
    Summer Squash Casserole, 192
    Thai Vegetable Curry, 163
    Zucchini Boats, 215
    Zucchini Bread, 83